7000 baby Names classic and modern

7000

baby
Names
classic and modern

foulsham
LONDON • NEW YORK • TORONTO • SYDNEY

foulsham

Capital Point, 33 Bath Road, Slough, Berkshire SL1 3UF, England

Foulsham books can be found in all good bookshops and direct from
www.foulsham.com

ISBN: 978-0-572-02647-9

Copyright © 2001 W. Foulsham & Co. Ltd
Last reprinted 2011

Cover photograph © The Stock Market

A CIP record for this book is available from the British Library

Printed in Great Britain by Thomson Litho Ltd, East Kilbride

Choosing your baby's name

When you are choosing a name for your new baby you want to be able to assess all the options so that your final selection is the one you feel is right for your child. It's not an easy decision as there are a lot of options to consider and you don't want to make a mistake. Very few people actually change their name later in life, so you are looking for something that your child will carry with them for the rest of their life and will come to define them as a unique individual.

With the help of this book, though, that whole process can become less daunting and instead become an enjoyable and exciting search for just the right name. Clearly organised in two main sections for girls and boys, this book offers a huge selection of names – with their meanings, origins and variations. Go through highlighting options to make your search easier, then draw up a short list for that final and all-important choice.

Things to think about when choosing a name

Here are a few things you might want to think about when choosing a name for your baby.

- Be adventurous, by all means, but do remember that a child might not enjoy too weird a name while he or she is growing up – if it is likely to cause teasing, it is not the best idea.

- Be careful to think about any negative associations of a name – Adolph and Cain, for example.

- Remember that the name will be used with your surname so make sure they work well together. Ida Down or Honey Comb could be misleading.

- Names beginning with the same letter as your surname can work, and can sound rather odd, so check that the combination has the effect you want.

- Rhyming names and surnames are not usually successful.

- Complement a long surname with a shorter first name, or vice versa: Tom Wilkinson rather than Templeton Wilkinson, for example.

- Similarly, team a common surname with a more unusual first name so that your child does not encounter too many people with the same name. Jacinta Smith will have fewer problems on that score than Ann Smith.

- Look at the initials of the chosen names together and remember that many documents have to be initialled, and that initials are often used as web site addresses and at other times. Barbara Ursula Markham would not be the best combination.

- If you have more than one child, you may not want their names to begin with the same letter, especially if they are the same sex. If a personal letter arrives for Mr M. Walker and there are three men of that name in the house, it could be confusing. If you do choose first names starting with the same letter, make sure the second names are different.

- Contractions of the first name which make an inappropriate combination with your surname are best avoided. Christopher Mass might not be the best choice.

- You do not have to give your child more than one name, but a second name can help avoid confusion, especially if you have a fairly common first or second name.

- Traditionally, you should register the full name, even if you plan to use the contraction, although this practice is now declining and Charlie, for example, is higher up the popularity list than Charles.

- Make sure you are happy with the familiar forms and contractions of the name, even if you intend to use the full name yourself.

- Nicknames are often associated with the child's name, so spare a thought for any obvious ones.

- The more popular the name you select, the greater the number of other children who will share the name.

- The more unusual the name you select, the more potential there is for mispronunciation or misspelling.

- Some names can be given both to girls and boys and you might prefer a name which is gender-specific.

- Spellings of most names vary considerably. Choose a spelling you are happy with and one which is least likely to be confusing to others.

- Names from countries or cultures other than your own are increasingly common and offer some excellent choices. Make sure the pronunciation does not cause problems in your native language.

- Most people make selections in advance for both a boy and a girl. Unless you are 100 per cent sure, don't be caught out by having only names for one or the other.

GIRLS

A

Aasta (TEUTONIC) 'Love'

Abbey *see* **Abigail**

Abbie *see* **Abigail**

Abeer (ARABIC) 'Fragrance'

Aberah *see* **Avera**

Abia (ARABIC) 'Great'

Abigail (HEBREW) 'A father's joy' (*Abagael, Abbe, Abbey, Abbie, Abby, Abigael, Gael, Gail, Gale, Gayla, Gayle, Gayleen, Gaylene*)

Abijah (HEBREW) 'God is my father' (*Abisha*)

Abnaki (NATIVE AMERICAN) 'Land of the morning'

Abra (HEBREW) 'Mother of multitudes'

Abrona (LATIN) 'Goddess of beginning journeys'

Acacia (GREEK) 'Innocent'. The symbol of immortality

Acantha (GREEK) 'Thorny'

Accalia (LATIN) Foster mother of Romulus and Remus, founders of Rome

Achala (SANSKRIT) 'Constant'

Acima (HEBREW) 'The Lord's judgement'

Acola (TEUTONIC) 'Cool'

Actia (GREEK) 'Ray of sunlight'

Ada (TEUTONIC) 'Prosperous and joyful'. A popular name in Victorian times (*Adda, Addia, Aida*)

Adabelle (LATIN) 'Joyous, happy and beautiful' (*Adabel, Adabela, Adabella*)

Adah (HEBREW) 'The crown's adornment'. One who gives lustre to the most eminent position

Adalia (TEUTONIC) An early Saxon tribal name, the origin of which is not known

Adaline *see* **Adelaide**

Adamina (LATIN) 'From the red earth', 'mortal'. Also feminine of Adam (*Addie, Addy, Mina*)

Adar (HEBREW) 'Fire'. A name sometimes given to Jewish daughters born in the sixth month of the Jewish year, which is known by the same name

Adara (GREEK) 'Beauty'

Addula (TEUTONIC) 'Noble cheer'

Adelaide (TEUTONIC) 'Noble and kind'. A gracious lady of noble birth. A name popular in 19th-century Britain as a compliment to the Queen Consort (*Adaline, Addi, Adela, Adelaida, Adele, Adelia, Adelina, Adelind, Adeline, Adelle, Dela, Della, Edelina, Edeline*)

Adelicia (TEUTONIC) 'Noble happiness'

Adelinda (FRENCH) 'Noble and sweet'

Adeline *see* **Adelaide**

Adelle *see* **Adelaide**

Adelphia (GREEK) 'Sisterly'. The eternal friend and sister to mankind (*Adelfia, Adelpha*)

Adena (GREEK) 'Accepted'

Aderyn (WELSH) 'Bird'

Adiba (ARABIC) 'Cultured'

Adicia (GREEK) 'Unjust'

Adiel (HEBREW) 'Ornament of the Lord'

Adila (ARABIC) 'Equal, like'

Adilah (ARABIC) 'Honest'

Adima (TEUTONIC) 'Noble, famous'

Adina (HEBREW) 'Voluptuous'. One of mature charm *see also* **Dena**

Adione (LATIN) Goddess of travellers

Adnette (FRENCH FROM OLD GERMAN) 'Noble'

Adolpha (TEUTONIC) 'The noble she-wolf'. Feminine of Adolf. The noble matriarch who will sacrifice everything, including life, for her young (*Adolfa, Adolfina, Adolphina*)

Adoncia (SPANISH) 'Sweet'

Adonia (GREEK) 'Beautiful goddess of the resurrection'

Adora (LATIN) 'Adored and beloved gift' (*Adorée*)

Adorabella (COMBINATION ADORA/BELLA) 'Beautiful gift'

Adorée see **Adora**

Adorna (LATIN) 'Adorned with jewels'

Adraima (ARABIC/HEBREW) 'Fruitful'

Adrienne (LATIN) 'Dark lady from the sea'. Feminine of Adrian. A dark, mysterious lady (*Adria, Adriana, Adriane, Adrianna, Adrianne, Hadria*)

Aeldra see **Aldora**

Aeldrida see **Eldrida**

Aelfreda see **Alfreda**

Aelwen (WELSH) 'Beautiful brow'

Aenea (HEBREW) 'Worthy of praise'

Aerona (WELSH) 'Like a berry'

Aeronwen (WELSH) 'Fair berry'

Afra (TEUTONIC) 'Peaceful leader' (HEBREW) 'Dust' see also **Aphra**

Africa (CELTIC) 'Pleasant'. 12th-century queen of the Isle of Man (*Affrica, Africah, Afrika, Afrikah*)

Afton (OLD ENGLISH) 'One from Afton'

Agace see **Agatha**

Agalia (GREEK) 'Brightness'

Agatha (GREEK) 'Of impeccable virtue' (*Agace, Agata, Agathe, Agathy, Aggie, Aggy, Agueda*)

Agave (GREEK) 'Illustrious and noble'

Agee (HEBREW) 'One who runs away'

Aglaia (GREEK) 'Splendour'

Agnella (GREEK) 'Pure'

Agnes (LATIN) 'Lamb', 'gentle and pure' (*Agna, Aigneis, Agneta, Agnola, Annis, Ina, Ines, Inessa, Inez, Nessa, Nessi, Nessie, Nesta, Neysa, Ynes, Ynez*)

Agneta *see* **Agnes**

Agnola (LATIN) 'Angel' *see* **Agnes**

Agrippa (LATIN) 'Born feet first' (*Agrippina*)

Agrippina *see* **Agrippa**

Agueda *see* **Agatha**

Ahuda (HEBREW) 'Praise', 'sympathetic'

Aida *see* **Ada**

Aidan (GAELIC) 'Little fire'. A girl with bright red hair *see also* **Edana**

Aiko (JAPANESE) 'Little love, beloved'

Aileen (GREEK) 'Light'. Also an Irish form of **Helen** (*Aila,* *Ailee, Ailey, Aili, Aleen, Alene, Eileen, Elene, Ileana, Ilene, Iline, Illeana, Illene, Illona, Ilona, Isleen*)

Ailsa (OLD GERMAN) 'Happy girl' (*Aillsa, Ailssa, Ilsa*)

Aili *see* **Aileen**

Aimee *see* **Amy**

Aindrea *see* **Andrea**

Ainsley (GAELIC) 'From one's own meadow' (*Ainslee, Ainslie*)

Ainslie *see* **Ainsley**

Aisha (AFRICAN) 'Life' (ARABIC) 'Living' (*Ashia*)

Aisleen (GAELIC) 'The vision' (*Helen*)

Aisling (OLD IRISH) 'Dream', 'vision'

Akasuki (JAPANESE) 'Bright helper'

Akela *see* **Akili**

Akili (TANZANIAN) 'Wisdom' (*Akela, Akeyla, Akeylah*)

Alaine *see* **Alana**

Alame (SPANISH) 'Stately poplar tree'

Alameda (SPANISH) 'Poplar tree', 'poplar grove'

Alana (CELTIC) 'Bright, fair one'. A term of endearment used by the Irish (*Alain, Alaine, Alanah, Alanna, Alayne, Alina, Allene, Allyn, Lana, Lanetta, Lanette*)

Alarice (TEUTONIC) 'Ruler of all'. Feminine of Alaric (*Alarica, Alarise*)

Alayne see Alana

Alba (LATIN) 'White'

Alberta (TEUTONIC) 'Noble and brilliant'. Feminine of Albert. A nobly born and highly intelligent girl. Popular name in Victorian times in compliment to the Prince Consort (*Albertina, Albertine, Alverta, Auberta, Berta, Berte, Bertie, Elberta, Elbertine*)

Albertina (ANGLO-SAXON) 'Illustrious' see also Alberta

Albina (LATIN) 'White lady'. One whose hair and colouring is of the fairest (*Albinia, Alvina, Aubina, Aubine*)

Albinia see Albina or Elvira

Alciana see Alcina

Alcina (GREEK) 'Strong-minded one'. The legendary Grecian lady who could produce gold from stardust. One who knows her own mind (*Alciana, Alcinette*)

Alcinette see Alcina

Alda (TEUTONIC) 'Wise and rich' (*Eada, Elda*)

Aldara (GREEK) 'Winged gift'

Aldis (OLD ENGLISH) 'From the old house'

Aldora (ANGLO-SAXON) 'Of noble rank' (*Aelda, Aeldra*)

Alegria (SPANISH) 'Happiness' see also Allegra

Alejandra see Alexandra

Alena (RUSSIAN) Form of Helen (*Aleen, Aleena, Alenah, Alene, Alenka, Allene, Alyna*)

Alenka see Alena

Aleria (LATIN) 'Eagle-like'

Alesha see Alice or Alisha

Alessandra see Alexandra

Alethea *see* **Alice** or **Althea**

Aletta (LATIN) 'Little wing', 'bird-like'

Alex *see* **Alexandra**

Alexandra (GREEK) 'The helper of mankind'. Popular in the early 20th century in Britain as a compliment to Queen Alexandra *(Alejandra, Alessandra, Alex, Alexa, Alexandrina, Alexia, Alexina, Alexine, Alexis, Alix, Lexie, Lexine, Sandy, Sandra, Sasha, Sashenka, Saskia, Zandra)*

Alexandrina *see* **Alexandra**

Alexia *see* **Alexandra**

Alexis *see* **Alexandra**

Alfonsine *see* **Alphonsine**

Alfreda (TEUTONIC) 'Wise counsellor'. Feminine of Alfred. A name popular in Britain in Anglo-Saxon times, but one which died out after the Norman conquest *(Aelfreda, Alfie, Allie, Elfreda, Elfreida, Elfrieda, Elfrida, Elfride, Elva, Elga, Freda)*

Alice (GREEK) 'Truth' *(Alecia, Aleece, Alesha, Aletha, Alethea, Alicea, Alicia, Alika, Alisa, Aliss, Alissa, Alithia, Alla, Allie, Allis, Ally, Allyce, Allys, Alyce, Alys, Alysia, Alyssa, Elisa, Elissa, Elke)*

Alicia *see* **Alice**

Alida *(Latin)* 'Little winged one'. One who is as small and lithe as the woodlark *(Aleda, Aleta, Alita, Leda, Lissie, Lita)*

Alika *see* **Alice**

Alima (ARABIC) 'Learned in music and dancing' ·

Alina *see* **Alana**

Alisha (SANSKRIT) 'Protected by god' (GREEK) 'Truthful' *(Aleesha, Alesha)*

Alison (GREEK) 'Alyssum flower' (TEUTONIC) 'Truthful warrior maid' *(Allie, Allison, Allyson)* see also **Louise**

Alix *see* **Alexandra**

Aliya (HEBREW) 'Ascend' (ARABIC) 'Sublime', 'exalted' *(Aliyah)*

Aliza (HEBREW) 'Joyful' *(Aleeza, Alieza, Aliezah, Alitza, Alizah)*

Alla *see* **Alice**

Allegra (LATIN) 'Cheerful'. As blithe as a bird *see also* **Alegria**

Allene *see* **Alena**

Alloula *see* **Alula**

Ally *see* **Alice**

Allyson *see* **Alison**

Alma (LATIN) 'Cherishing spirit'. Popular in Britain after the Battle of Alma in the Crimean War

Almeda (LATIN) 'Ambitious' *(Almeta)*

Almira (ARABIC) 'Truth without question', 'princess' *(Almeira, Almeria, Elmira)*

Alodie (ANGLO-SAXON) 'Wealthy, prosperous' *(Alodia)*

Aloha (HAWAIIAN) 'Greetings'. A romantic name from the Hawaiian islands

Aloisa (TEUTONIC) 'Feminine'

Alonza *see* **Alphonsine**

Alpha (GREEK) 'First one'. A suitable name for a first daughter

Alphonsine (TEUTONIC) 'Noble and eager for battle' *(Alfonsine, Alonza, Alphonica, Alphonsina)*

Alta (LATIN) 'Tall in spirit'

Althea (GREEK) 'The healer' *(Aletha, Alethea, Althee, Altheta, Thea)*

Altheda (GREEK) 'Flower-like'

Aludra (GREEK) 'Virgin'

Alula (ARABIC) 'The first' (LATIN) 'Winged one' *(Alloula, Allula, Aloula)*

Aluma (HEBREW) 'Girl'

Alura (ANGLO-SAXON) 'Divine counsellor'

Alva (LATIN) 'White lady'

Alverta *see* **Alberta**

Alvina (TEUTONIC) 'Beloved and noble friend' *(Alvine, Alvinia, Vina)* see also **Albina**

Alvine *see* **Alvina** or **Alviona**

Alviona (TEUTONIC) 'Loved and respected friend' *(Alvine, Vina)*

Alvira (TEUTONIC) 'Elfin arrow'

Alvita (LATIN) 'Vivacious'

Alyce *see* **Alice**

Alysia (GREEK) 'Unbroken chain' *see also* **Alice**

Alyssa (GREEK) 'Sane one'. The name of a white flower *see also* **Alice**

Alzena (ARABIC) 'Woman'. The embodiment of feminine charm and virtue

Am-ee *see* **Amy**

Ama (AFRICAN) 'Born on Saturday'

Amabel (LATIN) 'Sweet, lovable one'. A tender, loving, loyal daughter *(Amabella, Amabelle)*

Amadea (LATIN) 'The beloved of God'

Amadore (ITALIAN) 'Gift of love' *(Amadora)*

Amala (SANSKRIT) 'Pure one' (ARABIC) 'Hope' *(Amla)*

Amana (HEBREW) 'Faithful'

Amanda (LATIN) 'Worthy of being loved' *(Manda, Mandie, Mandy)*

Amanta (LATIN) 'Loving one'

Amany (ARABIC) 'Aspiration'

Amapola (ARABIC) 'Flower'

Amara (GREEK) 'Of eternal beauty' *(Amargo)*

Amarantha (GREEK) 'Unfading'

Amargo *see* **Amara**

Amaris (LATIN) 'Child of the moon' (HEBREW) 'Promised by God'

Amaryllis (GREEK) 'Fresh, new, sparkling'. The name of a flower *(Amarillis, Marilla)*

Amata (LATIN) 'Beloved'

Amber (SANSKRIT) 'The sky' (ARABIC) 'Jewel' *(Amberly, Ambur)*

Amberly *see* **Amber**

Ambrin (ARABIC) 'Fragrant'

Ambrosia *see* **Ambrosine**

Ambrosina *see* **Ambrosine**

Ambrosine (GREEK) 'Divine, immortal one'. Feminine of Ambrose *(Ambrosia, Ambrosina)*

Ambur *see* **Amber**

Ameerah (ARABIC) 'Princess'

Amelia (TEUTONIC) 'Industrious and hard-working' *(Amalee, Amalia, Amalie, Amealia, Amelea, Amelie, Ameline, Amelita, Emelda, Emelina, Emeline, Emily, Emmalee, Emmalynn, Mell, Mellie, Milicia, Mill, Millie)*

Amelinda (SPANISH) 'Beloved and pretty'

Amelita *see* **Amelia**

Amena (CELTIC) 'Honest'. One of incorruptible truth *(Amina)*

Amethyst (GREEK) Semi-precious stone which is said to be able to ward off intoxication

Amilia (LATIN) 'Affable'

Amina *see* **Amena** or **Amine**

Amine (ARABIC) 'Faithful' *(Amina)*

Aminta (GREEK) 'Protector'. The name of a shepherdess in Greek mythology *(Amintha, Aminthe)*

Amira (ARABIC) 'Princess', 'cultivated' (HEBREW) 'Speech'

Amity (OLD FRENCH) 'Friendship'

Amla *see* **Amala**

Amma (HINDI) 'God-like'. Another name for the goddess Shakti

Amorette (LATIN) 'Darling' *(Amarette, Amoret, Amorita, Morette)*

Amrit (SANSKRIT) 'Ambrosia'

Amy (FRENCH) 'Beloved friend' *(Aimee, Am-ee, Ami, Amie)*

Amyntas (GREEK) 'Helper'

Anaïs (FRENCH) 'Faithful' (HEBREW) 'Gracious'

Anal (SANSKRIT) 'Fiery' *(Anala)*

Anamari (BASQUE) Derivation of Anna Maria

Anastasia (GREEK) 'She who will rise again' *(Ana, Anstice, Stacey, Stacia, Stacie, Stacy)*

Anatholia *see* **Anatola**

Anatola (GREEK) 'Woman of the east', 'sunrise'. Feminine of Anatole *(Anatholia, Anatolia)*

Ancelin (LATIN) 'Fairest handmaid' *(Celine)*

Anchoret (WELSH) 'Much loved'

Ancita (HEBREW) 'Grace'

Andeana (SPANISH) 'Traveller on foot'

Andrea (LATIN) 'Womanly'. The epitome of feminine charm and beauty *(Aindrea, Andre, Andreana, Andree, Andria, Andriana) see also* **Edrea**

Andria *see* **Andrea**

Andromeda (GREEK) 'Ruler of men'. The princess rescued by Perseus in Greek mythology

Aneira (WELSH) 'Honourable' or 'golden'

Anemone (GREEK) 'Wind flower'. The nymph of Greek mythology who, when pursued by the wind, turned into the anemone flower

Angela (GREEK) 'Heavenly messenger'. The bringer of good news *(Angel, Angelina, Angeline, Angelita, Angie)*

Angelica (LATIN) 'Angelic one'. A name often used by medieval writers in Britain to typify the perfect woman *(Angelique)*

Angelique *see* **Angelica**

Angharad (WELSH) 'Free from shame'

Angie *see* **Angela**

Angwen (WELSH) 'Very beautiful'

Ani (HAWAIIAN) 'Beautiful'

Ania *see* **Anya**

Aniela (ITALIAN) 'Angel'

Anika (CZECH) 'Gracious'. A form of **Anne** *(Anneka, Annika)*

Anila (SANSKRIT) 'Wind'

Anita *see* **Anne**

Anitra *see* **Anne**

Ann *see* **Anne**

Anna *see* **Anne**

Annabelle (COMBINATION ANNE/ BELLE) *(Anabel, Annabel, Annabella, Annie, Bella, Belle)*

Anne (HEBREW) 'Full of grace'. One of the most popular feminine names in the UK and the name of a British queen and several queens consort *(Ana, Anita, Anitra, Ann, Anna, Annette, Annie, Nan, Nana, Nancy, Nanetta, Nanette, Nanice, Nanine, Nanna, Nanon, Nina, Ninette, Ninon, Nita)*

Anneka *see* **Anika**

Annette (FRENCH) 'Grace'. A familiar form of **Anne** *(Annetta)*

Annia *see* **Anya**

Annie *see* **Anne** or **Annabelle**

Annissa (ARABIC) 'Charming', 'gracious'

Annona (LATIN) 'Fruitful', 'annual crops'. The Roman goddess of crops *(Annora, Anona, Nona, Nonnie)*

Annunciata (LATIN) 'Bearer of news'. A suitable name for a girl born in March, particularly 24th March, as it derives from the 'Annunciation' – the announcement of the Virgin's conception *see also* **Nunciata**

Anora (ENGLISH) 'Light and graceful'

Anselma (NORSE) 'Divinely protected' *(Anselme, Selma, Zelma)*

Anstice *see* **Anastasia**

Anthea (GREEK) 'Flower-like'. One of delicate, fragile beauty *(Anthia, Bluma, Thea, Thia)*

Anthelia (GREEK) 'Facing the sun'

Antoinette *see* **Antonia**

Antonia (LATIN) 'Beyond price', 'excellent'. Feminine of Anthony. A jewel beyond compare *(Anthonia, Antoinette, Antoinietta, Antoni, Antonina, Netta, Nettie, Netty, Toinette, Toni, Tonia)*

Anusha (HINDI) 'A star'

Anwyl (WELSH) 'Precious'

Anya (HEBREW) 'Grace', 'mercy' *(Ania, Annia)*

Anysia (GREEK) 'Whole'

Anzonetta (TEUTONIC) 'Little holy one'

Aphra (HEBREW) 'Female deer' *(Afra)*

Appoline (GREEK) 'Sun' *(Apollene)*

April (GREEK) 'The beginning of spring'. The name of the first month of the Roman calendar and the fourth month of the Julian calendar

Aquilina (LATIN) 'Little eagle'

Ara (GREEK) 'Spirit of revenge'. The Greek goddddess of vengeance and destruction

Arabella (LATIN) 'Beautiful altar' *(Arabela, Arabelle, Aralia, Arbel, Arbele, Arbelia, Arbelle, Bel, Bella, Belle)*

Arabinda (SANSKRIT) *see* **Arvinda**

Aradhana (SANSKRIT) 'Worship'

Aramanta (HEBREW) 'Elegant lady' *(Aramenta)*

Araminta (GREEK) 'Beautiful, sweet-smelling flower'

Arbelia *see* **Arabella**

Arcadia (GREEK) 'Perfect place'

Arda *see* **Ardelle**

Ardana (SANSKRIT) 'Restless one'

Ardath (HEBREW) 'Field of flowers' *(Ardatha, Aridatha)*

Ardelle (LATIN) 'Enthusiasm, warmth' *(Arda, Arden, Ardelis, Ardella, Ardere)*

Arden (OLD ENGLISH) 'Eagle valley' *(Ardeen, Ardene)*

Ardere *see* **Ardelle**

Ardine (GREEK) 'One who quenches the thirst'

Ardis (LATIN) 'One who pleases'

Ardra (LATIN) 'Ardent'

Ardun (WELSH) 'Sublime'

Areta (GREEK) 'Of excellent virtue' *(Arete, Aretha, Aretta, Arette, Retha)*

Arethusa (GREEK) 'Virtuous'. A nymph who was turned into a fountain to escape her pursuers

Arezou (PERSIAN) 'Wishful'

Argenta (LATIN) 'Silvery one' *(Argente, Argentia)*

Aria (LATIN) 'Beautiful melody'

Ariadne (GREEK) 'Holy one'. The mythological maiden who told Theseus how he could escape from the labyrinth after he had killed the minotaur *(Ariadna, Ariane)*

Ariane *see* **Ariadne**

Arianwen (WELSH) 'Silvery one'

Aric *see* **Erica**

Ariella (HEBREW) 'God's lioness' *(Ariel, Arielle)*

Arilda (GERMAN) 'Hearth, home'

Ariminta (HEBREW) 'Lofty'

Arista (GREEK) 'The best'

Arlene (CELTIC) 'A pledge' *(Arlana, Arleas, Arleen, Arlen, Arlena, Arletta, Arlette, Arlina, Arline, Arlyne, Herleva)*

Arlina *see* **Arlene**

Armelle (FRENCH FROM CELTIC) 'Princess'

Armida (LATIN) 'Small warrior'

Armilla (LATIN) 'Bracelet' *(Armillette)*

Armina (TEUTONIC) 'Warrior maid' *(Armine, Arminia, Erminia, Erminie)*

Armorel (IRISH) 'Sea-dweller'

Arnalda (TEUTONIC) 'Eagle-like ruler'. Feminine of Arnold

Arnhilda (TEUTONIC) 'Maiden ready for battle'

Arnoldine (TEUTONIC) 'The eagle's mate'

Arpita (SANSKRIT) 'Dedicated'

Arselma (NORSE) 'Divine protective helmet'

Artemia (GREEK) The goddess of the moon

Artemisia (GREEK/SPANISH) 'Perfect'

Artis (GAELIC) 'Noble', 'lofty hill'

Aruna (SANSKRIT) 'Sunrise', 'reddish-brown'

Arva (LATIN) 'Pastureland', 'seashore'

Arvinda (SANSKRIT) 'Lotus blossom' *(Arabinda)*

Aseema *see* **Ashima**

Asha (SANSKRIT) 'Hope', 'desire'

Ashanti (SWAHILI) From the West African tribe

Ashima (SANSKRIT) 'Without limit' *(Aseema)*

Ashira (HEBREW) 'Wealthy'

Ashley (OLD ENGLISH) 'From the ash tree meadow'

Ashlyn (ENGLISH) 'Pool by the ash tree'

Ashna (SANSKRIT) 'Friend'

Asia (GREEK) 'Resurrection'

Asisa (HEBREW) 'Ripe'

Asma (ARABIC) 'More eminent', 'more prestigious'

Aspasia (GREEK) 'Welcome', 'radiant'

Aspen (ENGLISH) 'Aspen tree'

Asphodel (GREEK) 'The wild lily of Greece'

Assumpta *see* **Assunta**

Assunta (ITALIAN) From the Assumption of Mary *(Assumpta)*

Asta (GREEK) 'Star-like' *(Astera, Astra, Astrea)*

Astrea *see* **Asta**

Astrid (NORSE) 'Divine strength' *(Astred)*

Atalanta (GREEK) 'Might bearer'. The legendary Greek huntress *(Atalante, Atlanta)*

Atalia *see* **Athalia**

Atalya (SPANISH) 'Guardian'. One who protects hearth and home

Atara (HEBREW) 'Crown'

Athalia (HEBREW) 'God is exalted' *(Atalia, Athalea, Athalie, Athie, Attie)*

Athena (GREEK) The Greek goddess of wisdom *(Athene, Athenee)*

Athie *see* **Athalia**

Atiya (ARABIC) 'Gift'

Atlanta *see* **Atalanta**

Attie *see* **Athalia**

Auberta *see* **Alberta**

Aubrey (FRENCH) 'Blonde ruler' (TEUTONIC) 'Noble' *(Aubary, Auberi, Aubery, Aubre, Aubrea, Aubreah, Aubree, Aubrei, Aubreigh, Aubrette)*

Audie see **Audrey**

Audrey (ANGLO-SAXON) 'Strong and noble'. Derives from the Anglo-Saxon name Aethelthryth *(Audie, Audrie, Audry, Dee)*

Augusta (LATIN) 'Sacred and majestic'. Popular name in royal and noble families in the 18th and early 19th century *(Auguste, Augustina, Augustine, Austine, Gussie, Gusta)*

Aura (LATIN) 'Gentle breeze'. A name said to endow its owner with gentility *(Aure, Auria, Ora)* see also **Aurelia**

Aurelia (LATIN) 'Golden'. The girl of the dawn *(Aurea, Aurel, Aurelie, Aurie, Auristela, Aurora, Aurore, Ora, Oralia, Oralie, Oriel, Oriole)* see also **Aura**

Auria see **Aura**

Aurora see **Aurelia**

Autumn (LATIN) From the season

Ava see **Avis**

Avel (HEBREW) 'Breath'

Aveline (HEBREW) 'Pleasant' see also **Hazel**

Avena (LATIN) 'Oatfield'. A girl with rich, golden hair *(Avene)*

Avene see **Avena**

Avenida (CHILEAN) 'An avenue'

Avera (HEBREW) 'Transgressor' *(Aberah)*

Averil (OLD ENGLISH) 'Slayer of the boar' *(Averyl, Avril, Avyril)*

Avery (OLD FRENCH) 'To confirm' *(Averi)*

Averyl see **Averil**

Avice (FRENCH) 'War-like' *(Avisa, Hadwisa)* see also **Avis**

Avicia (GERMAN) 'Refuge in war'

Avis (LATIN) 'A bird' *(Ava, Avi, Avisa, Avissa)* see also **Avice**

Avishag (HEBREW) 'Father's delight'

Avital (HEBREW) 'God protects'

Aviva (HEBREW) 'Springtime' *(Avivah, Avrit)*

Avonwy (WELSH) 'Someone who lives by the river'

Avril *see* **Averil**

Avrit *see* **Aviva**

Awel (WELSH) 'Gentle breeze'

Awena (WELSH) 'Poetry', 'prophecy'

Aya (HEBREW) 'Swift flyer'

Ayala (HEBREW) 'Deer'

Ayanna (HINDI) 'Innocent one'

Ayesha (PERSIAN) 'Happy one'

Ayla (HEBREW) 'Oak tree'

Aylwen (WELSH) 'Fair brow'

Azalea (LATIN) 'Dry earth'. From the flower of the same name *(Azalee, Azalia, Azaliea)*

Azaria (HEBREW) 'Blessed by God' *(Azeria, Zaria)*

Azeria *see* **Azaria**

Azura (FRENCH) 'The blue sky'. One whose eyes are blue

B

Bab (ARABIC) 'From the gateway'
see also **Barbara**

Babette *see* **Barbara**

Babita *see* **Barbara**

Badriyah (ARABIC) 'Full moon'

Bailey (FRENCH) 'Steward'

Bala (SANSKRIT) 'Girl'

Balbina (LATIN) 'She who
hesitates' *(Balbine, Balbinia)*

Bambi (LATIN) 'The child'.
Suitable name for anyone of
tiny stature

Baptista (LATIN) 'Baptised'. A
name symbolic of man's
freedom from sin through
baptism *(Baptiste, Batista,
Battista)*

Barbara (LATIN) 'Beautiful
stranger'. The lovely but
unknown visitor *(Bab,
Babb, Babe, Babette, Babita,
Babs, Barb, Barbetta,
Barbie, Barbra, Bas)*

Barbie *see* **Barbara**

Barra (HEBREW) 'To choose'
(Bara)

Barrie (GAELIC) 'Markswoman'

Basia (HEBREW) 'Daughter of
God'

Basile Feminine of Basil

Basilia (GREEK) 'Queenly, regal'.
Feminine of Basil

Basima (ARABIC) 'Smiling'

Bathilda (TEUTONIC) 'Battle commander'. Traditionally one who fought for honour and truth *(Bathilde, Batilda, Batilde)*

Bathsheba (HEBREW) 'Seventh daughter'. Bathsheba was the wife of King David in Biblical times *(Batsheva)*

Batilda *see* **Bathilda**

Batista *see* **Baptista**

Bea *see* **Beata** or **Beatrice**

Beata (LATIN) 'Blessed, divine one', 'blessed and beloved of God' *(Bea)*

Beathag *see* **Sophia**

Beatrice (LATIN) 'She who brings joy' *(Bea, Beatrix, Bee, Beitris, Trix, Trixie, Trixy)*

Bebba (SWISS FROM HEBREW) 'God's oath'

Bebhin *see* **Bevin**

Becca *see* **Rebecca**

Becky *see* **Rebecca**

Beda (ANGLO-SAXON) 'Warrior maiden'

Bedelia (CELTIC) 'Mighty' *(Delia)*

Bee *see* **Beatrice**

Behira (HEBREW) 'Brilliant'

Beka (HEBREW) 'Half-sister'

Bel *see* **Arabella** or **Isabel**

Bela (SLAVONIC) 'White'

Belda (FRENCH) 'Beautiful lady'

Belicia (SPANISH) 'Dedicated to God'

Belinda (ITALIAN) 'Wise and immortal beauty' *(Bella, Belle, Linda, Lindie, Lindy)* *see also* **Linda**

Beline (FRENCH/OLD GERMAN) 'Goddess'

Belisama (LATIN) Roman divinity like Minerva, goddess of wisdom

Belita (SPANISH FROM LATIN) 'Beautiful'

Bella *see* **Annabelle, Arabella, Belinda, Clarabella** or **Isabel**

Bellance (ITALIAN) 'Blonde beauty' *(Blanca)*

Belle (FRENCH) 'Beautiful woman'. Can also be used as diminutive of **Belinda** and **Isabel** *(Bell, Bella, Bellina, Belva, Belvia) see also* **Annabelle, Arabella, Belinda** or **Isabel**

Bellina *see* **Belle**

Bellona (LATIN) 'War goddess'

Belva *see* **Belle**

Belvina (LATIN) 'Fair girl' *(Belvia)*

Bema (GREEK) 'Fair speech'

Bena (HEBREW) 'The wise one'. A woman whose charm is enhanced by wisdom

Benedicta (LATIN) 'Blessed one'. Feminine of Benedict *(Benedetta, Benecia, Benedikta, Benita, Bennie, Benoite, Binnie, Dixie)*

Benedikta *see* **Benedicta**

Benigna (LATIN) 'Gentle, kind and gracious'. A great lady

Benilda (LATIN) 'Well-intentioned'

Benita (SPANISH) 'Blessed'. *(Benitia) see also* **Benedicta**

Benoite *see* **Benedicta**

Berdine (TEUTONIC) 'Glorious one'

Berengaria (TEUTONIC) 'Spearer of bears'. A warrior huntress of renown

Berit (TEUTONIC) 'Glorious'

Berlynn (ENGLISH) Combination of Bertha and Lynn *(Berlin, Berlyn)*

Bernadette (FRENCH) 'Brave as a bear' *(Berna, Bernadene, Bernadina, Bernadine, Bernardina, Berneta, Berney, Bernie, Bernita)*

Berneen (CELTIC) 'Little one, brave as a bear'

Bernessa (TEUTONIC) 'With the heart of a bear'

Bernia (LATIN) 'Angel in armour' *(Bernie)*

Bernice (GREEK) 'Herald of victory' *(Berenice, Berny, Bunny, Burnice, Veronica)*

Bernie *see* **Bernadette** or **Bernia**

Berri *see* **Beryl**

Bertha (TEUTONIC) 'Bright and shining'. The Teutonic goddess of fertility *(Berta, Berthe, Bertie, Bertina, Berty)*

Berthelda (TEUTONIC) 'Girl who goes into battle'

Berthilda (ANGLO-SAXON) 'Shining warrior maid' *(Beertilda, Berthilde, Bertilde)*

Bertie *see* **Alberta**, **Bertha** or **Roberta**

Bertina *see* **Bertha**

Bertrade (ANGLO-SAXON) 'Shining adviser' *(Bertrada)*

Berura (HEBREW) 'Pure'

Beryl (GREEK) 'Precious jewel'. This stone, and therefore the name, is said to bring good luck *(Beril, Berri, Berrie, Berry, Beryle)*

Bess *see* **Elizabeth**

Beth *see* **Bethel** or **Elizabeth**

Bethany (ARAMAIC) 'House of poverty' *(Bethena, Bethina)*

Bethel (HEBREW) 'House of God' *(Beth)*

Bethia (HEBREW) 'Daughter of God'

Bethinn *see* **Bevin**

Bethseda (HEBREW) 'House of Mercy' *(Bethesda)*

Betina *see* **Elizabeth**

Betsy *see* **Elizabeth**

Bette *see* **Elizabeth**

Beulah (HEBREW) 'The married one'. The traditional wife *(Beula)*

Beverley (ANGLO-SAXON) 'Ambitious one' *(Berry, Bev, Beverlie, Beverly)*

Bevin (GAELIC) 'Melodious lady'. One whose voice is so beautiful that even the birds will cease singing to listen to her *(Bebhinn, Bethinn)*

Bianca (ITALIAN) 'White'

Bibi (ARABIC) 'Lady'

Bibiana (SPANISH) *see* **Vivian**

Biddie *see* **Bridget**

Bienvenida (SPANISH) 'Welcome'

Bijou (OLD FRENCH) 'Jewel'

Bik (CHINESE) 'Jade'

Billie (TEUTONIC) 'Wise, resolute ruler' *(Billy, Billye, Willa)* *see also* **Wilhelmina**

Bina (AFRICAN) 'To dance'

Binga (TEUTONIC) 'From the hollow'

Birdie (MODERN ENGLISH) 'Sweet little bird'

Birjis (ARABIC) 'Planet Jupiter'

Blaine (GAELIC) 'Thin' *(Blane, Blayne)*

Blair (GAELIC) 'Dweller on the plain' *(Blaire)*

Blake (OLD ENGLISH) 'Fair haired'

Blanca *see* **Bellance** or **Blanche**

Blanche (FRENCH) 'Fair and white'. A very popular name in medieval times when it was supposed to endow its user with all feminine virtues *(Bellanca, Blanca, Blanch, Blanka, Blinne, Blinnie, Bluinse, Branca)*

Blanda (LATIN) 'Seductive', 'flattering', 'caressing'

Blanka *see* **Blanche**

Blasia (LATIN) 'She who stammers' *(Blaise)*

Blayne *see* **Blaine**

Blenda (GERMAN) 'Glorious', 'dazzling'

Blessin (OLD ENGLISH) 'Consecrated' *(Blessing)*

Bliss (OLD ENGLISH) 'Gladness', 'joy' *(Blita, Blitha)*

Blithe *see* **Blyth**

Blodwen *see* **Blodwyn**

Blodwyn (WELSH) 'White flower' *(Blodwen)*

Blondelle (FRENCH) 'Little fair one' *(Blondie)*

Blossom (OLD ENGLISH) 'Fragrant as a flower'

Bluinse *see* **Blanche**

Blyth (ANGLO-SAXON) 'Joyful and happy' *(Blith, Blithe, Blythe)*

Bo (CHINESE) 'Precious'

Bobbie *see* **Roberta**

Bobina *see* **Roberta**

Bodgana (POLISH) 'God's gift'

Bonfilia (ITALIAN) 'Good daughter'

Bonita (LATIN) 'Sweet and good' *(Bona, Bonne, Bonnibelle, Bonnie, Nita)*

Bonnie *see* **Bonita**

Bradley (OLD ENGLISH) 'From the broad meadow' *(Bradlee, Bradleigh)*

Brandice *see* **Brandy**

Brandy (DUTCH) 'Brandy' *(Brandais, Brandea, Brandice)*

Branwen (WELSH) 'Beautiful raven'

Breanna (IRISH) 'Strong and honourable' *(Breana, Breann, Breanne, Breighann)*

Breena (IRISH) 'Fairy palace' *(Breina, Brena, Brina)*

Breina *see* **Breena**

Brenda (TEUTONIC) 'Fiery' (IRISH) 'Raven' *(Bren)*

Brenna (IRISH) 'Raven-haired beauty'

Brett *see* **Brittany**

Briallen (WELSH) 'Primrose'

Briana (CELTIC) 'Strength', 'virtue', 'honour' *(Breona, Bria, Brianna, Brienne, Briona, Bryana) see also* **Bryna**

Briar (FRENCH) 'Heather' *(Bryar)*

Bridget (IRISH/CELTIC) 'Strong and mighty' *(Biddie, Biddy, Birkita, Breita, Bridey, Bridie, Brie, Brieta, Brietta, Brigette, Brigid, Brigida, Brigitte, Brita, Brydie)*

Brier (FRENCH) 'Heather'

Brieta *see* **Bridget**

Brigette *see* **Bridget**

Brigid *see* **Bridget**

Brina *see* **Breena** or **Sabrina**

Briona *see* **Briana**

Briony *see* **Bryony**

Brissa *see* **Bryssa**

Britney *see* **Brittany**

Brittany (LATIN) 'Britain' *(Britannia, Britney, Britta)*

Bronwen (WELSH/CELTIC) 'White bosomed' *(Bronwyn)*

Bronya (RUSSIAN) 'Armour'

Brook (OLD ENGLISH) 'Living near the brook' *(Brooke)*

Brooklyn (AMERICAN) Place name

Brucie (FRENCH) 'From the thicket'. Feminine of Bruce

Brunella (ITALIAN) 'One with brown hair.' The true brunette *(Bruella, Bruelle, Brunelle)*

Brunetta (FRENCH) 'Dark-haired maiden'

Brunhilda (TEUTONIC) 'Warrior heroine' *(Bronhilde, Brunhild, Brunhilde)*

Bryana *see* **Briana**

Bryna (IRISH) 'Strength with virtue'. Feminine of Brian

Bryony (OLD ENGLISH) 'A twining vine' *(Briony)*

Bryssa (SPANISH) 'Beloved' *(Brisa, Brissa)*

Buena (SPANISH) 'The good one' *(Buona)*

Buffy (AMERICAN) 'From the plains', 'buffalo' *(Buffee, Buffey, Buffie, Buffye Buffye)*

Bunny (ENGLISH) 'Little rabbit' *see also* **Bernice**

Buona *see* **Buena**

Burgundy (FRENCH) Name of French wine

Burnetta (FRENCH) 'Little brown one'

GIRLS

Cachée *see* Cachet

Cachet (FRENCH) 'Desirous'
(Cachée)

Cadena *see* Cadence

Cadence (LATIN) 'Rhythmic'.
One who is graceful and
charming *(Cadena, Cadenza)*

Caera (GAELIC) 'Spear', 'ruddy'

Cai (VIETNAMESE) 'Feminine'
(Cae, Cay, Caye)

Cailey *see* Cayla

Caileen *see* Colleen

Caireen *see* Catherine

Cairistiona *see* Christine

Caitlin (GAELIC) 'Pure girl'.
Form of **Catherine**

Caitrin *see* Catherine

Cal *see* Calandra or Calantha

Cala (ARABIC) 'Castle'

Calandra (GREEK) 'Lark'. One
who is as light and gay as a
lark *(Cal, Calandre,
Calandria, Callie, Cally)*

Calandre *see* Calandra

Calandria *see* Calandra

Calantha (GREEK) 'Beautiful
blossom'. A woman of
child-like beauty and
innocence *(Cal, Calanthe,
Callie, Cally, Kalantha,
Kalanthe)*

Caldora (GREEK) 'Beautiful
present'

Caledonia (LATIN) 'Scottish lassie'. One who comes from the part of Scotland formerly known as Caledonia *(Caledonie)*

Calida (SPANISH) 'Ardently loving'. A woman capable of great affection

Calista (GREEK) 'Most beautiful of women'. A name for a girl thought to be beautiful beyond the ordinary *(Callista, Calisto, Kallista, Kallisto)*

Calla (GREEK) 'Beautiful' *(Calli)*

Callena (TEUTONIC) 'One who talks a lot'

Callidora (GREEK) 'Gift of beauty'

Calligenia (GREEK) 'Daughter of beauty'

Calliope (GREEK) 'The music of poetry'

Callista *see* **Calista**

Callula (LATIN) 'Little beautiful one'

Calosa (GREEK) 'Beautiful to look at'

Caltha (LATIN) 'Yellow flower'

Calvina (LATIN) 'Bald'. Feminine of Calvin. A name sometimes used in strongly Calvinistic families

Calypso (GREEK) 'Concealer'. The legendary sea nymph who held Odysseus captive *(Kalypso)*

Cam (VIETNAMESE) 'Sweet citrus fruit'

Camelia *see* **Camilla**

Cameo (ITALIAN) 'Sculptured jewel'

Cameron (SCOTTISH) 'Crooked nose' *(Cam, Cameran, Cameren)*

Camilla (LATIN) 'Noble and righteous'. The name given to the young and beautiful handmaiden in pagan ceremonies *(Cam, Camala, Camelia, Camella, Camellia, Camile, Camille, Cammi)*

Canace (LATIN) 'The daughter of the wind' *(Kanaka, Kanake)*

Candace (LATIN) 'Pure', 'glittering', 'brilliant white'. One whose purity and virtue is beyond suspicion *(Candice, Candida, Candie, Candy)*

Candra (LATIN) 'Luminescent'
  see also **Chandra**

Candy *see* **Candace**

Cantara (ARABIC) 'Small bridge'

Caprice (ITALIAN) 'Fanciful'
  (Capriccia)

Capucine (FRENCH) 'Cape'

Cara (CELTIC) 'Friend' (ITALIAN)
  'Dearest one'. A term of
  endearment *(Caralie,
  Cariad, Carina, Carine,
  Kara, Karine, Karina)*

Caragh (IRISH) 'Friend'

Caralie *see* **Cara**

Caressa *see* **Carissa**

Carey *see* **Caroline**

Cari (TURKISH) 'Flows like water'

Carina (LATIN) 'Keel' *(Karina)*
  see also **Cara**

Carine *see* **Cara** or **Catherine**

Carissa (LATIN) 'Most dear one'
  (Caressa, Caresse, Carisse)

Carita (LATIN) 'Beloved little
  one' *(Karita)*

Carla *see* **Charlotte**

Carlie *see* **Charlotte**

Carliss *see* **Corliss**

Carlotta *see* **Charlotte**

Carly *see* **Caroline** or
  Charlotte

Carma (SANSKRIT) 'Destiny'.
  From the Buddhist 'Karma'
  meaning 'fate' *see also*
  Carmel or **Carmen**

Carmel (HEBREW) 'God's fruitful
  vineyard' *(Carma, Carmela,
  Carmelina, Carmeline,
  Carmelita, Carmella,
  Carmie, Melina)*

Carmen (LATIN) 'Songstress'.
  One who has a beautiful
  voice *(Carma, Carmacita,
  Carmelita, Carmencita,
  Carmia, Carmina, Carmine,
  Carmita, Charmaine)*

Carmie *see* **Carmel**

Carmine *see* **Carmen**

Carnation (FRENCH) 'Fresh
  colour'. One with perfect
  features and colouring

Carol *see* **Caroline**

Carolina *see* **Caroline**

Caroline (TEUTONIC) 'Little woman born to command'. The power behind the throne; the hand which rocks the cradle and rules the world. One who is all that is feminine but who rules and controls. Also used as the feminine of Charles *(Carey, Carilla, Carlin, Carline, Carly, Caro, Carol, Carola, Carole, Carolina, Caryn, Cazzie, Charleen, Charlene, Charline, Lena, Lina, Line, Sharleen, Sharlene, Sharline) see also* **Charlotte**

Caron *see* **Cheron**

Caronwen (WELSH) 'Little fair love'

Carrie *see* **Caroline**

Caryl (WELSH) 'Beloved' *(Carryl, Carys)*

Caryn *see* **Catherine**

Casey (IRISH) 'Brave' *(Cacy, Casie)*

Casilda (SPANISH) 'The solitary one' *(Casilde)*

Casimira (LATIN) 'Bringer of peace'

Casmira *see* **Kasmira**

Cassandra (GREEK) Prophetess ignored by men *(Cass, Cassandre, Cassie, Kassandra)*

Cassia (GREEK) 'Spicy cinnamon'

Cassidy (IRISH) 'Clever'

Cassiopeia (GREEK) 'Scent of flowers'

Casta (LATIN) 'Of pure upbringing' *(Caste)*

Catalina *see* **Catherine**

Caterina *see* **Catherine**

Catherine (GREEK) 'Pure maiden'. The saint who was martyred on a spiked wheel *(Caireen, Caitlin, Caitrin, Carine, Caryn, Catalina, Caterina, Catharina, Catharine, Cathelle, Cathie, Cathleen, Cathy, Catriona, Kaitlyn, Kate, Katerine, Kateryn, Katharina, Katharine, Katherina, Katherine, Kathryn, Kathy, Katie, Katrina, Katrine, Katy, Kit, Kitty)*

Cathlin (CELTIC) 'One with beautiful eyes'

Cathy *see* **Catherine**

Catriona (SCOTTISH) 'Pure maiden'. Scottish variation of **Catherine**

Cattima (LATIN) 'Delicate reed'

Cay *see* **Cai**

Cayla (HEBREW) 'Crown of laurel leaves' *(Kayla, Caily)*

Cazzie *see* **Caroline**

Ceara (IRISH) 'Spear'. A warrior who fought with a spear

Cecilia (LATIN) The patron saint of music *(Cecelia, Cecil, Cecile, Cecily, Cele, Celia, Cicely, Ciel, Cissie, Sileas, Sisile, Sisle, Sisley, Sissie)*

Cecily *see* **Cecelia**

Cedrella (LATIN) 'Silver fir tree'

Cein (CELTIC) 'Jewel'

Ceinlys (WELSH) 'Sweet gems'

Ceinwen (WELSH) 'Beautiful gems'

Ceiridwen (WELSH) The goddess of bardism *(Ceri, Kerridwen)*

Celandine (GREEK) 'Swallow', 'yellow water flower' *(Celandon)*

Celene *see* **Selena**

Celeste (LATIN) 'Heavenly'. A woman of divine beauty *(Cele, Celesta, Celestina, Celestine, Celestyna, Celia, Celina, Celinda, Celinka)*

Celia *see* **Cecelia** or **Celeste**

Celine *see* **Ancelin**

Celinka *see* **Celeste**

Celo (GREEK) 'Flame-like'

Celosia (GREEK) 'Burning flame' *(Kelosia)*

Cerelia (LATIN) 'Spring-like'. A woman of spring-blossom beauty *(Cerealia, Cerelie, Cerellia)*

Cerella (LATIN) 'Springtime'

Ceri *see* **Ceridwen**

Cerian (WELSH) 'Loved one'

Ceridwen (WELSH) 'Fair poetry' *(Ceri, Ceiridwen, Kerridwen)*

Cerrita (SPANISH) 'Closed', 'silent'

Cerys (WELSH) 'Love'

Chakra (SANSKRIT) 'Circle of energy' *(Chakara, Shakra)*

Champa (SANSKRIT) 'Flower' *(Champak)*

Chan (CAMBODIAN) 'Sweet-smelling tree'

Chandni (SANSKRIT) 'Moonlight'

Chandra (SANSKRIT) 'The moon which outshines the stars' *(Candra, Candre, Chandre)*

Chanel (OLD FRENCH) 'Wine jar'

Chantelle (FRENCH) 'Little singer' *(Chantal, Chantel)*

Chantesuta (NATIVE AMERICAN) 'Resolute'

Chantrea (CAMBODIAN) 'Moonbeam' *(Chantria)*

Chantrice (FRENCH) 'Singer'

Charis (GREEK) 'Grace'

Charity (LATIN) 'Benevolent and loving'. One who gives with generosity and affection *(Charissa, Charita, Charry, Cherry)*

Charlene *see* **Caroline**

Charlie *see* **Charlotte**

Charlotte (TEUTONIC) A form of **Caroline** *(Carla, Carlie, Carly, Carlotta, Charlie,*
Charlotta, Charmian, Charo, Charyl, Cheryl, Sharleen, Sherry, Sheryl and all the variations of *Caroline)*

Charma (GREEK) 'Delight'

Charmaine (LATIN) 'Little song' *(Carmen, Charmain, Charmian) see also* **Carmen**

Charmian *see* **Charlotte** or **Charmaine**

Charmian (GREEK) 'Little joy'

Charyl *see* **Charlotte**

Chastity (LATIN) 'Purity'

Chatura (SANSKRIT) 'Clever one'

Chaya (HEBREW) 'Life-giving' *(Chayra)*

Chelsea (OLD ENGLISH) 'A port of ships' *(Chelsey, Chelsy, Cheslie, Kelsie)*

Chenoa (NATIVE AMERICAN) 'White bird'

Cher (FRENCH) 'Beloved', 'dearest' *(Chere, Sher)*

Cherie (FRENCH) 'Dear, beloved one'. A term of endearment *(Cheri, Cherida, Cherry, Cheryl, Sherrie, Sherry, Sheryl)*

Cherise (OLD FRENCH) 'Cherry-like'

Cherish (ENGLISH) 'Precious'

Cheron (FRENCH) 'Beloved' *(Caron)*

Cherry *see* **Charity** or **Cherie**

Cheryl *see* **Charlotte** or **Cherie**

Chesna (SLAVIC) 'Peaceful'

Cheyenne (AMERICAN) Tribal name

Chiara (ITALIAN) 'Famous, light'

Chika (JAPANESE) 'Near', 'thousand rejoicings'

Chilali (NATIVE AMERICAN) 'Snow bird'

Chimalis (NATIVE AMERICAN) 'Blue bird'

Chinika (SWAHILI) 'God receives'

Chiquita (SPANISH) 'Little one'. A term of endearment for a small girl

Chispa (SPANISH) 'Spark from a fire'

Chitsa (NATIVE AMERICAN) 'Beautiful one'

Chlarimonde *see* **Clarimond**

Chloe (GREEK) 'Fresh young blossom'. The Greek goddess of unripened grain *(Chlöe, Cloe, Kloe)*

Chlora (GREEK) 'Spring freshness'

Chloris (GREEK) 'Goddess of the flowers' *(Chloras, Chlores, Chlori, Loris) see also* **Clarice**

Cho (KOREAN) 'Beautiful' (JAPANESE) 'Butterfly'

Cholena (NATIVE AMERICAN) 'Bird'

Chris *see* **Christine**

Chrissie *see* **Christine**

Christabel (LATIN) 'Beautiful bright-faced Christian' *(Christabella, Christabelle, Kristabel, Kristabella, Kristabelle)*

Christalle *see* **Crystal**

Christanta (COLOMBIAN) 'A chrysanthemum'

Christian *see* **Christine**

Christine (FRENCH) 'Christian one' *(Cairistiona, Cairstine, Chris, Chrissie, Chrissy, Christan, Christian, Christiana, Christiane, Christina, Christye, Christyna, Chrystal, Cristina, Cristine, Crissie, Crissy, Cristen, Cristiona, Crystal, Kristen, Krystina, Tina)*

Chryseis (LATIN) 'Golden daughter'

Chrysilla (GREEK) 'One with golden hair'

Chrystal *see* **Christine** or **Crystal**

Chun (CHINESE) 'Springtime'

Cilla (FRENCH) 'The cilla flower' *see also* **Priscilla**

Cinderella (FRENCH) 'Girl of the ashes'. From the French fairy tale

Cindy *see* **Cinderella** or **Cynthia**

Cirilla *see* **Cyrilla**

Cissie *see* **Cecelia**

Claire *see* **Clara**

Clairine (LATIN) 'Bright girl'

Clanenda (LATIN) 'Becoming brighter'

Clara (LATIN) 'Bright, shining girl'. One of clear, outstanding beauty *(Claire, Clare, Clareta, Clarette, Clarine, Klara) see also* **Clarabella**

Clarabella (LATIN/FRENCH) 'Bright, shining beauty' *(Bella, Clara, Clarabelle)*

Claramae (ENGLISH) 'Brilliant beauty' *(Chlarinda, Chlorinda, Clarinda, Clorinda)*

Clare *see* **Clara**

Claresta (ENGLISH) 'The most shining one'. A woman to outshine all others *(Clarista)*

Claribel (LATIN) 'Fair and bright'

Clarice (FRENCH) 'Little, shining one'. French form of **Clara** *(Chlaris, Clariss, Clarissa, Clarisse) see also* **Chloris**

Clarimond (TEUTONIC) 'Brilliant protector' *(Chlarimonda, Chlarimonde, Clarimonda, Clarimonde)*

Clarissa *see* **Clarice**

Claudette see **Claudia**

Claudia (LATIN) 'The lame one'. Feminine of Claud (Claude, Claudell, Claudette, Claudie, Claudina, Claudine, Gladys)

Claudine see **Claudia**

Clea (LITERARY) A name perhaps coined by Lawrence Durrell in The Alexandria Quartet

Cleantha see **Cliantha**

Clearests (GREEK) 'Pinnacle of achievement'

Clematis (GREEK) 'Sweet wine'

Clemence (LATIN) 'Merciful and kind'. One who tempers justice with mercy (Clemency, Clementia, Clementina, Clementine)

Clementina see **Clemence**

Cleopatra (GREEK) 'Her father's glory'. A girl who will add lustre to her father's name (Cleo)

Cleophila (GREEK) 'Lover of glory'

Cleosa (GREEK) 'Famous'

Cleva (OLD ENGLISH) 'Cliff dweller'. Feminine of Clive

Cliantha (GREEK) 'Flower of glory' (Cleantha, Cleanthe, Clianthe)

Clianthe see **Cliantha**

Clio (GREEK) 'She who proclaims'. The Greek muse of history

Clodagh (IRISH) A river in Ireland

Cloe see **Chloe**

Clorinda (LATIN) 'Famed for her beauty' (Chlorinda, Chlorinde, Clarinda, Clarinde, Clorinde) see also **Claramae**

Clotilda (TEUTONIC) 'Famous battle maiden'. A warrior who fought alongside her father and brothers (Clothilda, Clothilde, Clotilde)

Clover (ENGLISH) 'Meadow blossom'. From the flower (Clovie)

Clydia (GREEK) 'Glorious' Clydina

Clymene (GREEK) 'Fame and renown'

Clytie (GREEK) 'Splendid daughter'. The mythical nymph who was turned into a heliotrope, so that she could worship the sun

Cocheta (NATIVE AMERICAN) 'Unknown one'

Cody (OLD ENGLISH) 'A cushion'

Colette (LATIN) 'Victorious'. A form of Nicolette, a diminutive form of Nicole (Collete, Collette)

Coline see Colleen or Columba

Colinette (LATIN) 'Tiny dove'

Colleen (GAELIC) 'Girl'. The name given to a young girl in Ireland (Cailin, Coleen, Colene, Coline, Colline, Collete)

Columba (LATIN) 'The dove'. One of a peaceful disposition (Coline, Colly, Colombe, Columbia, Columbine)

Columbine see Columba

Comfort (FRENCH) 'One who gives comfort'. One of the virtue names popular with English and American Puritan families

Con see Constance

Conception (LATIN) 'Beginning' (Concepcion, Conceptia, Concha, Conchita)

Concessa (LATIN) 'One who grants a favour'

Concetta (ITALIAN) 'An ingenious thought'

Concordia (LATIN) 'Harmony and peace' (Concordie, Concordina, Concordy)

Connal (LATIN) 'Faithful one'

Connie see Conradine, Constance or Consuela

Conradine (TEUTONIC) 'Bold and wise'. Feminine of Conrad (Connie, Conrada, Conradina)

Consolata (LATIN) 'One who consoles' (Consolation)

Constance (LATIN) 'Constant'. One who is firm and unchanging (Con, Connie, Constancy, Constanta, Constantia, Constantina, Constantine, Constanze)

Consuela (SPANISH) 'Consolation'. A friend in need (Connie, Consuelo)

Cora (GREEK) 'The maiden'. From Kore, the daugher of the Greek goddess Demeter *(Corella, Corett, Coretta, Corette, Corin, Corina, Corinna, Corinne, Correna, Coretta, Corie, Corin, Corina, Corrie, Corrina, Corrine)*

Corabella (COMBINATION CORA/ BELLA) 'Beautiful maiden' *(Corabelle)*

Coral (LATIN) 'Sincere', 'from the sea' *(Corale, Coralie, Coraline)*

Coraline *see* **Coral**

Corazon (SPANISH) 'Heart'

Cordana (TEUTONIC) 'Harmony'

Cordelia (WELSH) 'Jewel of the sea'. The daughter of Lear, the sea king *(Cordelie, Cordie, Cordula, Delia)*

Cordie *see* **Cordelia**

Corella *see* **Cora**

Corette *see* **Cora**

Corinna *see* **Cora**

Corey (GAELIC) 'From the hollow'

Corissa (LATIN/GREEK) 'Most modest maiden' *(Corisse)*

Corla (OLD ENGLISH) 'Curlew'

Corliss (ENGLISH) 'Cheerful and kind-hearted' *(Carliss, Carlissa, Corlissa)*

Cornelia (LATIN) 'Womanly virtue' *(Cornela, Cornelie, Cornelle, Cornie, Nela, Nelie, Nelli)*

Cornelle *see* **Cornelia**

Corolla (LATIN) 'Tiny crown'

Corona (SPANISH) 'Crowned maiden' *(Coronie)*

Correna *see* **Cora**

Cosette (FRENCH) 'Victorious army' *(Cosetta)*

Cosina (GREEK) 'World harmony' *(Cosima)*

Cottins (GREEK) 'Crown of wild flowers'

Coulava (CELTIC) 'One with soft hands'

Courtney (OLD ENGLISH) 'From the court' *(Courtenay)*

Coyetta (TEUTONIC) 'Caged'

Coyne (FRENCH) 'Modest'

Crescent (FRENCH) 'The creative one'

Cressida (GREEK) 'The golden one' *(Cresseide)*

Crisiant (WELSH) 'Crystal'

Crispina (LATIN) 'Curly haired'. Feminine of Crispin *(Crispine)*

Cristen *see* **Christine**

Crystal (LATIN) 'Clear' *(Christalle, Cristal, Chrystal, Krystal) see also* **Christine**

Cybil *see* **Sybil**

Cynara (GREEK) 'Artichoke'. A beautiful maiden, protected by thorns

Cynthia (GREEK) 'Moon goddess'. Another name for Diana, Goddess of the Moon, born on Cynthos *(Cindy, Cyn, Cynth, Cynthie)*

Cypris (GREEK) 'Born in Cyprus' *(Cipressa, Cypress, Cypressa)*

Cyra (PERSIAN) 'The Sun God'

Cyrena (GREEK) 'From Cyrene'. A water nymph loved by Apollo, the sun god *(Cyrenia, Kyrena, Kyrenia)*

Cyrene (GREEK) 'River nymph'

Cyrenia *see* **Cyrena**

Cyrilla (LATIN) 'Lordly one'. Feminine of Cyril *(Cirila, Cirilla)*

Cytherea (GREEK) 'From Cythera'. Another name for Aphrodite, goddess of love *(Cytherere, Cytheria, Cytherine)*

D

GIRLS

Dacey (GAELIC) 'Southerner'

Dacia (GREEK) 'From Dacia'

Daffodil (GREEK) 'Golden spring flower'

Dagania (HEBREW) 'Ceremonial grain' *(Daganya)*

Dagmar (NORSE) 'Glory of the Danes'

Dahlia (GREEK) 'Of the valley'. From the flower of the same name

Dai (JAPANESE) 'Great'

Daina (TEUTONIC) 'Disdainful'

Daisy (ANGLO-SAXON) 'The day's eye'. Also a nickname for **Margaret** from Marguerite, French for the daisy flower

Dakapaki (NATIVE AMERICAN) 'Blossom'

Dakota (AMERICAN) 'Friend, partner'. Tribal name

Dale (TEUTONIC) 'From the valley'. An earlier form of **Dahlia** *(Dael, Daile)*

Dallas (GAELIC) 'Wise'

Dalta (GAELIC) 'Favourite child'

Damara (GREEK) 'Gentle girl' *(Damaris, Mara, Maris)*

Damasa (FRENCH) 'Maiden'

Damia (GREEK) 'Goddess of forces of nature'

Damiana (GREEK) 'Soothing one'. Feminine of Damian *(Damiann, Damianna, Damianne)*

Damica (FRENCH) 'Friendly' *(Damika)*

Damika *see* **Damica**

Damita (SPANISH) 'Little noble lady'

Dana (SCANDINAVIAN) 'From Denmark' *(Dayna)*

Danae (GREEK) Mother of Perseus

Danica (NORSE) 'The morning star' *(Danika)*

Danielle (HEBREW) 'God is my judge'. Feminine of Daniel *(Danella, Danelle, Danice, Daniela, Danielea, Danila, Danita, Danya, Danyelle)*

Danuta (POLISH) 'Young deer'

Daphne (GREEK) 'Bay tree'. Symbol of victory. The nymph who was turned into a laurel bush to escape the attentions of Apollo

Dara (HEBREW) 'Charity, compassion and wisdom' *(Darya)*

Daraka (SANSKRIT) 'Gentle and shy'

Daralis (OLD ENGLISH) 'Beloved'

Darcie (FRENCH) 'From the fortress'. Feminine of D'Arcy *(D'Arcie)*

Darcy (CELTIC) 'Girl with dark hair' *(Darcia, Dercia, Dercy)*

Darea *see* **Darlene**

Dareece *see* **Darice**

Darel (ANGLO-SAXON) 'Little dear one'. Another form of **Darlene** *(Darelle, Darrelle, Darry, Daryl)*

Daria (PERSIAN) 'Wealthy queen'. Feminine of Darius

Darice (PERSIAN) 'Queenly' *(Dareece, Darees)*

Darlene (ANGLO-SAXON) 'Little darling' *(Darea, Dareen, Darel, Darleen, Darline, Daryl)*

Daron (GAELIC) 'Great'

Darya *see* **Dara**

Dasha (RUSSIAN) 'Gift of God'

Davina (HEBREW) 'Beloved'. Feminine of David *(Daveen, Davida, Davita)*

Davita *see* **Davina**

Dawn (ANGLO-SAXON) 'The break of day'. One who lightens the darkness

Dea (LATIN) 'Goddess'

Deanna *see* **Diana**

Debbie *see* **Deborah**

Deborah (HEBREW) 'The bee'. An industrious woman who looks only for what is sweet in life *(Debbie, Debby, Debor, Debora, Debra, Debs, Devora)*

Decima (LATIN) 'Tenth daughter', 'dark beauty' *see also* **Diana**

Dee (WELSH) 'Black, dark'

Deiphila (GREEK) 'Divine love'

Deirdre (GAELIC) 'Sorrow'. A legendary Irish beauty *(Deerdre, Deidre)*

Deja (FRENCH) 'Before'

Delfine (GREEK) 'The larkspur or delphinium flower' *(Delfina, Delphina, Delphine, Delveen)*

Delia (GREEK) 'Visible'. Another name for the moon goddess *see also* **Bedelia** or **Cordelia**

Delicia (LATIN) 'Delightful maiden', 'spirit of delight'

Delie (FRENCH) 'Slim and delicate'

Delight (FRENCH) 'Pleasure'. One who brings happiness to her family

Delilah (HEBREW) 'The gentle temptress'. The woman who betrayed the Biblical Samson *(Dalila, Delila, Lila)*

Delinda (TEUTONIC) 'Gentle'

Delizea (LATIN) 'Delight'

Delma (SPANISH) 'Of the sea' *(Delmar, Delmare)*

Delora (LATIN) 'From the seashore'

Delores *see* **Dolores**

Delorita *see* **Dolores**

Delphine (GREEK) 'Calmness and serenity' *see also* **Delfine**

Delta (GREEK) 'Fourth daughter'. The fourth letter of the Greek alphabet

Delveen *see* **Delfine**

Delwen (WELSH) 'Neat, fair'

Delyth (WELSH) 'Neat, pretty'

Demelza (ENGLISH) 'Hill-fort'

Demetria (GREEK) 'Fertility'. The Greek goddess of fertility *(Demi, Demeter)*

Demi *see* **Demetria**

Dena (ANGLO-SAXON) 'From the valley' *(Deana, Deane) see also* **Adina**

Denaneer (ARABIC) 'Piece of gold'

Denise (FRENCH) 'Wine goddess'. Feminine of Dionysus, god of wine *(Denice, Denny, Denys)*

Dercia *see* **Darcy**

Derede (GREEK) 'Gift of God'

Derika (TEUTONIC) 'Ruler of the people'

Derora (HEBREW) 'Brook'

Derry (IRISH) 'Red-haired girl'

Derryth (WELSH) 'Of the oak'

Dervia (OLD IRISH) 'Daughter of the poet'

Desdemona (GREEK) 'One born under an unlucky star'. After the heroine of Shakespeare's *Othello (Desmona)*

Desiree (FRENCH) 'Desired one'

Desma (GREEK) 'A pledge'

Desta *see* **Modesty**

Destinee (OLD FRENCH) 'Destiny'

Destiny (FRENCH) 'Fate'

Deva (SANSKRIT) 'Divine'. The moon goddess

Devi (HINDU) Name of a Hindu goddess

Devin (GAELIC) 'Poet'

Devnet (CELTIC) 'White wave'

Devona (TEUTONIC) 'Brave girl' (ENGLISH) 'From Devon'. Someone born in the English country of Devon, the name of which means 'people of the deep valley' *(Devondra)*

Dextra (LATIN) 'Skilful, adept'

Di *see* **Diana**

Diadema (GREEK) 'Jewel'

Diamanta (FRENCH) 'Diamond-like'. One who is as precious as the rarest jewel

Diamond (LATIN) 'Precious jewel'

Diana (LATIN) 'Divine moon goddess'. Roman goddess of the moon and of hunting *(Deanna, Dee, Decima, Di, Diahann, Dian, Diandra, Diane, Dianna, Dianne, Dyana, Dyane, Dyanna)*

Diane *see* **Diana**

Diantha (GREEK) 'Divine flower of Zeus' *(Dianthe, Dianthia)*

Diaphenia (GREEK) 'Shedding light'

Dicentra (GREEK) 'Flower'. Flower commonly known as bleeding heart

Dicky *see* **Ricarda**

Didi (HEBREW) 'Beloved'

Didiane (FRENCH) Feminine of Didier *(Didière)*

Dido (GREEK) 'Teacher'

Diella (LATIN) 'One who worships God'

Dilys (WELSH) 'Perfect'

Dimphia *see* **Dymphia**

Dinah (HEBREW) 'Judgement'. One whose understanding is complete

Dione (GREEK) 'The daughter of heaven and earth' *(Dionia, Dionne)*

Dior (FRENCH) 'Golden'

Disa (GREEK) 'Double' (NORSE) 'Lively spirit'

Divya (HINDI) 'Divine, heavenly' *(Divia)*

Dixie (FRENCH) 'The tenth' *(Dixey, Dixil, Dixy) see also* **Benedicta**

Dixil *see* **Dixie**

Docie *see* **Endocia**

Docila (LATIN) 'Gentle teacher'

Dodi *see* **Doris**

Dodie (HEBREW) 'Beloved'

Dolly *see* **Dolores** or **Dorothy**

Dolores (SPANISH) 'Lady of sorrow' *(Delora, Delores, Deloris, Delorita, Dolly, Doloritas, Lola, Lolita)*

Domina (LATIN) 'The lady'. One of noble birth

Dominica (LATIN) 'Child born on a Sunday', 'belonging to the Lord'. Feminine of Dominic *(Domenica, Domeniga, Dominga, Domini, Dominique)*

Dominique *see* **Dominica**

Donabella (SPANISH) 'Beautiful woman'

Donalda (GAELIC) 'Ruler of the world'. Feminine of Donald

Donata (LATIN) 'The gift'

Donella (SPANISH) 'Little girl'

Donna (ITALIAN) 'Noble lady' *(Dona)*

Dora *see* **Doreen, Doris, Dorothy, Eudora, Isadora** or **Theodora**

Dorcas (GREEK) 'Graceful'. One with the grace of a gazelle

Dore (FRENCH) 'Golden maiden' *see also* **Dorothy**

Dorea (GREEK) 'Gift'

Doreen (GAELIC) 'Golden girl' or 'the sullen one' *(Dora, Dorene, Dori, Dorie, Dori, Dorie, Dorine, Dory)*

Doretta *see* **Doreen**

Dorhissa (HEBREW) 'Gift of the promise'

Dori *see* **Doreen** or **Isadora**

Dorianne (GREEK) 'From Doria'

Dorice *see* **Doris**

Dorinda (GREEK/SPANISH) 'Beautiful golden gift'

Doris (GREEK) 'From the sea'. The daughter of Oceanus *(Dodi, Dora, Dorice, Dorise, Dorita, Dorris)*

Dorleta (BASQUE) Name for the Virgin Mary

Dorothy (GREEK) 'Gift of God' *(Deel, Dolley, Dollie, Dolly, Dora, Dore, Doretta, Dorothea, Dorothi, Dorothoe, Dorthea, Dot, Theodora) see also* **Theodora**

Dorymene (GREEK) 'Brave, courageous'

Dot *see* **Dorothy**

Douce (FRENCH) 'Sweet'

Douna (SLAVIC) 'Valley'

Dove (ENGLISH) 'Bird of peace'

Doxie *see* **Endocia**

Drew (GREEK) 'Courageous'

Dromicia (GREEK) 'Fast'

Druella (TEUTONIC) 'Elfin vision' *(Druilla)*

Drusilla (LATIN) 'The strong one'. One with patience and fortitude

Duana (GAELIC) 'Little dark maiden' *(Duna, Dwana)*

Duena (SPANISH) 'Chaperone'. Women of good birth who were responsible for the manners of young girls in their charge *(Duenna)*

Dulcibella *see* **Dulcie**

Dulcie (LATIN) 'Sweet and charming'. One who believes that love is the sweetest thing *(Delcine, Dulce, Dulcea, Dulciana, Dulcibella, Dulcibelle, Dulcine, Dulcinea)*

Durene (LATIN) 'Enduring one'

Duretta (SPANISH) 'Little reliable one'

Durga (HINDI) Mythological figure, wife of Siva

Duscha (RUSSIAN) 'Soul'

Dyani (NATIVE AMERICAN) 'Deer'

Dymphia (LATIN) 'Nurse' *(Dimphia, Dympha)*

Dympna (IRISH) 'Eligible' *(Dymphna)*

Dyna (GREEK) 'Powerful'

Dyota (SANSKRIT) 'Sunshine'

Dysis (GREEK) 'Sunset'

Eada *see* **Alda** or **Eda**

Eadith *see* **Edith**

Eadrea *see* **Edrea**

Eadwina *see* **Edwina**

Eady see Edith

Earlene (ANGLO-SAXON) 'Noble woman'. Feminine of Earl *(Earley, Earlie, Earline, Erlene, Erline)*

Eartha (OLD ENGLISH) 'Of the earth' *(Erda, Ertha, Herta, Hertha)*

Easter (OLD ENGLISH) 'Born at Easter'. Derivation of Eostre, the pre-Christian goddess of spring *see also* **Eostre**

Ebba (ANGLO-SAXON) Form of **Eve**

Eberta (TEUTONIC) 'Brilliant'

Ebony (GREEK) 'A hard, dark wood'

Echo (GREEK) 'Repeating sound'. A Greek nymph who pined away for love

Eda (ANGLO-SAXON) 'Poetry' (GREEK) 'Loving mother of many', 'prosperous' *(Eada, Edda) see also* **Edith**

Edana (GAELIC) 'Little fiery one'. A warmly loving child whose ardent nature is said to have been given by God *(Aidan, Aiden, Eidann)*

Edelina *see* **Adelaide**

Eden (HEBREW) 'Enchanting'. The epitome of all female charm

Edia (TEUTONIC) 'Rich friend'

Edina (SCOTTISH) Another form of **Edwina**

Edith (TEUTONIC) 'Rich gift' *(Eadie, Eadith, Eaidie, Eady, Eda, Edythe, Ede, Edie, Editha, Edithe, Ediva, Edythe)*

Ediva *see* **Edith**

Edla (TEUTONIC) 'Woman of noble birth'

Edlyn (ANGLO-SAXON) 'Noble maiden'

Edmee (ANGLO-SAXON) 'Fortunate protector'

Edmonda (ANGLO-SAXON) 'Rich protector'. Feminine of Edmund *(Edmunda)*

Edna (HEBREW) 'Rejuvenation'. One who knows the secret of eternal youth *(Ed, Eddie, Edny)*

Edra (HEBREW) 'Mighty'

Edrea (ANGLO-SAXON) 'Powerful and prosperous'. Feminine of Edric *(Eadrea) see also* **Andrea**

Edwardina (ANGLO-SAXON) 'Rich guardian'. Feminine of Edward

Edwina (ANGLO-SAXON) 'Rich friend' *(Eadwina, Eadwine, Edina, Edwine, Win, Wina, Winnie)*

Edythe *see* **Edith**

Effie (GREEK) 'Famous beauty'

Effy *see* **Euphemia**

Efrat (HEBREW) 'Honoured' *(Efrata)*

Egberta (ANGLO-SAXON) 'Bright, shining sword'. Feminine of Egbert *(Egberte, Egbertha, Egberthe, Egbertina, Egbertine)*

Eglantine (FRENCH) 'The wild rose' *(Eglantina, Eglintyne, Eglyntine)*

Eiblin (GAELIC) 'Pleasant' *(Eveleen)*

Eidann *see* **Edana**

Eileen *see* **Aileen** or **Helen**

Eilien (GREEK) 'Light'

Eilwen (WELSH) 'Fair brow'

Eir (NORSE) 'Peace and mercy'. The goddess of healing

Eirene *see* **Irene**

Eirian (WELSH) 'Silver'

Eiric *see* **Henrietta**

Eirlys (WELSH) 'Snowdrop'

Eirwen (WELSH) 'Snow-white'

Ekata (SANSKRIT) 'Unity'

Ekaterina *see* **Catherine**

Elaine (FRENCH) French form of **Helen** *(Lainey) see also* **Helen**

Elama (GREEK) 'From the mountains'

Elana (HEBREW) 'Oak tree'

Elane *see* **Helen**

Elata (LATIN) 'Lofty, noble'. A woman of high birth and beauty

Elberta (TEUTONIC) 'Brilliant' *see also* **Alberta**

Elbertine *see* **Alberta**

Elda (ANGLO-SAXON) 'Princess' *see also* **Alda**

Eldora (SPANISH) 'Gilded one'. From El Dorado, the land of gold

Eldreda (ANGLO-SAXON) 'Wise companion' *(Eldrida)*

Eldrida (TEUTONIC) 'Old and wise adviser'. Feminine of Eldred *(Aeldrida) see also* **Eldreda**

Eleanor (FRENCH) A medieval form of **Helen** *(Eleanora, Eleanore, Elinor, Elinora, Elinore, Eleonor, Eleonora, Eleonore, Ellie, Lenora, Leonora, Nora)*

Electra (GREEK) 'Brilliant one'

Elefteria (GREEK) 'Freedom'

Eleta (SPANISH) 'Astonished'

Eleuneria (GREEK) Daughter of Jupiter and Juno

Elfrida *see* **Alfreda**

Elga (SLAV) 'Consecrated' *(Olga) see also* **Alfreda**

Elicia *see* **Elysia**

Elinel (CELTIC) 'Shapely'

Eliora (HEBREW) 'God is my light' *(Eleora)*

Elisa *see* Alice or Elizabeth

Elisabeth *see* Elizabeth

Elise *see* Elizabeth or Elysia

Elita (OLD FRENCH) 'Chosen' *see also* Melita

Eliza *see* Elizabeth

Elizabeth (HEBREW) 'Consecrated to God' *(Bess, Bessie, Bessy, Beth, Betina, Betsy, Betta, Bette, Betty, Elisa, Elisabeth, Elise, Elissa, Eliza, Ellissa, Eloise, Elsa, Elsbeth, Else, Elsie, Elspeth, Elysa, Elyse, Helsa, Ilse, Libb, Libby, Lisa, Lisbeth, Liza, Lizabeta, Lizbeth, Lizzy) see also* Elsa or Isabel

Elkana (HEBREW) 'God has acquired'

Ella (TEUTONIC) 'Beautiful fairy maiden'. Beauty bestowed by fairies as a birth gift *see also* Cinderella and Helen

Ellen *see* Helen

Ellenis (GREEK) 'Priestess'

Ellice (GREEK) 'Jehovah is God'. Feminine of Elias *(Ellis)*

Ellie *see* Eleanor

Ellora (GREEK) 'Happy one'

Ellyn *see* Helen

Elma (GREEK) 'Pleasant and amiable'

Elmina (OLD GERMAN) 'Awe-inspiring fame'

Elmira *see* Almira

Elna *see* Helen

Elodie (GREEK) 'Fragile flower'

Eloine (LATIN) 'Worthy to be chosen'

Eloise (FRENCH) 'Noble one' *see also* Louise or Elizabeth

Elora (GREEK) 'Light'

Elrica *see* Ulrica

Elsa (OLD GERMAN) 'Noble' *see also* Elizabeth

Elsbeth *see* Elizabeth

Else *see* Elizabeth

Elsie *see* Elizabeth

Elspeth *see* Elizabeth

Elswyth (OLD ENGLISH) 'Noble strength'

Eluned (WELSH) 'Idol'

Elva (ANGLO-SAXON) 'Friend of the elves' *(Elfie, Elvia, Elvie, Ivina)* see also **Alfreda**

Elvina (TEUTONIC) 'Wise and friendly'

Elvira (LATIN) 'White woman' *(Albinia, Alinia, Elvera, Elvire, Elwira)*

Elvita (LATIN) 'Life'

Elwy (WELSH) 'Benefit'

Elwyn (WELSH) 'One with brown hair'

Elyse see **Elizabeth**

Elysia (LATIN) 'Blissful sweetness'. From Elysium *(Elicia, Elise)*

Emanuela (HEBREW) 'God is with you'

Embla (SCANDINAVIAN) The first woman in Norse mythology

Emeline see **Amelia** or **Emma**

Emer (IRISH) 'Gifted'

Emerald (FRENCH) 'The bright green jewel' *(Emerande, Emerant, Eneraude, Esme, Esmeralda, Esmeralde)*

Emily (TEUTONIC) 'Hard-working'

Emina (LATIN) 'Highly born maiden'. Daughter of a noble house

Emma (TEUTONIC) 'One who heals the universe'. A woman of command *(Ema, Emelina, Emeline, Emmeline)*

Emmanuela (HEBREW) 'God with us'

Emmeranne (FRENCH/OLD GERMAN) 'Raven'

Emogene see **Imogen**

Emrys (CELTIC) 'Immortal' *(Emryss)*

Ena (GAELIC) 'Little ardent one' see also **Eugenia**

Enda (SANSKRIT) 'The last one'

Endocia (GREEK) 'Of spotless reputation' *(Docie, Doxie, Doxy, Eudoxia)* see also **Eudosia**

Endora (FRENCH/OLD GERMAN) 'Noble'

Enfys (WELSH) 'Rainbow'

Engacia see **Grace**

Engelberta (TEUTONIC) 'Bright angel'. One of the bright defenders of legend *(Engelberga, Engelbert, Engelbertha, Engelberthe)*

Engracia (SPANISH) 'Graceful' *see also* **Grace**

Enid (CELTIC) 'Purity of the soul'

Ennata (FRENCH/GREEK) 'Goddess'

Enona (GREEK) Nymph of Mount Ida, who married Paris

Enone (GREEK) 'Flower in the hedgerow'

Enora (FRENCH/GREEK) 'Light'

Enrica (ITALIAN) Italian form of **Henrietta**

Enya (IRISH) 'Kernel'

Eostre (OLD ENGLISH) The pre-Christian goddess of spring *(Easter, Eastra)*

Ephratah (HEBREW) 'Fruitful'

Eranthe (GREEK) 'Flower of spring'

Erica (NORSE) 'Powerful ruler'. Symbol of royalty. Feminine of Eric *(Aric, Erika)*

Erin (GAELIC) 'From Ireland'. One born in the Emerald Isle *(Erina)*

Erlina (OLD ENGLISH) 'Little elf'

Erma (TEUTONIC) 'Army maid' *(Ermina, Erminia, Erminie, Hermia, Hermina, Hermione) see also* **Irma**

Erna (ANGLO-SAXON) 'Eagle'

Ernestine (ANGLO-SAXON) 'Purposeful one' *(Erna, Ernesta)*

Erwina (ANGLO-SAXON) 'Friend from the sea'

Esha (SANSKRIT) 'One who desires' *(Eshita)*

Esme *see* **Emerald**

Esmeralda *see* **Emerald**

Essylt (WELSH) 'Beautiful to behold'

Esta (ITALIAN) 'From the East'

Estaphania (GREEK) 'Crown'

Estelle (FRENCH) 'Bright star' *(Estella, Estrelita, Estrella, Stella, Stelle)*

Esther (HEBREW) 'The star' *(Eister, Essa, Etty, Hessy, Hester, Hesther, Hetty)*

Estra (ANGLO-SAXON) Goddess of spring

Estrella *see* **Estelle**

Eswen (WELSH) 'Strong one'

Etain (IRISH) 'Shining'

Ethel (TEUTONIC) 'Noble maiden'. The daughter of a princely house *(Ethelda, Etheline, Ethyl, Ethylyn) see also* **Ethelinda**

Ethelinda (TEUTONIC) 'Noble serpent'. The symbol of immortality *see also* **Ethel**

Etoile (FRENCH) 'Star'

Etsu (JAPANESE) 'Delight'

Etta *see* **Henrietta**

Euclea (GREEK) 'Glory'

Eudine (FRENCH/OLD GERMAN) 'Noble'

Eudora (GREEK) 'Generous gift' *(Dora, Eudore)*

Eudosia (GREEK) 'Esteemed' *(Eudocia) see also* **Endocia**

Eugenia (GREEK) 'Well born'. A woman of noble family *(Ena, Eugenie, Gena, Gene, Genie, Gina)*

Eulalia (GREEK) 'Fair spoken one' *(Eula, Eulalie, Lallie)*

Eunice (GREEK) 'Happy and victorious'

Euphemia (GREEK) 'Of good reputation' *(Effie, Effy, Euphemie, Phemie)*

Euphrasia (GREEK) 'Delight'

Eurielle (CELTIC/FRENCH) 'Angel'

Eurwen (WELSH) 'Fair and golden'

Eurydice (GREEK) 'Broad'

Eustacia (LATIN) 'Tranquil maiden', 'fruitful' *(Eustacie, Stacey, Stacie, Stacy)*

Eva *see* **Eve**

Evadne (GREEK) 'Fortunate'

Evangelina *see* **Evangeline**

Evangeline (GREEK) 'Bearer of glad tidings' *(Eva, Evangelina, Vancy, Vangie)*

Evania (GREEK) 'Tranquil, untroubled' *(Evanne)*

Evanthe (GREEK) 'Lovely flower'

Eve (HEBREW) 'Life-giver' *(Ebba, Eva, Eveleen, Evelina, Eveline, Evelyn, Evie, Evita, Evonne)*

Evelyn *see* **Eve**

Everilde (FRENCH FROM OLD GERMAN) 'Honour in battle'

Evette *see* **Yvonne**

Evita *see* **Eve** or **Vita**

Evodie (GREEK) 'One who follows the right path'

Evonne *see* **Eve** or **Yvonne**

Ezara (HEBREW) 'Little treasure'

Fabia (LATIN) 'Bean-grower' *(Fabiana, Fabianna, Fabienne)*

Fabienne *see* **Fabia**

Fabiola (LATIN) 'Woman who does good works'

Fabrianne (LATIN) 'Girl of resourcefulness' *(Fabrianna, Fabrienne, Frabriane)*

Fadilla *see* **Frances**

Faida (ARABIC) 'Abundant'

Faine (OLD ENGLISH) 'Joyful'

Faith (TEUTONIC) 'Trust in God'. One who is loyal and true *(Fae, Fay, Faye)*

Faline (LATIN) 'Cat-like'

Fallon (GAELIC) 'Grandchild of the ruler'

Fanchon (FRENCH) 'Free being'

Fania (TEUTONIC) 'Free'

Fanny *see* **Frances**

Fanshom (TEUTONIC) 'Free'

Farha (SANSKRIT) 'Happiness' *(Farhad, Farhat)*

Farhanna (ARABIC) 'Joyful'

Farica (TEUTONIC) 'Peaceful rule' *see also* **Frederica**

Farida (ARABIC) 'Unique and precious gem'

Farideh (PERSIAN) 'Glorious'

Fariha (ARABIC) 'Happy'

Farrah (MIDDLE ENGLISH) 'Beautiful' *(Farah)*

Faten (ARABIC) 'Fascinating, charming'

Fathia (ARABIC) 'My conquest'

Fatima (ARABIC) 'Unknown'

Fausta (ITALIAN/SPANISH) 'Fortunate' *see also* **Faustine**

Faustine (LATIN) 'Lucky omen' *(Fausta, Faustina)*

Favor (FRENCH) 'The helpful one' *(Favora)*

Fawn (FRENCH) 'Young deer'. A lithe, swift-footed girl *(Faun, Faunia, Fawnia)*

Fay (IRISH) 'A raven' (FRENCH) 'A fairy'. A fairy-like person *(Fae, Faye, Fayette, Fayina)* *see also* **Faith**

Fayme (FRENCH) 'Of high reputation'. Beyond reproach

Fayola (NIGERIAN) 'Lucky'

Fayre (OLD ENGLISH) 'Beautiful'

Fe (SPANISH) 'Faith'

Fealty (FRENCH) 'Faithful one'. One who is loyal to God, sovereign, country and friend

Felda (TEUTONIC) 'From the field'. For one born at harvest time

Felicia (LATIN) 'Joyous one'. Feminine of Felix *(Felice, Felicidad, Felicie, Felicity, Felis, Felise, Feliza)*

Felipa (GREEK) 'One who loves horses'

Felita (LATIN) 'Happy little one'

Fenella (GAELIC) 'White-shouldered' *(Finella, Fionnula)*

Feodora *see* **Theodora**

Feride (TURKISH) 'Unique'

Feriga (ITALIAN/TEUTONIC) 'Peaceful ruler'

Fern (ANGLO-SAXON) 'Fern-like'

Fernanda (TEUTONIC) 'Adventurous'. One who is daring and courageous *(Ferdinanda, Fernandina)*

Feronia (LATIN) A goddess of the forests

Ffion (WELSH) 'Foxglove flower'

Fidela (LATIN) 'Faithful one' *(Fidele, Fidelia, Fidelity)*

Fifi *see* **Josephine**

Filana *see* **Philana**

Filantha *see* **Philantha**

Filberta *see* **Philberta**

Filida *see* **Phyllis**

Filma (ANGLO-SAXON) 'Misty veil'. An ethereal type of beauty *(Philmen, Pholma)*

Finette (HEBREW) 'Little addition'

Fingal (CELTIC) 'Beautiful stranger'

Finley (GAELIC) 'Sunbeam'

Finna (CELTIC) 'White'

Fiona (GAELIC) 'Fair one' *(Fionn, Fionna)*

Fionnula *see* **Fenella**

Fiore *see* **Florence**

Firoenza *see* **Florence**

Flanna (GAELIC) 'Red-haired'

Flavia (LATIN) 'Yellow-haired'

Fleta (ANGLO-SAXON) 'The swift one' *(Fleda)*

Fleur (FRENCH) 'A flower'. The French version of **Florence** *(Fleurette)*

Fleurdelice (FRENCH) 'Iris', 'lily'

Flora *see* **Florence**

Florence (LATIN) 'A flower' *(Fiora, Firoenza, Fleur, Flo, Flor, Flora, Florance, Flore, Florella, Florencia, Florentia, Florenza, Floria, Florinda, Florine, Floris, Florrie, Florry, Flossie, Flower)*

Florette (FRENCH) 'Little flower' *(Floretta)*

Florida (LATIN) 'Flowery'

Florimel (GREEK) 'Flower honey'

Floris *see* **Florence**

Flossie *see* **Florence**

Flower (ENGLISH) The English version of **Florence**

Fonda (ENGLISH) 'Affectionate'

Fontanna (FRENCH) 'Fountain'

Fortune (LATIN) 'Fate'. The woman of destiny *(Fortuna)*

Fossetta (FRENCH) 'Dimpled'

Fran *see* **Frances**

Frances (LATIN) 'Free' or 'girl from France' *(Fadilla, Fan, Fanchon, Fanny, Fran, Francesca, Francine, Francisca, Franciska, Françoise, Frankie, Frannie, Franny)*

Francesca *see* **Frances**

Francine *see* **Frances**

Françoise *see* **Frances**

Frankie *see* **Frances**

Freda (TEUTONIC) 'Peace'. One who is calm and unflurried *(Freddie, Freida, Frida, Frieda, Friedie)* see also **Alfreda**, **Halfrida** or **Wilfreda**

Frederica (TEUTONIC) 'Peaceful ruler' *(Farica, Freddie, Freddy, Fredericka, Frederika, Frederique, Frerika, Frerike, Friederik)*

Fredicia (TEUTONIC) 'Peaceful leader'

Freida *see* **Freda** or **Halfrida**

Fresa (TEUTONIC) 'One with curly hair'

Freya (NORSE) 'Noble goddess of love'. The Norse goddess of love

Fritzi *see* **Frederica**

Frodine (TEUTONIC) 'Wise companion'

Frodis *see* **Fronde**

Froma (TEUTONIC) 'Holy one'

Fronde (LATIN) 'Leaf of the fern' *(Frodis, Frond)*

Fulca (LATIN) 'Accomplished'

Fulvia (LATIN) 'Golden girl'. The daughter born at high summer

Gabinia (LATIN) Famous Roman family. City in central Italy

Gabrielle (HEBREW) 'Woman of God'. The bringer of good news *(Gabbie, Gabriel, Gabriela, Gabriele, Gabriella, Gabrila, Gaby, Gavrielle)*

Gabrila *see* **Gabrielle**

Gaea (GREEK) 'The earth'. The Goddess of the Earth *(Gaia)*

Gael *see* **Abigail**

Gaerwen (WELSH) 'White castle'

Gail *see* **Abigail**

Galane (FRENCH) 'Flower name' *(Galliane)*

Galatea (GREEK) 'Milky white'

Galia (HEBREW) 'God has redeemed'

Galiena (TEUTONIC) 'Lofty maiden'. A tall, statuesque girl *(Galiana)*

Galilah (HEBREW) Place name in Galiliee

Galina *see* **Helen**

Garda *see* **Gerda**

Gardenia (LATIN) 'White, fragrant flower'

Garland (FRENCH) 'Crown of blossoms'

Garlanda (LATIN) 'Decorated with flowers'

Garnet (ENGLISH) 'Deep-red-haired beauty' *(Garnette)*

Gaviota (SPANISH) 'Seagull'

Gavra (HEBREW) 'God is my rock'

Gavrila (HEBREW) 'Heroine'

Gay (FRENCH) 'Lively' *(Gai, Gaye)*

Gayle *see* **Abigail**

Gaynor *see* **Genevieve** or **Guinevere**

Gazella (LATIN) 'The antelope'. One who is graceful and modest

Gedalia (HEBREW) 'God is great'

Geena (SANSKRIT) 'Silvery'

Geeta (SANSKRIT) The holy book of advice from Lord Krishna to Arjuna

Gelasia (GREEK) 'Laughing water'. One who is like a fresh and gurgling stream *(Gelasie)*

Gemini (GREEK) 'Twin'

Gemma *(Latin)* 'Precious stone' *(Gemmel)*

Gena *see* **Eugenia**

Genesia (LATIN) 'Newcomer' *(Genesa, Genisia, Jenesia)*

Geneva (FRENCH) 'Juniper tree' *(Genevre, Genvra, Ginerva) see also* **Genevieve** and **Guinevere**

Genevieve (FRENCH) 'Pure white wave' *(Gaynor, Geneva, Genevra, Genevre, Genovera, Ginette, Ginevra, Guenevere, Guinevere, Jennifer, Jenny, Vanora)*

Genie *see* **Eugenia**

Genna *see* **Jena**

Georgette *see* **Georgina**

Georgia (GREEK) 'Farm girl' *see also* **Georgina**

Georgina (GREEK) 'Girl from the farm'. Feminine of George *(Georgana, Georganne, Georgene, Georgette, Georgia, Georgiana, Georgianna, Georgie, Georgine, Georgy, Girogia)*

Geraldine (TEUTONIC) 'Noble spear-carrier' *(Geralda, Geraldina, Gerhardine, Geri, Gerianna, Gerrilee, Gerry, Giralda, Jeraldine, Jeri, Jerri, Jerry)*

Geranium (GREEK) 'Bright red flower'

Gerda (NORSE) 'Protected one'. One who has been brought up strictly *(Garda) see also* **Gertrude**

Geri *see* **Geraldine**

Gerianna *see* **Geraldine**

Germaine (FRENCH) 'From Germany' *(Germain)*

Gertrude (TEUTONIC) 'Spear maiden'. One of the Valkyrie *(Gartred, Gerda, Gert, Gertie, Gertrud, Gertruda, Gertrudis, Gerty, Trudie, Trudy)*

Gervaise (FRENCH FROM TEUTONIC) 'Eager for battle'

Giacinta *see* **Hyacinth**

Gianina (HEBREW) 'The Lord's grace'

Gigi *see* **Gilberta**

Gilah (HEBREW) 'Joy'

Gilberta (TEUTONIC) 'Bright pledge'. Feminine of Gilbert *(Gigi, Gilberte, Gilbertha, Gilberthe, Gilbertina, Gilbertine, Gillie, Gilly)*

Gilda (CELTIC) 'God's servant'

Gillian (LATIN) 'Young nestling' *(Gill, Gillie, Jill, Jillian, Jillie)*

Gina *see* **Eugenia** or **Regina**

Ginger *see* **Virginia**

Ginny *see* **Virginia**

Giselle (TEUTONIC) 'A promise'. One who stands as a pledge for her family *(Gisela, Gisele, Gisella, Gizela)*

Gita (HINDI) 'Song'

Gitana (SPANISH) 'The gypsy' *(Gipsy, Gypsy) see also* **Tizane**

Gittle (HEBREW) 'Innocent flatterer' *(Gytle)*

Gladys (CELTIC) 'Frail, delicate flower' *(Glad, Gladdie, Gladine, Gladis, Gleda, Gwladys, Gwyladys) see also* **Claudia**

Gleda (ANGLO-SAXON) Old English version of **Gladys**

Glenda *see* **Glenna**

Glenna (CELTIC) 'From the valley'. One of the oldest names on record *(Glenda, Glenine, Glenn, Glennis, Glynis)*

Glenys (WELSH) 'Holy'

Glinys (WELSH) 'Little valley'

Gloria (LATIN) 'Glorious one'. An illustrious person. This name was often used of Queen Elizabeth I of Britain by her sycophantic courtiers *(Gloire, Glori, Gloriana, Gloriane, Glorianna, Glorianne, Glory)*

Glynis *see* **Glenna**

Goda *see* **Guda**

Godine (TEUTONIC) 'Friend of God'

Godiva (ANGLO-SAXON) 'Gift of God' *(Godgifu)*

Goldie (ANGLO-SAXON) 'Pure gold' *(Golda, Goldina)*

Gondoline (TEUTONIC) 'Brave and wise'

Goneril (LATIN) 'Honoured'

Gorvena (TEUTONIC) 'One who lives in the forest'

Grace (LATIN) 'The graceful one' *(Engacia, Engracia, Giorsal, Gracia, Gracie, Gratiana, Grayce, Grazia)*

Gracienne (LATIN) 'Small one'

Graciosa (SPANISH) 'Graceful and beautiful'

Grainne (IRISH) 'Love' *(Graine, Grania)*

Grazina (ITALIAN) 'Grace, charm'

Gredel (TEUTONIC) 'Pearl'

Greer (GREEK) 'The watchful mother'. The eternal matriarch *(Gregoria)*

Greta *see* **Margaret**

Gretchen *see* **Margaret**

Grimonia (LATIN) 'Wise old woman'

Griselda (TEUTONIC) 'Grey heroine' *(Griselde, Grishelda, Grishelde, Grishilda, Grishilde, Grizelda, Selda, Zelda)*

Guadalupe (ARABIC) 'River of black stones'

Guda (ANGLO-SAXON) 'The good one' *(Goda)*

Gudila (TEUTONIC) 'God is my help'

Gudrid (TEUTONIC) 'Divine impluse'

Gudrun (GERMAN) 'War', rune'

Guenna *see* **Guinevere** or **Gwendoline**

Guida (LATIN) 'The guide'

Guinevere (CELTIC) 'White phantom' *(Gaynor, Ginerva, Guenna, Guinivere, Guenevere, Gwenhwyvar, Jennifer) see also* **Genevieve**

Gundred (TEUTONIC) 'Courageous and wise'

Gunhilda (NORSE) 'Warrior maid' *(Gunhilde)*

Gustava (SCANDINAVIAN) 'Staff of the Goths' *(Gussie, Gussy, Gustave)*

Gwendoline (CELTIC) 'White-browed maid' *(Guenna, Gwenda, Gwendolen, Gwendolene, Gwendolyn, Gwendolyne, Gwen, Gwennie, Gwyn, Wendy)*

Gwendydd (WELSH) 'Morning star'

Gweneal (CELTIC) 'White angel'

Gweneira (WELSH) 'Pure white snow'

Gwenhwyvar *see* **Guinevere**

Gwenllian (WELSH) 'Fair', 'flaxen'

Gwennie *see* **Gwendoline**

Gwennol (WELSH) 'Swallow'

Gwenog (WELSH) 'Smiling one'

Gwenonwyn (WELSH) 'Lily of the valley'

Gwylfai (WELSH) May festival

Gwyn *see* **Gwendoline**

Gwyneth (WELSH) 'Blessed'

Gwynne (OLD WELSH) 'White or fair one'

Gyda (TEUTONIC) 'Gift'

Gypsy (ANGLO-SAXON) 'The wanderer' *(Gipsy) see also* **Gitana**

Gytha (ANGLO-SAXON) 'War-like' *(Githa)*

Habiba (SANSKRIT) 'Beloved'

Hadria *see* **Adrienne**

Hadwisa *see* **Avice**

Hafwen (WELSH) 'Beautiful as the summer'

Hagar (HEBREW) 'Forsaken'

Haidee (GREEK) 'Modest, honoured'. A girl well-known for her natural modesty

Hailey *see* **Hayley**

Halcyone (GREEK) 'The kingfisher'. The mythological Greek who was turned into a bird when she drowned herself *(Halcyon)*

Haldana (NORSE) 'Half Danish'

Haldis (TEUTONIC) 'Resolute'

Haley (SCANDINAVIAN) 'Hero' *(Haleigh)*

Halfrida (TEUTONIC) 'Peaceful heroine'. A diplomat not a warrior *(Halfreida, Halfrieda, Hallie, Halliee, Freida, Frida, Frieda) see also* **Freda**

Halima (ARABIC) 'Kind', 'humane'

Halimeda (GREEK) 'Sea thoughts'. One who is drawn to the sea *(Hallie, Meda)*

Halla (AFRICAN) 'Unexpected gift'

Hallie (GREEK) 'Thinking of the sea' *(Halette, Hali, Halley)* *see also* **Halfrida** or **Halimeda**

Halona (NATIVE AMERICAN) 'Fortunate'

Hameline (TEUTONIC) 'Homely'

Hana (JAPANESE) 'Flower' *(Hanako)*

Hannah (HEBREW) 'Full of grace'

Hanusia (HEBREW) 'Grace of the Lord

Happy (ENGLISH) 'Happy'

Haralda (NORSE) 'Army ruler'. Feminine of Harold *(Haraldina, Harolda, Haroldina)*

Harika (TURKISH) 'Most beautiful'

Harley (OLD ENGLISH) 'From the long field' *(Harlene, Harlie)*

Harmony (LATIN) 'Concord and harmony' *(Harmonia, Harmonie)*

Harriet *see* **Henrietta**

Harshada (SANSKRIT) 'Bringer of joy'

Harshita (SANSKRIT) 'Happy' *(Harshini)*

Haru (JAPANESE) 'Springtime'

Hasina (SANSKRIT) 'Beautiful one'

Hasita (SANSKRIT) 'Laughing one'

Hasna (ARABIC) 'Beautiful'

Hatsu (JAPANESE) 'First born'

Hattie *see* **Henrietta**

Hayfa (ARABIC) 'Slender'

Hayley (ENGLISH) From the surname *(Hailey, Haylie) see also* **Haley**

Hazar (ARABIC) 'Nightingale'

Hazel (ENGLISH) 'The hazel tree' *(Aveline)*

Heather (ANGLO-SAXON) 'Flower of the moors'

Hebe (GREEK) Goddess of youth

Hedda (TEUTONIC) 'War'. A born fighter *(Heddi, Heddy, Hedy)*

Hedia (GREEK) 'Pleasing'

Hedva (GREEK) 'Industrious worker'

Hedwig (TEUTONIC) 'Safe place in time of trouble'

Heera (SANSKRIT) 'Diamond'

Heidi *see* **Hilda**

Helbona (HEBREW) 'Fruitful'

Helen (GREEK) 'Light'. According to tradition, the most beautiful woman, Helen of Troy. There are so many variations of this name that it is not possible to list them all, but we have included a representative selection *(Aileen, Aisleen, Alena, Alleen, Eileen, Elaine, Elane, Eleanor, Eleanore, Elena, Elenora, Elenore, Elinor, Elinora, Elinore, Ella, Ellen, Ellene, Ellyn, Galina, Helena, Helene, Ileane, Ilena, Illonna, Illone, Ilona, Isleen, Lana, Lena, Lenora, Leona, Leonora, Leonore, Leora, Lina, Lora, Nell, Nora, Norah) see also* **Aileen**

Helga (TEUTONIC) 'Pious, religious and holy' *see also* **Olga**

Helia (GREEK) 'Sun'

Helianthe (GREEK) 'Bright flower', 'sunflower'

Helice (GREEK) 'Spiral' *(Helixa)*

Helixa *see* **Helice**

Helma (TEUTONIC) 'A helmet'

Heloise *see* **Louise**

Helonia (GREEK) 'Marsh lily'

Helvitia (LATIN) 'Home on the hill'

Hendrika *see* **Henrietta**

Henrietta (TEUTONIC) 'Ruler of home and estate'. Feminine of Henry *(Eiric, Enrica, Etta, Harriet, Harriette, Harriot, Harriotte, Hattie, Hatty, Henriette, Hendrika, Henrika, Hettie, Hetty, Minette, Netie, Netta, Yetta)*

Hephzibah (HEBREW) 'My delight'

Hera (LATIN) 'Queen of the heaven'. The wife of the Greek ruler of heaven, Zeus

Hermione (GREEK) 'Of the earth'. Daughter of Helen of Troy *(Hermia, Hermina, Hermine, Herminia) see also* **Erma**

Hermosa (SPANISH) 'Beautiful'

Hernanda (SPANISH) 'Adventuring life'

Hero (GREEK) Mythological lover of Leander

Herta *see* **Eartha**

Hesper (GREEK) 'The evening star' *(Hespera, Hesperia)*

Hester *see* **Esther**

Hesther *see* **Esther**

Hestia (GREEK) 'A star'

Heulwen (WELSH) 'Sunshine'

Heutte (OLD ENGLISH) 'Brilliant' *(Huetta, Hugette, Hughette)*

Hiberna (LATIN) 'Girl from Ireland' *(Hibernia)*

Hibiscus (LATIN) 'The marshmallow plant'

Hidé (JAPANESE) 'Excellent', 'fruitful', 'superior'

Hilary (LATIN) 'Cheerful one'. One who is always happy *(Hilaire, Hilaria)*

Hilda (TEUTONIC) 'Battle maid'. A handmaiden of the warriors of Valhalla *(Heidi, Heidy, Hidie, Hild, Hilde, Hildie, Hildy)*

Hildegarde (TEUTONIC) 'Battle stronghold' *(Hildagard, Hildegarde)*

Hildemar (TEUTONIC) 'Battle celebrated'

Hildreth (TEUTONIC) 'Battle adviser' *(Hildretha)*

Hilma *see* **Helma**

Hina (HEBREW) 'Female deer'

Hippolyta (GREEK) 'Horse destruction'

Holda (NORSE) 'Muffled' *(Holde, Holle, Hulda)*

Holly (ANGLO-SAXON) 'Bringer of good luck'. A child born during the Christmas season *(Hollie)*

Honesta (LATIN) 'Honourable'

Honey (ENGLISH) 'Sweet one'. A term of endearment, especially in the USA *see also* **Honora**

Honi (HEBREW) 'Gracious'

Honora (LATIN) 'Honour' *(Honey, Honor, Honoria, Honour, Nora, Norah, Noreen, Norine, Norrey, Norrie, Norry)*

Hope (ANGLO-SAXON) 'Cheerful optimism'

Horatia (LATIN) 'Keeper of the hours'. Feminine of Horace *(Haracia, Horacia)*

Hortense (LATIN) 'Of the garden'. One with green fingers *(Hortensia)*

Hoshi (JAPANESE) 'Star'

Howin (CHINESE) 'Loyal swallow'

Huberta (TEUTONIC) 'Brilliant girl' *(Hubertha, Huberthe)*

Huda (ARABIC) 'Guidance'

Huette (ANGLO-SAXON) 'Brilliant thinker'. Feminine of Hugh *(Huetta, Hugette)*

Hugette *see* **Heutte** or **Huette**

Huguette (TEUTONIC) 'Intellectual'

Huriyah (ARABIC) 'Virgin of paradise'

Hyacinth (GREEK) 'Hyacinth flower' *(Cynthie, Cynthis, Giacinta, Hyacintha, Hyacinthia, Jacinda, Jacinth, Jacintha, Jacinthia, Jackie, Jakinda)*

Hypatia (GREEK) 'Highest'

I

GIRLS

Ianira (GREEK) 'Enchantress'

Ianthe (GREEK) 'Violet-coloured flower' *(Iantha, Ianthina, Janthina, Janthine)*

Icasia (GREEK) 'Happy'

Ida (TEUTONIC) 'Happy'. The name comes from Mount Ida in Crete, where Jupiter is supposed to have been hidden *(Idalia, Idalina, Idaline, Idalle, Idelea, Idelia, Idella, Idelle) see also* **Idalia** or **Idelia**

Idalia (SPANISH) 'Sunny' *see also* **Ida**

Idelia (TEUTONIC) 'Noble' *see also* **Ida**

Idelle *see* **Ida**

Idmonia (GREEK) 'Skilful'

Iduna (NORSE) 'Lover'. The keeper of the golden apples of youth *(Idonia, Idonie)*

Ierne (LATIN) 'From Ireland'

Ignatia (LATIN) 'Fiery ardour'. Feminine of Ignatius

Ignes (LATIN) 'Pure'

Ila (FRENCH) 'From the island' *(Ilde)*

Ilana (HEBREW) 'Tree'

Ilde *see* **Ida**

Ileana (GREEK) 'Of Ilion (Troy)' *see also* **Aileen**

Ilena *see* **Helen**

Ilene *see* **Eileen**

Ilka (SLAVIC) 'Flattering'

Ilsa *see* **Ailsa**

Iluminada (SPANISH) 'Illuminated'

Ilythia (GREEK) Goddess of childbirth

Imani (ARABIC) 'Believer'

Imelda (LATIN) 'Wishful' *(Imalda, Melda)*

Immaculada (SPANISH) 'Immaculate conception'

Imogen (LATIN) 'Image of her mother' *(Imogene)*

Imperial (LATIN) 'Imperial one' *(Imperia)*

Ina *see* **Agnes**

India (HINDI) 'From India'

Indira (HINDI) 'Beauty', 'splendid'

Inez *see* **Agnes**

Inger *see* **Ingrid**

Ingrid (NORSE) 'Hero's daughter'. Child of a warrior *(Inga, Ingaberg, Ingeborg, Ingebiorg, Inger, Ingibiorg, Ingunna)*

Iniga (LATIN) 'Fiery ardour' *(Ignatia)*

Inocencia (SPANISH) 'Innocence'

Intisar (ARABIC) 'Triumph'

Iola (GREEK) 'Colour of the dawn cloud' *(Iole)*

Iolana (HAWAIIAN) 'Soaring like a hawk'

Iolanthe (GREEK) 'Violet flower' *(Eolande, Yolanda, Yolande)* *see also* **Violet**

Ione (GREEK) 'Violet-coloured stone' *(Iona)*

Iorwen (WELSH) 'Beautiful'

Iphigenia (GREEK) 'Sacrifice'. In mythology the daughter of the Greek leader Agamemnon. In one myth she was sacrificed to a goddess; in another she was saved

Irene (GREEK) 'Peace'. The goddess of peace *(Eirena, Eirene, Erena, Irena, Irenna, Irina, Rena, Renata, Rene, Reini, Rennie, Renny)*

Ireta (LATIN) 'Enraged one' *(Irete, Iretta, Irette)*

Iris (GREEK) 'The rainbow'. The messenger of the gods *(Irisa)*

Irma (LATIN) 'Noble person' *(Erma, Erme, Irme, Irmina, Irmine)*

Irma (TEUTONIC) 'Strong' *(Erma, Erme, Irmina, Irmine, Irme)*

Irvette (ENGLISH) 'Sea friend' *(Irvetta)*

Isa (TEUTONIC) 'Lady of the iron will'. A determined girl

Isabel (HEBREW) Spanish form of **Elizabeth** *(Bel, Bella, Belle, Isabeau, Isabella, Isabelle, Isbel, Ishbel, Isobel, Ysabeau, Ysabel, Ysabella, Ysabelle, Ysobel, Ysobella, Ysobelle)*

Isadora (GREEK) 'The gift of Isis' *(Dora, Dori, Dory, Isadore, Isidora, Isidore, Issie, Issy, Izzy)*

Iseult *see* **Isolde**

Isis (EGYPTIAN) 'Supreme goddess'. The goddess of fertility

Isla (LATIN/FRENCH) 'Island'

Islamey (ARABIC) 'Obedient to Allah'

Ismena (GREEK) 'Learned'

Isoda *see* **Isolde**

Isola (LATIN) 'The isolated one'. A loner

Isolabella (COMBINATION ISOLA/BELLA) 'Beautiful lonely one' *(Isolabelle)*

Isolde (CELTIC) 'The fair one' *(Esyllt, Iseult, Isoda, Yseult, Ysolda, Ysolde)*

Ita (GAELIC) 'Desire for truth' *(Ite)*

Iva (FRENCH) 'The yew tree' *(Ivanna, Ivanne)*

Iverna (LATIN) An old name for Ireland

Ivory (WELSH) 'High-born lady'

Ivy (ENGLISH) 'A vine'. The sacred plant of the ancient religions

Ixia (GREEK) 'Mistletoe'

Izora (ARAB) 'Dawn'

GIRLS

Jacinda (GREEK) 'Beautiful and comely' *(Jacenta) see also* **Hyacinth**

Jacintha *see* **Hyacinth**

Jackie *see* **Hyacinth** or **Jacqueline**

Jacoba (LATIN) 'The supplanter'. The understudy who is better than the star *(Jacobina, Jacobine)*

Jacqueleine *see* **Jacqueline**

Jacqueline (HEBREW) 'The supplanter' *(Jackeline, Jackelyn, Jacketta, Jackie, Jacklyn, Jacky, Jacobina, Jacqueleine, Jacquelyn, Jacquetta, Jacqui, Jamesina, Jaquith)*

Jade (SPANISH) 'Daughter'. A mother's most precious jewel *(Jada)*

Jaea *see* **Jaya**

Jaffa (HEBREW) 'Beautiful'

Jagoda (SLAVONIC) 'Strawberry'

Jahanara (SANSKRIT) 'Queen of the world'

Jahola (HEBREW) 'Dove'

Jaia *see* **Jaya**

Jaime (FRENCH) 'I love' *(Jaimee, Jaimey, Jamey, Jamie, Jaymee)*

Jakinda *see* **Hyacinth**

Jala (ARABIC) 'Clarity'

Jalaya (SANSKRIT) 'Lotus blossom'

Jalila (ARABIC) 'Great'

Jamie *see* **Jaime**

Jamila (MUSLIM) 'Beautiful'

Jamuna (SANSKRIT) 'Holy river'

Jan *see* **Jane**

Jane (HEBREW) 'God's gift of grace'. With Mary, one of the most consistently popular girl's names, with a huge range of variations *(Jan, Jana, Janet, Janette, Janetta, Janice, Janina, Janna, Jayne, Jaynell, Jean, Jeanette, Jeanne, Jenda, Jenete, Jeniece, Joan, Joana, Joanna, Joanne, Johanna, Johanne, Joni, Juana, Juanita, Nita, Sean, Seon, Seonaid, Sheena, Shena, Siän, Sine, Sinead, Siobhan, Yoanna, Zaneta)*

Janette *see* **Jane**

Jarita (HINDI) 'Legendary bird'

Jarmila (SLAVIC) 'Spring'

Jarvia (TEUTONIC) 'Keen as a spear'

Jasmine (PERSIAN) 'Fragrant flower' *(Jasmin, Jasmina, Jessamie, Jessamine, Jessamy, Jessamyn, Yasmin, Yasmina, Yasmie)*

Jaspreet (PUNJABI) 'Virtuous' *(Jasprit)*

Jawahir (ARABIC) 'Jewels'

Jaya (HINDI) 'Victory' *(Jaea, Jaia, Jayla)*

Jayati (SANSKRIT) 'Victorious' *(Jayata)*

Jayne (SANSKRIT) 'God's victorious smile' *see also* **Jane**

Jean *see* **Jane**

Jeanette *see* **Jane**

Jelena (GREEK) 'Light'

Jemina (HEBREW) 'The dove'. Symbol of peace *(Jemie, Jemmie, Mina)*

Jena (ARABIC) 'A small bird' *(Genna, Jenna)*

Jenette *see* **Jane**

Jeniece *see* **Jane**

Jenna *see* **Jena**

Jennifer *see* **Genevieve** or **Guinevere**

Jeraldine *see* **Geraldine**

Jeremia (HEBREW) 'The Lord's exalted'. Feminine of Jeremiah *(Jeri, Jerrie, Jerry)*

Jeri *see* **Geraldine** or **Jeremia**

Jerri *see* **Geraldine**

Jerusha (HEBREW) 'The married one'. The perfect wife *(Yerusha)*

Jessamine *see* **Jasmine**

Jessica (HEBREW) 'The rich one' *(Jessalyn)*

Jessie (HEBREW) 'God's grace'

Jevera (HEBREW) 'Life'

Jewel (LATIN) 'Most precious one'. The ornament of the home

Jill *see* **Julia** or **Gillian**

Jinx (LATIN) 'Charming spell'. A girl who can enchant others with her beauty and grace *(Jynx)*

Joakima (HEBREW) 'The Lord's judge' *(Joachima)*

Joan *see* **Jane**

Joanna *see* **Jane**

Jobina (HEBREW) 'The afflicted'. 'Persecuted'. Feminine of Job *(Joby, Jobyna)*

Jocasta (GREEK) 'Shining moon'

Joccoaa (LATIN) 'The humorous one'. Girl with a lively wit

Jocelyn (LATIN) 'Fair and just'. Feminine of Justin *(Jocelin, Joceline, Jocelyne, Joscelin, Josceline, Joscelyn, Joscelyne, Joselen, Joselene, Joselin, Joseline, Joselyn, Joselyne, Josilen, Josilene, Josilin, Josiline, Josilyn, Josilyne, Joslin, Josline, Justina, Justine, Lyn, Lynne)*

Jocunda (LATIN) 'Full of happiness'

Jodette (LATIN) 'Active and sporty'

Jody *see* **Judith**

Joelle (HEBREW) 'The Lord is willing'

Jofrid (TEUTONIC) 'Lover of horses'

Joicelyn *see* **Joyce**

Jolene (MIDDLE ENGLISH) 'He will increase' *(Joleen, Jolyn)*

Joletta *see* Joliette

Jolie (FRENCH) 'Pretty' *(Jolee, Joly)*

Joliette (FRENCH) 'Violet' *(Joletta)*

Jonquil (LATIN) From the name of the flower

Jordana (HEBREW) 'The descending' *(Jordan)*

Joselyne *see* Jocelyn

Josephine (HEBREW) 'She shall add'. Feminine of Joseph *(Fifi, Jo, Joette, Josepha, Josephina, Josetta, Josette, Josie, Pepita, Yosepha, Yusepha)*

Josie *see* Josephine

Jovanna (LATIN) 'Majestic'

Jovita (LATIN) 'The joyful one'. The feminine of Jove. Bringer of jollity

Joy *see* Joyce

Joyce (LATIN) 'Gay and joyful' *(Joice, Joicelin, Joicelyn, Joy, Joycelin, Joycelyn, Joyous)*

Juana *see* Jane or June

Juanita *see* Jane

Judith (HEBREW) 'Admired, praised'. One whose praises cannot be over emphasised *(Jodie, Jody, Judie, Juditha, Judy, Siobhan, Siuban)*

Julia (GREEK) 'Youthful'. Young in heart and mind *(Jill, Juli, Juliana, Juliane, Julianna, Julianne, Julie, Juliet, Julietta, Julina, Juline, Sile, Sileas)*

Juliana *see* Julia

Julie *see* Julia

Jumanah (ARABIC) 'Pearl'

Jun (CHINESE) 'Truthful'

June (LATIN) 'Summer's child'. One born in the early summer *(Juana, Juna, Junia, Juniata, Junette, Junine)*

Junko (JAPANESE) 'Obedient'

Juno (LATIN) 'Heavenly being'. The wife of Jupiter, Greek ruler of the heavens

Jurisa (SLAVONIC) 'Storm'

Justine *see* Jocelyn

Jutta (LATIN) 'Near'

Jyoti (HINDI) 'Light'

Jyotsna (SANSKRIT) 'Moonlight'

K

GIRLS

Kabira (ARABIC) 'Powerful'

Kachina (NATIVE AMERICAN) 'Sacred dance'

Kaela (HEBREW) 'Sweetheart' *(Kaelah, Kayla, Kaylah, Keyla, Keylah)*

Kaelah *see* **Kaela**

Kagami (JAPANESE) 'Mirror'

Kai (HAWAIIAN) 'Sea'

Kairos (GREEK) 'Goddess born last to Jupiter'

Kaitlyn *see* **Catherine**

Kaja *see* **Kaya**

Kala (HINDI) 'Black', 'time'

Kalama (NATIVE AMERICAN) 'Wild goose'

Kalamit (HEBREW) 'Flower'

Kaldora (GREEK) 'Lovely gift'

Kaleena *see* **Kalinda**

Kali (SANSKRIT) 'Energy'

Kalika (SANSKRIT) 'A bud'

Kalila (ARABIC) 'Beloved' *(Kally, Kaylee, Kayleigh, Kylila)*

Kalinda (SANSKRIT) 'Sun' *(Kaleena, Kalindi)*

Kally *see* **Kalila**

Kalma (TEUTONIC) 'Calm'

Kalonice (GREEK) 'Beauty's victory'

Kalwa (FINNISH) 'Heroic'

Kalya (SANSKRIT) 'Healthy'

Kalyana (SANSKRIT) 'Virtuous one'

Kalyca (GREEK) 'Rosebud'

Kama (SANSKRIT) 'Love'. The Hindu god of love, like Cupid

Kamakshi (SANSKRIT) *see* **Kamalakshi**

Kamalakshi (SANSKRIT) 'Girl whose eyes are as beautiful as the lotus flower' *(Kamakshi)*

Kamama (NATIVE AMERICAN) 'Butterfly'

Kamana (SANSKRIT) 'Desire'

Kameko (JAPANESE) 'Child of the tortoise'. The tortoise is a symbol of long life

Kamilah (ARABIC) 'The perfect one' *(Kamila)*

Kamra (ARABIC) 'Moon'

Kanakabati (SANSKRIT) 'Fairy-tale princess'

Kanake *see* **Canace**

Kanda (NATIVE AMERICAN) 'Magical power'

Kane (JAPANESE) 'Ambidextrous'

Kanya (THAI) 'Young lady'

Kara *see* **Cara** or **Katherine**

Karabel (SPANISH) 'Lovely face'

Karen *see* **Katherine**

Karima (ARABIC) 'Generous'

Karma (SANSKRIT) 'Destiny'

Karyn *see* **Katherine**

Kasia (GREEK) 'Pure'

Kasmira (SLAVIC) 'Commands peace' *(Casmira)*

Kate *see* **Katherine**

Katharine *see* **Katherine**

Katherine (GREEK) 'Pure maiden' *(Kara, Karen, Karena, Karin, Karyn, Kate, Katharina, Katharine, Katherina, Katheryn, Kathie, Kathleen, Kathlene, Kathryn, Kathy, Katie, Katrin, Katrina, Katrine, Katryn, Kay, Ketti, Kitty) see also* **Catherine**

Kathleen *see* **Katherine**

Kathryn *see* **Katherine**

Katrin *see* **Katherine**

Katrina *see* **Catherine** or **Katherine**

Kaulana (HAWAIIAN) 'Famous' *(Kaula, Kauna, Kahuna)*

Kaumudi (SANSKRIT) 'Moonlight'

Kavita (SANSKRIT) 'A poem'

Kay *see* **Katherine**

Kaya (JAPANESE) 'Resting place' *(Kaja, Kayia)*

Kayla (HEBREW) 'Crown'

Kayleigh (MODERN FROM ARABIC) 'Beloved'. Modern name derived from **Kalila**

Kazia *see* **Keziah**

Keara (IRISH) 'Dark' *(Kiara)*

Keely (GAELIC) 'The beautiful one'

Keena (IRISH) 'Brave' *(Keenya, Kina)*

Keenya *see* **Keena**

Kei (JAPANESE) 'Reverent' *(Keiana, Keikann, Keikanna, Keionna)*

Keikann *see* **Kei**

Keiko (JAPANESE) 'Happy child'

Keile (HAWAIIAN) 'Gardenia blossom' *(Kiela, Kieli)*

Kelda (NORSE) 'Bubbling spring' *(Kelly)*

Kelila (HEBREW) 'Crown, laurel' *(Kelula)*

Kelly (IRISH GAELIC) 'Warrior maid'

Kelsey (SCANDINAVIAN) 'From the island of the ships' *(Kelci, Kelsi, Kesley)*

Kelsie (SCOTTISH) Scottish form of **Chelsea** *(Kelula Kelila)*

Kendall (ENGLISH) 'Ruler of the valley' *(Kendell, Kendyll)*

Kendra (OLD ENGLISH) 'Knowledgeable' *(Kenna)*

Kenzie (SCOTTISH) 'Light-skinned'

Keren (HEBREW) 'Horn of antimony'

Kerridwen *see* **Ceiridwen**

Kerry (GAELIC) 'Dark one' *(Kerri, Kerrianne)*

Keshena (NATIVE AMERICAN) 'Swift in flight'

Keshina (SANSKRIT) 'Girl with beautiful hair'

Kesi (SWAHILI) 'Born during difficult times'

Kesia (AFRICAN) 'Favourite'

Kessie (ASHANTI) 'Chubby baby'

Ketura (HEBREW) 'Incense'

Kevin (GAELIC) 'Gentle and lovable' *(Kelvina, Kevyn)*

Keylah *see* **Kaela**

Keyne (CELTIC) 'Jewel'

Keziah (HEBREW) 'Like cinnamon' *(Kaziah, Kezia)*

Khalida (ARABIC) 'Immortal, everlasting'

Khalipha (ARABIC) 'Successor'

Ki (KOREAN) 'Arisen'

Kia (AFRICAN) 'The beginning of the season'

Kiah (AFRICAN) 'Season's beginning'

Kiku (JAPANESE) 'Chrysanthemum'

Kim (ORIGIN NOT KNOWN) 'Noble chief'

Kimberley (ENGLISH) 'From the royal meadow'

Kimi (JAPANESE) 'Righteous' *(Kimia, Kimiko)*

Kimiko *see* **Kimi**

Kina (GREEK) 'Christian'

Kineta (GREEK) 'Active and elusive'

Kinnereth (HEBREW) 'From the Sea of Galilee'

Kinsey (ENGLISH) 'Relative'

Kiona (NATIVE AMERICAN) 'Brown hills'

Kira (PERSIAN) 'Sun'

Kirby (OLD ENGLISH) 'From the church town' *(Kirbee, Kirbie)*

Kirima (ESKIMO) 'A hill'

Kirstin (NORSE) 'The annointed one' *(Kirsten, Kirstie, Kirstina, Kirsty, Kirstyn)*

Kirsty *see* **Kirstin**

Kishi (JAPANESE) 'Long and happy life'

Kita (JAPANESE) 'North'

Kitty *see* **Catherine** or **Katherine**

Kohana (JAPANESE) 'Little flower'

Kolfinna (CELTIC) 'Cool, white lady'

Kolina (GREEK) 'Pure'

Kolotosa (NATIVE AMERICAN) 'Star'

Komala (SANSKRIT) 'Charming', 'tender' *(Komal)*

Kora (GREEK) 'Young girl, maiden' *(Korella, Koressa)*

Koren (GREEK) 'Beautiful maiden'

Koto (JAPANESE) 'Harp'

Kotsasi (NATIVE AMERICAN) 'White flower'

Krishna (SANSKRIT) Hindu god

Kristabelle *see* **Christabel**

Kristen *see* **Christine**

Krystal *see* **Crystal**

Krystina *see* **Christine**

Kuki (JAPANESE) 'Snow'

Kundanika (SANSKRIT) 'Flower'

Kuni (JAPANESE) 'Born in the countryside'

Kuntala (SANSKRIT) 'Girl with beautiful hair' *(Kuntal)*

Kurva (JAPANESE) 'Mulberry tree'

Kwai (CHINESE) 'Rose-scented'

Kyla (GAELIC) 'Pretty one' *(Kilah, Kylah, Kylie)*

Kyna (GAELIC) 'Great wisdom'

Kyoko (JAPANESE) 'Mirror'

L

GIRLS

La Roux (FRENCH) 'Red-haired one' *(Larousse, Roux)*

Labhaoise *see* **Louise**

Labiba (ARABIC) 'Wise'

Lacey *see* **Larissa**

Lada (RUSSIAN) 'Mythological goddess of beauty'

Ladonna (FRENCH) 'The lady'

Laetitia *see* **Letitia**

Laila *see* **Layla**

Lakia (ARABIC) 'Discovered treasure'

Lala (SLAVIC) 'The tulip flower'

Lalage (GREEK) 'Gentle laughter'

Lalana (SANSKRIT) 'Beautiful one' *(Lalan)*

Laleh (PERSIAN) 'Tulip'

Lalita (SANSKRIT) 'Beautiful', 'without guile' *(Lalit)*

Lallie *see* **Eulalia**

Lalota (SANSKRIT) 'Pleasing'

Lamya (ARABIC) 'Dark lips'

Lana *see* **Alana** or **Helen**

Lane (MIDDLE ENGLISH) 'From the narrow road'

Lanelle (OLD FRENCH) 'From the little lane'

Lani (HAWAIIAN) 'The sky'

Lara (LATIN) 'Famous'

Larentia (LATIN) 'Foster mother'
(Laurentia)

Larine (LATIN) 'Girl of the sea'
(Lareena, Larene, Larianna)
see also Lorraine

Larissa (GREEK) 'Cheerful maiden'.
One who is as happy as a lark
(Lacee, Lacey, Laris)

Lark (ENGLISH) 'Singing bird'

Lasca (LATIN) 'Weary one'

Lassie (SCOTTISH) 'Little girl'

Latonia (LATIN) 'Belonging to
Latona'. The mother of the
Greek goddess Diana
(Latona, Latoya)

Laura (LATIN) 'Laurel wreath'.
The victor's crown of
laurels (Laure, Laureen,
Laurel, Lauren, Laurena,
Laurene, Lauretta, Laurette,
Laurie, Lora, Loralie, Loree,
Lorelie, Loren, Lorena,
Lorene, Lorenza, Loretta,
Lorette, Lori, Lorie, Lorinda,
Lorine, Lorita, Lorna, Lorne,
Lorrie)

Lauren (LATIN) 'Laurel wreath'.
Familiar form of Laura

Laveda (LATIN) 'One who is
purified' (Lavetta, Lavette)

Lavelle (LATIN) 'Cleansing'

Lavena (CELTIC) 'Joy'

Lavender (ENGLISH) 'Sweet-
smelling flower' (Lavvie)

Laverne (FRENCH) 'Spring-like',
'alder tree' (Laverna, Vern,
Verna, Verne)

Lavette see Laveola

Lavinia (LATIN) 'Lady of Rome'
(Lavina, Vina, Vinia)

Layla (ARABIC) 'Night' (Laila)
see also Leila

Leah (HEBREW) 'The weary one'
(Lea, Lee, Leigh)

Leala (FRENCH) 'The true one'.
One who is true to home,
family and friends

Leana see Liana

Leandra (LATIN) 'Like a lioness'
(Leodora, Leoline, Leonelle)

Leatrice (HEBREW) 'Tired but
joyful'. Combination of
Leah and Beatrice (Leatrix)

Lechsinska (POLISH) 'Woodland spirit'

Leda (GREEK) 'Mother of beauty'. The mother of Helen of Troy *see also* **Alida, Letha** or **Letitia**

Lee (ENGLISH) 'From the fields'. Also a variation of **Leah** *(Leanna, Leeann) see also* **Leah** or **Leila**

Leena (SANSKRIT) 'Devoted one'

Lefa (TEUTONIC) 'The heart of the tree'

Leigh (OLD ENGLISH) 'From the meadow' *see also* **Leah**

Leila (ARABIC) 'Black as the night' *(Layla, Lee, Leela, Leilah, Leilia, Lela, Leyla, Lila, Lilah, Lilia) see also* **Lilian**

Leilani (HAWAIIAN) 'Heavenly blossom'. The tropical flower of the islands *(Lillani, Lullani)*

Lela *see* **Leila** or **Lilian**

Lelah *see* **Lilian**

Lemma (ETHIOPIAN) 'Developed'

Lemuela (HEBREW) 'Dedicated to God'. A daughter dedicated to the service of God *(Lemuella)*

Lena (LATIN) 'Enchanting one' *(Lenette, Lina) see also* **Caroline, Helen, Madeleine** or **Selena**

Lenette *see* **Lena**

Lenis (LATIN) 'Smooth and white as the lily' *(Lene, Leneta, Lenita, Lenta, Lenos)*

Lenita *see* **Lenis**

Lenora *see* **Eleanor** or **Helen**

Lentula (CELTIC) 'Gentle one'

Leocadia (SPANISH FROM GREEK) 'Lion-like'

Leoda (TEUTONIC) 'Woman of the people' *(Leola, Leota)*

Leola *see* **Leoda** or **Leona**

Leoma (ANGLO-SAXON) 'Bright light'. One who casts radiance around her

Leona (LATIN) 'The lioness' *(Lennie, Lenny, Leola, Leone, Leonelle, Leoni, Leonie) see also* **Helen**

Leonarda (FRENCH) 'Like a lion' *(Leonarde, Leonardina, Leonardine)*

Leonora *see* **Eleanor** or **Helen**

Leontine (LATIN) 'Like a lion' *(Leontina, Leontyne)*

Leopoldina (TEUTONIC) 'The people's champion'. Feminine of Leopold *(Leopolda, Leopoldine)*

Leor (HEBREW) 'I have light'

Leora (GREEK) 'Light' *see also* **Helen**

Les *see* **Lesley**

Lesham (HEBREW) 'Precious stone'

Lesley (CELTIC) 'Keeper of the grey fort' *(Les, Lesli, Leslie, Lesly)*

Letha (GREEK) 'Sweet oblivion'. Lethe was the river of forgetfulness in Greek mythology *(Leda, Leta, Leithia, Lethia, Lethitha)*

Letitia (LATIN) 'Joyous gladness' *(Laetitia, Leda, Leshia, Leta, Leticia, Letisha, Letizia, Lettice, Lettie, Loutitia, Tish)*

Lettice *see* **Letitia**

Levana (LATIN) 'The sun of the dawn'. The goddess of childbirth *(Levania)*

Levina (ENGLISH) 'A bright flash'. One who passes like a comet

Lewanna (HEBREW) 'As pure as the white moon' *(Luanna)*

Lexine *see* **Alexandra**

Leya (SPANISH) 'Loyalty to the law'. A strict upholder of morals and principles

Leyla (TURKISH) 'Born at night'

Lia (GREEK) 'The bringer of good news'

Lian (CHINESE) 'The graceful willow'

Liana (FRENCH) 'The climbing vine' *(Leana, Leane, Leanna, Lianna, Lianne)*

Libby *see* **Elizabeth**

Liberata (LATIN) 'Freed'

Libusa (RUSSIAN) 'Beloved'

Lida (SLAVIC) 'Beloved of the people'

Lien (CHINESE) 'Lotus blossom' *(Lienne)*

Ligia (GREEK) 'Silver voice'

Lila *see* **Delilah, Leila** or **Lilian**

Lilac (PERSIAN) 'Dark mauve flower'

Lilian (LATIN) 'A lily'. One who is pure in thought, word and deed *(Lela, Lelah, Lelia, Leila, Lila, Lilah, Lilais, Lili, Lilia, Liliana, Liliane, Lilias, Lilla, Lilli, Lillian, Liliana, Lilliane, Lillis, Lily, Lilly, Lilyan, Lillyan)*

Lilith (ARABIC) 'Woman of the night'. According to Eastern belief, Lilith was the first wife of Adam and the first woman in the world; Eve was his second wife

Lily *see* **Lilian**

Lin (CHINESE) 'Beautiful jade'

Lina *see* **Caroline, Helen** or **Lena**

Linda (SPANISH) 'Pretty one'. Also diminutive of **Belinda, Rosalinda**, etc *(Lind, Linde, Lindie, Lindy, Lynd, Lynda see also Belinda)*

Lindsay (OLD ENGLISH) 'From the linden tree island' *(Lindsey)*

Lindy *see* **Belinda** or **Linda**

Line *see* **Caroline**

Linette *see* **Linnet**

Ling (CHINESE) 'Delicate' or 'dainty'

Linnea (NORSE) 'The lime blossom' *(Lynnea)*

Linnet (FRENCH) 'Sweet bird' *(Linetta, Linette, Linnetta, Linnette, Lynette, Lynnette)*

Liorah (HEBREW) 'I have light'

Lira (GREEK) 'Lyre'

Liria (GREEK) 'Tender one'

Lisa *see* **Elizabeth** or **Melissa**

Lisandra (GREEK) Feminine variation of Alexander

Lisbeth *see* **Elizabeth**

Lisha (ARABIC) 'The darkness before midnight' *(Lishe)*

Livia *see* **Olga** or **Olive**

Liyna (ARABIC) 'Tender'

Liza *see* **Elizabeth**

Lizbeth *see* **Elizabeth**

Llawela (WELSH) 'Like a ruler' *(Llawella)*

Lodema (ENGLISH) 'Leader or guide'

Lodie *see* **Melody**

Loella *see* **Luella**

Logan (CELTIC) 'Little hollow'

Loietu (NATIVE AMERICAN) 'Flower'

Lola (SPANISH) 'Strong woman' *(Loleta, Lolita, Lollie, Lulita) see also* **Dolores** or **Theola**

Lolita *see* **Dolores** or **Lola**

Lomasi (NATIVE AMERICAN) 'Pretty flower'

Lona (ANGLO-SPANISH) 'Solitary watcher'

Loralie *see* **Laura**

Lorelei (TEUTONIC) 'Siren of the river'. The Rhine maiden who lured unwary mariners to their death *(Lorelia, Lorelie, Lorilyn, Lurleen)*

Lorelle (LATIN/OLD GERMAN) 'Little'

Lorna *see* **Laura**

Lorraine (TEUTONIC) 'Renowned in battle' (FRENCH) 'The Queen' *(Laraine, Larayne, Larina, Larine, Larraine, Loraine)*

Lotus (GREEK) 'Flower of the sacred Nile'

Louella (TEUTONIC) 'Shrewd in battle' *see also* **Luella**

Louise (TEUTONIC) 'Famous battle maid'. One who leads victorious armies into battle *(Alison, Allison, Aloisa, Aloisia, Aloysia, Eloisa, Eloise, Heloise, Labhaoise, Liusade, Lois, Loise, Louisa, Louisitte, Loyce, Luise)*

Love (ENGLISH) 'Tender affection'

Loveday (ENGLISH) 'Reconciliation'

Lowena (ENGLISH) 'Joy'

Loyce *see* **Louise**

Luana (TEUTONIC) 'Graceful army maiden' *(Luane, Louanna, Louanne, Luwana, Luwanna, Luwanne)*

Luba (RUSSIAN) 'Love' *(Lubmila)*

Lubna (ARABIC) 'Flexible'

Lucette *see* **Lucy**

Lucille *see* **Lucy**

Lucinda *see* **Lucy**

Lucretia (LATIN) 'A rich reward' *(Lucrece, Lucrecia, Lucrezia)*

Lucy (LATIN) 'Light'. One who brings the lamp of learning to the ignorant *(Lacinia, Lucette, Lucia, Luciana, Lucida, Lucie, Lucile, Lucille, Lucinda, Lucita, Luighseach, Luisadh)*

Ludella (ANGLO-SAXON) 'Pixie maid'

Ludmilla (SLAVIC) 'Beloved of the people' *(Ludmila)*

Luella (ANGLO-SAXON) 'The appeaser' *(Loella, Louella, Luelle)*

Lulu (ARABIC) 'Pearl'

Luneda (CELTIC) 'With a beautiful figure'

Lunetta (LATIN) 'Little Moon' *(Luna, Luneta)*

Lupe (SPANISH) 'She wolf'. A fierce guardian of the home

Lurline (TEUTONIC) 'Siren' *(Lura, Lurleen, Lurlene, Lurlette, Lurlina) see also* **Lorelei**

Luvena (LATIN) 'Little beloved one'

Lycoris (GREEK) 'Twilight'

Lydia (GREEK) 'Cultured one' *(Lidia, Lidie, Lydie)*

Lyn *see* **Jocelyn** or **Lynette**

Lynette (ENGLISH) 'Idol' *(Linnet, Lyn, Lynn, Lynne)*

Lynn (CELTIC) 'A waterfall'. Also diminutive of **Carolyn**, **Evelyn**, etc

Lynne *see* **Jocelyn** or **Lynette**

Lyonelle (OLD FRENCH) 'Young lion'

Lyris (GREEK) 'She who plays the harp' *(Lyra)*

Lysandra (GREEK) 'The liberator'. The prototype of feminism

M

GIRLS

Mab (GAELIC) 'Mirthful joy' *(Mave, Mavis, Meave)*

Mabel (LATIN) 'Amiable and loving'. An endearing companion *(Mable, Maible, Maybelle, Moibeal)*

Mackenzie (GAELIC) 'Handsome'

Madeleine (GREEK) 'Tower of strength'. A girl of great physical and moral courage who will support others in difficult times *(Lena, Mada, Madalaine, Madaleine, Madalena, Madaline, Maddalena, Maddalene, Maddy, Madel, Madelaine, Madelia, Madeline, Madella, Madelle, Madelon, Madlin, Magdaa, Magdala, Magdalane, Magdalen, Magdalene, Magdalyn, Maighdlin, Mala, Malena, Malina, Marleen, Marlena, Marlene, Marline, Melina)*

Madge *see* **Margaret**

Madhuk (SANSKRIT) 'Honey bee'

Madhulika (SANSKRIT) 'Honey'

Madhur (HINDI) 'Sweet' *(Madhura)*

Madhur (SANSKRIT) 'Sweetness' *(Madhura, Madhuri)*

Madison (TEUTONIC) 'Child of Maud'

Madra (SPANISH) 'The matriarch'

Madonna (LATIN) 'Mother'

Maeve (IRISH) The warrior queen of Connaught *(Mave, Meave)*

Mag *see* Magnilda or Magnolia

Magaski (NATIVE AMERICAN) 'White swan'

Magdi (ARABIC) 'My glory'

Magena (NORTH AMERICAN INDIAN) 'The coming moon'

Maggie *see* Magnilda, Magnolia or Margaret

Magnilda (TEUTONIC) 'Great battle maid' *(Mag, Maggie, Magnhilda, Magnhilde, Magnilde, Nilda, Nillie)*

Magnolia (LATIN) 'Magnolia flower' *(Mag, Maggie, Nola, Nolie)*

Maha (ARABIC) 'Wild oxen'

Mahala (HEBREW) 'Tenderness' *(Mahalah, Mahalia)*

Mahira *see* Mehira

Maida (ANGLO-SAXON) 'The maiden' *(Mady, Maidel, Maidie, Mayda, Mayde, Maydena)*

Maighdlin *see* Madeleine

Maigrghread *see* Margaret

Maisie *see* Margaret

Majesta (LATIN) 'Majestic one'

Makala (HAWAIIAN) 'Myrtle'

Makana (HAWAIIAN) 'Gift'

Makani (HAWAIIAN) 'Wind'

Makara (HINDI) 'Born under the constellation of Capricorn'

Malika (SANSKRIT) 'Garland of flowers'

Malini (HINDI) 'Gardener'

Malise (GAELIC) 'Servant of God'

Mallika (SANSKRIT) 'Jasmine flower'

Mallory (FRENCH) 'Unlucky'

Malva (GREEK) 'Soft and tender' *(Melba, Melva) see also* Malvina or Mauve

Malvie *see* Malvina

Malvina (GAELIC) 'Polished chieftain' *(Malva, Malvie, Melva, Melvina, Melvine)*

Mandy *see* Amanda

Mani (CHINESE) 'Mantra'

Manpreet (PUNJABI) 'Full of love'

Manuela (SPANISH) 'God with us' *(Manuella)*

Mara *see* **Damara** or **Mary**

Maraam (ARABIC) 'Aspiration'

Marcella (LATIN) 'Belonging to Mars' *(Marcela, Marcelia, Marcelle, Marcelline, Marchella, Marchelle, Marchelline, Marchita, Marcia, Marcie, Marcile, Marcille, Marcy, Marilda, Marquita, Marsha)*

Mardi (FRENCH) 'Born on Tuesday'

Marelda (TEUTONIC) 'Famous battle maiden'

Mareria (LATIN) 'Of the sea' *(Maralla)*

Margaret (LATIN) 'A pearl' *(Daisy, Greta, Grete, Gretchen, Grethe, Maggie, Maigrghread, Maisie, Margalo, Margao, Margareta, Margaretha, Margarethe, Margaretta, Margarita, Marge, Margerie, Margerita, Margery, Marget, Margethe, Margetta, Margette, Margharita, Margo, Margorie, Margory, Margot, Marguerita, Marguerite, Margueritta, Marjery, Marjorie, Meg, Meta, Pearl, Peggy, Rita)*

Marian (HEBREW) 'Bitter and graceful' *(Mariam, Mariana, Marianna, Marianne, Mariom, Marion, Maryanne)*

Marie *see* **Mary**

Marigold (ENGLISH) 'Golden flower girl' *(Marygold)*

Mariko (JAPANESE) 'Circle'

Marina (LATIN) 'Lady of the sea' *(Marnie)*

Marini (SWAHILI) 'Healthy and pretty'

Mariposa (SPANISH) 'Butterfly'

Maris (LATIN) 'Of the sea'

Maritza (ARABIC) 'Blessed'

Marola (LATIN) 'Woman who lives by the sea'

Marola (LATIN) 'Little dark girl'

Marquita *see* **Marcella**

Marsha *see* **Marcella**

Martha (ARABIC) 'The mistress' *(Marta, Martella, Marthe, Marti, Martie, Martita, Marty, Martynne, Mattie, Matty)*

Marthe *see* **Martha**

Marti *see* **Martha**

Martina (LATIN) 'War-like one'. Feminine of Martin *(Marta, Martine, Tina)*

Marvel (LATIN) 'A wondrous miracle' *(Marva, Marvela, Marvella, Marvelle)*

Mary (HEBREW) 'Bitterness'. One of the most consistently popular girl's names in Christian countries *(Maire, Mairi, Mamie, Manette, Manon, Mara, Maretta, Marette, Maria, Mariah, Marie, Mariel, Marietta, Mariette, Marilla, Marilyn, Marla, Marya, Marylin, Marylyn, Maryse, Maureen, May, Mearr, Mimi, Miriam, Mitzi, Molly, Moya, Polly)*

Marya (ARABIC) 'Purity, whiteness' *see also* **Mary**

Maryam (ARABIC) 'Purity'

Marybelle A combination of **Mary** and **Belle** *(Maribell)*

Maryellen A combination of **Mary** and **Ellen**

Maryjo A combination of **Mary** and **Joanne**

Marylou A combination of **Mary** and **Louise**

Masa (JAPANESE) 'Straightforward', 'upright'

Massa (ARABIC) 'Uplifting'

Massima (ITALIAN/LATIN) 'Greatest'

Mathena (HEBREW) 'Gift from God'

Mathilda (TEUTONIC) 'Brave little maid'. One as courageous as a lion *(Maitilde, Matelda, Mathilde, Matilda, Matilde, Mattie, Tilda, Tilly)*

Matsu (JAPANESE) 'Pine tree' *(Matsuko)*

Mattea (HEBREW) 'Gift of God'. Feminine of Matthew *(Mathea, Mathia, Matthea, Matthia)*

Mattie *see* **Mathilda** or **Martha**

Maud (TEUTONIC) 'Brave girl' *(Maude)*

Maurilla (LATIN) 'Sympathetic woman' *(Mauralia, Maurilia)*

Maurise (FRENCH) 'Dark skinned'

Mauve (LATIN) 'Lilac-coloured bird' *(Malva)*

Mave *see* **Mab** or **Maeve**

Mavis (FRENCH) 'Song thrush' *see also* **Mab**

Maxine (FRENCH) 'The greatest'. Feminine of Maximilian *(Maxene, Maxie, Maxima)*

May (LATIN) 'Born in May' *(Maia, May) see also* **Mary**

Maya (SANSKRIT) 'Illusion'

Mead (GREEK) 'Honey wine' *(Meade)*

Meara (GAELIC) 'Mirth'

Medea (GREEK) 'The middle child', 'enchantress' *(Madora, Media, Medora)*

Medora (LITERARY) Poetic character of Lord Byron *see also* **Medea**

Medwenna (WELSH) 'Maiden', 'princess' *(Modwen, Modwenna)*

Meena (HINDI) 'Bird'. Blue semi-precious stone

Meg *see* **Margaret**

Megan (CELTIC) 'The strong one'. A popular name in Wales *(Meagan, Meaghan, Meghan, Meghann)*

Megara (GREEK) 'First'. Hercules' first wife

Mehira (HEBREW) 'Energetic and quick' *(Mahira)*

Mehitabel (HEBREW) 'Favoured of God' *(Hetty, Hitty, Mehetabel, Mehetabelle, Mehetabie, Mehitabelle, Mehitable, Metabel)*

Mehri (PERSIAN) 'Lovable and kind

Meinwen (WELSH) 'Slim'

Meira (HEBREW) 'Light' *(Meera)*

Meiying (CHINESE) 'Beautiful flower' *(Mei)*

Melada (GREEK) 'Honey'

Melanie (GREEK) 'Clad in darkness'. Lady of the night *(Malan, Mel, Melan, Melania, Melany, Mellie, Melloney, Melly)*

Melantha (GREEK) 'Dark flower' *(Melanthe)*

Melda *see* **Imelda**

Melia (GREEK) 'The ash tree'

Melina (LATIN) 'Yellow canary' *see also* **Carmel** or **Madeleine**

Melinda (GREEK) 'Mild and gentle'. A quiet, home-loving girl *(Malinda)*

Melior (LATIN) 'Better'

Melissa (GREEK) 'Honey bee' or 'nymph of the forest' *(Lisa, Mel, Melisa)*

Melita (GREEK) 'Little honey flower' *(Elita, Malita, Melitta)*

Melle (CELTIC/FRENCH) 'Princess'

Melody (GREEK) 'Like a song' *(Lodie, Melodia, Melodie)*

Meraud (GREEK) 'Emerald'

Mercedes (SPANISH) 'Compassionate', 'merciful'. One who forgives and does not condemn *(Merci, Mercy)*

Mercia (ANGLO-SAXON) 'Lady of Mercia'. One from the old Saxon kingdom in central England

Mercy (MIDDLE ENGLISH) 'Compassion', 'mercy' *see also* **Mercedes**

Meredith (CELTIC) 'Protector from the sea'. A popular name for both boys and girls in Wales *(Meredeth, Meredydd, Meredyth, Merideth, Meridith, Meridyth, Merrie, Merry)*

Meriel *see* **Muriel**

Meris (LATIN) 'Of the sea'

Merle (LATIN) 'The blackbird' *(Merl, Merla, Merlina, Merline, Merola, Merula, Meryl, Myrlene)*

Merlyn (CELTIC/SPANISH) 'Sea hill' *(Merlina)*

Merrie (ANGLO-SAXON) 'Mirthful, joyous' *(Meri, Merri, Merry) see also* **Meredith**

Merrila (GREEK) 'Fragrant'

Merrilees (OLD ENGLISH) 'St Mary's field'

Merritt (ANGLO-SAXON) 'Worthy, of merit' *(Meritt, Meritta, Merrit, Merritta)*

Merry *see* **Meredith** or **Merrie**

Mertice (ANGLO-SAXON) 'Famous and pleasant'. One who has not been spoiled by praise or fame *(Merdyce, Mertyce) see also* **Myrtle**

Merula *see* **Merle**

Meryl *see* **Merle**

Mesha (HINDI) 'Born under the constellation of Aries'

Messina (LATIN) 'The middle child'

Meta (LATIN) 'Ambition achieved' *see also* **Margaret**

Metea (GREEK) 'Gentle'

Metis (GREEK) 'Wisdom and skill' *(Metys)*

Mevena (CELTIC/FRENCH) 'Agile'

Mia (LATIN) 'Mine'

Michaela (HEBREW) 'Likeness to God'. Feminine of Michael *(Micaela, Michaelina, Michaeline, Michaella, Michel, Micheline, Michella, Michelle, Michelline, Mikaela)*

Michal (HEBREW) 'God is perfect'

Michi (JAPANESE) 'The way'

Michiko (JAPANESE) 'Three thousand'

Midori (JAPANESE) 'Green'

Mignon (FRENCH) 'Little, dainty darling'. A kitten-like girl of charm and grace *(Mignonette)*

Mihewi (NATIVE AMERICAN) 'Woman of the sun'

Miki (JAPANESE) 'Stem'

Mildred (ANGLO-SAXON) 'Gentle counsellor'. The diplomatic power behind the throne *(Mildrid, Milli, Millie, Milly)*

Millicent (TEUTONIC) 'Strong and industrious'. The hard-working girl *(Melicent, Melisanda, Melisande, Melisandra, Melisenda, Melisende, Mellicent, Milicent, Milisent, Milissent, Milli, Millie, Milly)*

Mimi *see* **Mary**

Mimosa (LATIN) 'Imitative'

Mina *see* **Adamina, Jemina, Minta** or **Wilhelmina**

Minda (INDIAN) 'Knowledge' *see also* **Minta**

Mindora (TEUTONIC) 'Gift of love'

Mindy *see* **Minta**

Minerva (LATIN) 'Wise, purposeful one'. The goddess of wisdom

Minette (FRENCH) 'Little kitten' *(Minetta) see also* **Henrietta**

Minna (OLD GERMAN) 'Tender affection'

Minta (GREEK/TEUTONIC) 'Remembered with love'. From the plant *(Mina, Minda, Mindy, Minetta, Minnie, Mintha, Minthe) see also* **Araminta**

Mione (GREEK) 'Small'

Mira (LATIN) 'Wonderful one' *(Mireilla, Mireille, Mirella, Mirilla, Myra, Myrilla)*

Mirabel (LATIN) 'Admired for her beauty' *(Mirabella, Mirabelle)*

Miranda (LATIN) 'Greatly admired' *(Randa)*

Mireille *see* **Mira**

Miriam *see* **Mary**

Mirta (GREEK/SPANISH) 'Crown of beauty' *(Mirtala, Myrta)*

Misty (OLD ENGLISH) 'Shrouded with mist'

Mitra (PERSIAN) 'Name of angel'

Mitzi *see* **Mary**

Miya (JAPANESE) 'Temple'

Miyuki (JAPANESE) 'Snow'

Mocita (SANSKRIT) 'The one who is set free'

Modana (SANSKRIT) 'One who makes people happy'

Modesty (LATIN) 'Shy, modest'. The retiring and bashful girl *(Desta, Modesta, Modeste, Modestia, Modestine)*

Mohala (HAWAIIAN) 'Flowers in bloom'

Moina (CELTIC) 'Soft' *see also* **Myrna**

Moira *see* **Morag**

Molly *see* **Mary**

Mona *see* **Monica** or **Ramona**

Monica (LATIN) 'Advice giver' *(Mona, Monca, Monika, Monique, Moyna)*

Mora (GAELIC) 'Sun'

Morag (CELTIC) 'Great' *(Moira, Moyra)*

Morgana (WELSH) 'From the sea shore' *(Morgan, Morgen)*

Morwena (WELSH) 'Maiden'

Moselle (HEBREW) 'Taken from the water'. Feminine of Moses *(Mosella, Mozel, Mozella, Mozelle)*

Mosera (HEBREW) 'Bound to men'

Motaza (ARABIC) 'Proud'

Moto (JAPANESE) 'Source'

Moya *see* **Mary**

Moyna *see* **Monica** or **Myrna**

Moyra *see* **Morag**

Moza (HEBREW) 'Fountain'

Mozel *see* **Moselle**

Mozella *see* **Moselle**

Mozelle *see* **Moselle**

Muire *see* **Muriel**

Munira (ARABIC) 'Illuminating', 'light'

Muriel (CELTIC) 'Sea bright' *(Meriel, Muire, Murielle)*

Murielle *see* **Muriel**

Musa (LATIN) 'Song'

Musetta (FRENCH) 'Child of the Muses' *(Musette)*

Musette *see* **Musetta**

Musidore (GREEK) 'Gift of the Muses'

Mwynen (WELSH) 'Gentle'

Mya (BURMESE) 'Emerald'

Myfanwy (WELSH) 'My rare one' *(Myvanwy)*

Myla (ENGLISH) 'Merciful'

Myra (LATIN) 'Admired', 'wonderful one' *see also* **Mira**

Myrilla *see* **Mira**

Myrlene *see* Merle

Myrna (GAELIC) 'Beloved' *(Merna, Mirna, Moina, Morna, Moyna)*

Myrta *see* Mirta or Myrtle

Myrtia *see* Myrtle

Myrtis *see* Myrtle

Myrtle (GREEK) 'Victorious crown'. The hero's laurel wreath *(Mertice, Mertle, Mirle, Myrta, Myrtia, Myrtis)*

Myvanwy *see* Myfanwy

N

GIRLS

Naamah (HEBREW) 'Pleasant', 'beautiful' *(Nama, Namah, Namana)*

Naashom (HEBREW) 'Enchantress' *(Nashom, Nashoma)*

Naava (HEBREW) 'Beautiful'

Nabeela (ARABIC) 'Noble' *(Nabila)*

Nabila *see* **Nabeela**

Nabrissa (FRENCH/GREEK) 'Peace'

Nada *see* **Nadine**

Nadda *see* **Nadine**

Nadeen *see* **Nadine**

Nadia *see* **Nadine**

Nadine (FRENCH) 'Hope' *(Nada, Nadda, Nadeen, Nadia)*

Nadira (ARABIC) 'Rare, precious'

Nafisa (ARABIC) 'Precious'

Nahtanha (NATIVE AMERICAN) 'Cornflower'

Naiada *see* **Naida**

Naida (LATIN) 'The water nymph'. From the streams of Arcadia *(Naiada)*

Naima (ARABIC) 'Contented'

Nairne (GAELIC) 'From the river'

Najila (ARABIC) 'One with beautiful eyes'

Nalani (HAWAIIAN) 'Calmness of the heavens'

Nama *see* Naamah

Namah *see* Naamah

Namana *see* Naamah

Nana *see* Anne

Nancy *see* Anne

Nandelle (GERMAN)
'Adventuring life'

Nandita (SANSKRIT) 'Happy'

Nanette *see* Anne

Nani (HAWAIIAN) 'Beautiful'

Nanice *see* Anne

Nanine *see* Anne

Nanna *see* Anne

Nanon *see* Anne

Naoma *see* Naomi

Naomi (HEBREW) 'The pleasant
one' *(Naoma, Noami, Nomi,
Nomie)*

Napaea *see* Napea

Napea (LATIN) 'Girl of the
valley' *(Napaea, Napia)*

Nara (ENGLISH) 'Nearest and
dearest' *see also* Narda

Narda (LATIN) 'Fragrant
perfume' *(Nara)*

Narelle (AUSTRALIAN) 'Woman
from the sea'

Narmada (HINDI) 'Gives
pleasure'

Nashoma *see* Naashom

Nasiba (ARABIC) 'Love, poetry'

Nasima (ARABIC) 'Gentle breeze'

Nastasya *see* Natalie

Nasya (HEBREW) 'Miracle of
God'

Nata (SANSKRIT) 'Dancer'

Natacha *see* Natalie

Natala *see* Natalie

Natalie (LATIN) 'Born at
Christmas tide' *(Nastasya,
Natacha, Natala, Natale,
Natalia, Natalina, Natasha,
Nathalie, Natica, Natika,
Natividad, Nattie, Netta,
Nettie, Netty, Noel, Noelle,
Novella)*

Natalina *see* Natalie

Natasha *see* Natalie

Natene *see* Nathania

Natesa (HINDI) 'God-like'. Another name for the Hindu goddess Shakti

Nathalie *see* **Natalie**

Nathania (HEBREW) 'Gift of God' *(Natene, Nathane, Nathene)*

Natica *see* **Natalie**

Natividad *see* **Natalie**

Natsu (JAPANESE) 'Summer'

Nattie *see* **Natalie**

Nayana (SANSKRIT) 'Lovely eyes'

Nazima (SANSKRIT) 'Beautiful song'

Neala (GAELIC) 'The champion'. Feminine of Neal *(Neale)*

Nebula (LATIN) 'A cloud of mist'

Neda (SLAV) 'Born on Sunday' *(Nedda, Nedi)*

Neila (IRISH) 'Champion'

Nela *see* **Cornelia** or **Nila**

Nelda (ANGLO-SAXON) 'Born under the elder tree'

Nelie *see* **Cornelia**

Nell *see* **Helen**

Nelli *see* **Cornelia**

Nellwyn (GREEK) 'Bright friend and companion'

Neola (GREEK) 'The young one'

Neoma (GREEK) 'The new moon'

Nerice *see* **Nerima**

Nerima (GREEK) 'From the sea' *(Nerice, Nerine, Nerissa, Nerita)*

Nerine *see* **Nerima**

Nerissa (GREEK) 'Of the sea' *(Nerita)*

Nerita *see* **Nerima** or **Nerissa**

Nerys (WELSH) 'Lordly one'

Nessa *see* **Agnes**

Nessie *see* **Agnes**

Nesta *see* **Agnes**

Netania (HEBREW) 'Gift of God'

Netie *see* **Henrietta**

Netta *see* **Antonia, Henrietta, Natalie**

Nettie *see* **Antonia** or **Natalie**

Neva (SPANISH) 'As white as the moon' *(Nevada)*

Nevada *see* **Neva**

Nevina (IRISH) 'Worshipper of Saint Nevin'

Neysa see **Agnes**

Niamh (IRISH) 'Brightness'

Nichola see **Nicole**

Nicholina see **Nicole**

Nicky see **Nicole**

Nicol see **Nicole**

Nicola see **Nicole**

Nicole (GREEK) 'The people's victory' *(Nichola, Nicholina, Nickie, Nicky, Nicol, Nicola, Nicolette, Nicolina, Nicoline, Nikki, Nikola, Nikoletta)*

Nicolina see **Nicole**

Nidia (LATIN) 'Nest'

Nieta (SPANISH) 'Granddaughter'

Nigella (LATIN) 'Black'

Nike (GREEK) 'Victorious'

Nikhita (SANSKRIT) 'The earth'

Nikki see **Nicole**

Nikola see **Nicole**

Nikoletta see **Nicole**

Nila (LATIN) 'From the Nile' *(Nela)*

Nilaya (SANSKRIT) 'Home'

Nilda see **Magnilda**

Nillie see **Magnilda**

Nima (HEBREW) 'Thread'

Nina (SPANISH) 'The daughter' *(Nineta, Ninetta, Ninette)* see also **Anne**

Nineta see **Nina**

Ninetta see **Nina**

Ninette see **Anne** or **Nina**

Ninon see **Anne**

Nipha (GREEK) 'Snowflake'

Nirah (HEBREW) 'Light'

Nirel (HEBREW) 'Light of God'

Nisha (SANSKRIT) 'Night'

Nissa (SCANDINAVIAN) 'Friendly elf'. A fairy who can be seen only by lovers

Nissie see **Nixie**

Nita see **Anne, Jane** or **Bonita**

Nixie (TEUTONIC) 'Water sprite' *(Nissie, Nissy)*

Nizana (HEBREW) 'Flower bud'

Noami see **Naomi**

Noel *see* **Natalie**

Noelle *see* **Natalie**

Nokomis (AMERICAN INDIAN) 'The grandmother'. From the legend of Hiawatha

Nola (GAELIC) 'Famous one' *see also* **Magnolia** or **Olive**

Noleta (LATIN) 'Unwilling' *(Nolita)*

Nolie *see* **Magnolia**

Nolita *see* **Noleta**

Nollie *see* **Olive**

Nomie *see* **Naomi**

Nona (LATIN) 'Ninth-born'

Nonnie *see* **Annona**

Nora *see* **Eleanor, Helen** or **Honora**

Norah *see* **Helen** or **Honora**

Norberta (TEUTONIC) 'Bright heroine' *(Norberte, Norbertha, Norberthe)*

Norberte *see* **Norberta**

Norbertha *see* **Norberta**

Norberthe *see* **Norberta**

Nordica (TEUTONIC) 'Girl from the North' *(Nordika)*

Nordika *see* **Nodica**

Noreen *see* **Honora** or **Norma**

Norine *see* **Honora**

Norma (LATIN) 'A pattern or rule'. The template of the perfect girl *(Noreen, Normi, Normie)*

Norna (NORSE) 'Destiny'. The goddess of fate

Norrie *see* **Honora**

Nova *see* **Novia**

Novella *see* **Natalie**

Novia (LATIN) 'The newcomer' *(Nova)*

Nuala (GAELIC) 'One with beautiful shoulders'

Numidia (LATIN) 'The traveller'

Nuna (NATIVE AMERICAN) 'Our land'

Nunciata (ITALIAN) 'She has good news' *see also* **Annunciata**

Nuru (SWAHILI) 'Daylight'

Nydia (LATIN) 'A refuge', 'nest'

Nyssa (GREEK) 'Starting point'

Nyx (GREEK) 'White-haired'

GIRLS

Obelia (GREEK) 'A pointed pillar'

Octavia (LATIN) 'The eighth child' *(Octavie, Ottavia, Ottavie, Tavi, Tavia, Tavie, Tavy)*

Oda (TEUTONIC) 'Rich'

Odele *see* **Odelia**

Odelette (FRENCH) 'A small lyric' *(Odelet)*

Odelia (TEUTONIC) 'Prosperous one' *(Odele, Odelie, Odelinda, Odella, Odilia, Odilla, Otha, Othilla, Ottilie)*

Odessa (GREEK) 'A long journey'

Odette (FRENCH) 'Home-lover'. One who makes a house a home

Odile (FRENCH/GERMAN) 'Rich' *(Odeline, Odila)*

Odilia *see* **Odelia**

Ofelia *see* **Ophelia**

Ofrah (HEBREW) 'Young mind, lively maiden'

Ola (SCANDINAVIAN) 'Descendant'. The daughter of a chief *(Olaa)*

Olaathe (NATIVE AMERICAN) 'Beautiful'

Olatta (NATIVE AMERICAN) 'Lagoon'

Olave (TEUTONIC) 'Ancestor's relic'

Olenka *see* **Olga**

Oleta *see* **Olethea**

Olethea (LATIN) 'Truth'
(*Alethea, Oleta*)

Olga (TEUTONIC) 'Holy'. One
who has been annointed in
the service of God (*Helga,
Livi, Livia, Livie, Livvi,
Olenka, Olive, Olivia, Ollie,
Olva see also Elga*)

Olien (RUSSIAN) 'Deer'

Olimpie *see* **Olympia**

Olina (HAWAIIAN) 'Filled with
happiness'

Olinda (LATIN) 'Fragrant herb'

Olive (LATIN) 'Symbol of peace'
(*Livia, Nola, Nollie,
Olivette, Olivia, Ollie, Olva*)
see also **Olga**

Olivette *see* **Olive**

Olivia *see* **Olga** or **Olive**

Ollie *see* **Olga** or **Olive**

Olva *see* **Olga** or **Olive**

Olwyn (WELSH) 'White clover'
(*Olwen*)

Olympia (GREEK) 'Heavenly one'
(*Olimpie, Olympe, Olympie*)
see also **Pia**

Oma (HEBREW) 'Reverent'.
Feminine of Omar

Ona *see* **Una**

Onawa (AMERICAN INDIAN)
'Maiden who is wide awake'

Ondine (LATIN) 'Wave', 'wave of
water' (*Ondina, Undine*)

Oneida (NATIVE AMERICAN)
'Expected' (*Onida*)

Onida *see* **Oneida**

Oola *see* **Ula**

Oona *see* **Una**

Oonagh *see* **Una**

Opal (SANSKRIT) 'Precious jewel'
(*Opalina, Opaline*)

Opalina *see* **Opal**

Ophelia (GREEK) 'Wise and
immortal' (*Ofelia, Ofilia,
Phelia*)

Ora (LATIN) 'Golden one'
  (Orabel, Orabella, Orabelle)
  see also **Aura, Aurelia** or
  Ursula

Orabella *see* **Ora**

Oralee (HEBREW) 'My light'
  (Orali, Orli)

Oralia *see* **Aurelia**

Orane (FRENCH) 'Rising'

Ordelia (TEUTONIC) 'Elf's spear'

Orea (GREEK) 'Of the mountain'.
  The original maid of the
  mountains

Orel (LATIN) 'Small one'

Orela (LATIN) 'Divine
  pronouncement'. The oracle

Orella (LATIN) 'Girl who listens'

Orenda (AMERICAN INDIAN)
  'Magic power'

Oria *see* **Oriana**

Oriana (LATIN) 'Golden one'
  (Oria, Oriane)

Oriole *see* **Aurelia**

Orla (IRISH) 'Golden lady'

Orlanda *see* **Rolanda**

Orlena (FRENCH) 'Gold'

Orli *see* **Oralee**

Orna (GAELIC) 'Pale-coloured'

Orpah (HEBREW) 'A fawn'. From
  The Song of Solomon in the
  Bible

Orquidea (SPANISH) 'Orchid'

Orsa *see* **Ursula**

Orsola *see* **Ursula**

Ortrud (TEUTONIC) 'Golden girl'

Orva (TEUTONIC) 'Spear friend'

Orvala (LATIN) 'Worthy of gold'

Osanna (LATIN) 'Filled with
  mercy'

Osnat (HEBREW) 'Favourite of
  the deity'

Otha *see* **Odelia**

Othilla *see* **Odelia**

Ottavia *see* **Octavia**

Ottilie *see* **Odelia**

Ovina (LATIN) 'Like a lamb'

Owena (WELSH) 'Well-born'

Owissa (NATIVE AMERICAN) 'Bluebird'. The bringer of spring

Ozana (HEBREW) 'Treasure', 'wealth'

Ozora (HEBREW) 'Strength of the Lord'

P

GIRLS

Paciane (FRENCH FROM LATIN) 'Peace'

Pacifica (LATIN) 'Peaceful one'

Page *see* **Paige**

Paige (ANGLO-SAXON) 'Young child' *(Page)*

Paka (SWAHILI) 'Kitten'

Pakhi *see* **Pakshi**

Pakshi (SANSKRIT) 'Bird' *(Pakhi)*

Pallas (GREEK) 'Wisdom and knowledge'

Palma (LATIN) 'Palm tree' *(Palmer, Palmira)*

Palmira *see* **Palma**

Paloma (SPANISH) 'The dove'. Gentle, tender *(Palometa, Palomita)*

Palometa *see* **Paloma**

Pam *see* **Pamela**

Pamela (GREEK) 'All sweetness and honey'. A loving person of great kindness *(Pam, Pamelina, Pamella, Pammie, Pammy)*

Pamelina *see* **Pamela**

Pamella *see* **Pamela**

Pammy *see* **Pamela**

Pamphila (GREEK) 'All loving'. One who loves all humanity

Pandora (GREEK) 'Talented, gifted one'

Pansy (GREEK) 'Fragrant like a flower'

Panthea (GREEK) 'Of all the Gods' *(Panthia)*

Panthia *see* Panthea

Panya (SWAHILI) 'Little mouse'

Paola (ITALIAN) 'Little' *see also* Paula

Parasha *see* Paschasia

Parnella (FRENCH) 'Little rook' *(Parnelle, Pernella, Pernelle)*

Parnelle *see* Parnella

Parthenia (GREEK) 'Sweet virgin'

Parvaneh (PERSIAN) 'Butterfly'

Paschasia (LATIN) 'Born at Easter' *(Parasha)*

Pat *see* Patricia

Patience (LATIN) 'Patient one' *(Patienza, Pattie, Patty)*

Patienza *see* Patience

Patrice *see* Patricia

Patricia (LATIN) 'Well-born girl' *(Pat, Patrice, Patrizia, Patsy, Patti, Patty)*

Patrizia *see* Patricia

Patsy *see* Patricia

Patti *see* Patricia

Pattie *see* Patience

Patty *see* Patience or Patricia

Paula (LATIN) 'Little'. Feminine of Paul *(Paola, Paule, Paulena, Pauletta, Paulette, Pauli, Paulie, Paulina, Pauline, Paulita, Pavla)*

Paulena *see* Paula

Paulette *see* Paula

Paulie *see* Paula

Pauline *see* Paula

Paulita *see* Paula

Pavla *see* Paula

Peace (LATIN) 'Tranquillity', 'calm'

Pearl (LATIN) 'Precious jewel'. One of unmatched beauty *(Pearle, Pearlie, Perl, Perle, Perlie, Perlina, Perline) see also* Margaret

Pearlie *see* Pearl

Peggy *see* Margaret

Peirrette *see* **Petrina**

Pelagia (GREEK) 'Mermaid'

Pen *see* **Penelope**

Penelope (GREEK) 'The weaver'.
The patient wife of Ulysses
(Pen, Penny)

Peni *see* **Peninah**

Peninah (HEBREW) 'Pearl' *(Peni, Penina, Peninnah)*

Penny *see* **Penelope**

Penta *see* **Penthea**

Penthea (GREEK) 'Fifth child'
(Penta, Penthia)

Peony (LATIN) 'The gift of
healing'

Pepita *see* **Josephine**

Perdita (LATIN) 'The lost one'

Perfecta (SPANISH) 'The most
perfect being'

Perizada (PERSIAN) 'Born of the
fairies'

Perlina *see* **Pearl**

Pernella *see* **Parnella**

Peronel (LATIN) 'A rock'
(Peronelle)

Perpetua (LATIN) 'Everlasting'

Perrine *see* **Petrina**

Persephone (GREEK) 'Goddess of
the Underworld'

Persis (LATIN) 'Woman from
Persia'

Peta (GREEK) 'A rock'

Petica (LATIN) 'Noble one'

Petra *see* **Petrina**

Petrina (GREEK) 'Steadfast as a
rock'. Feminine of Peter
*(Perrine, Petra, Petronella,
Petronelle, Petronia,
Petronilla, Petronille, Petula,
Pierette, Pierrette, Pietra)*

Petronella *see* **Petrina**

Petula (LATIN) 'Seeker' *see also*
Petrina

Petunia (INDIAN) 'Reddish
flower'

Phaidra *see* **Phedra**

Phebe *see* **Phoebe**

Phedra (GREEK) 'Bright one'.
The daughter of King
Minos of Crete *(Phaidra,
Phedre)*

Phelia *see* Ophelia

Phemie *see* Euphemia

Philadelphia (GREEK) 'Brotherly love'

Philana (GREEK) 'Friend of humanity' *(Filana)*

Philantha (GREEK) 'Lover of flowers'. Child of the blossoms *(Filantha, Philanthe)*

Philberta (TEUTONIC) 'Exceptionally brilliant' *(Filberta, Filberte, Filbertha, Filberthe, Philberthe, Philertha)*

Philippa (GREEK) 'Lover of horses'. Feminine of Philip *(Filipa, Filippa, Phillie, Phillipa, Phillippa, Pippa)*

Philis *see* Phyllis

Phillida (GREEK) 'Loving woman' *see also* Phyllis

Phillie *see* Philippa

Phillis *see* Phyllis

Philmen *see* Filma

Philomela (GREEK) 'Lover of song'

Philomena (GREEK) 'Lover of the moon'. The nightingale

Philothra (GREEK) 'Pious'

Phoebe (GREEK) 'Bright, shining sun'. Feminine of Phoebus (Apollo) *(Phebe)*

Phoenix (GREEK) 'The phoenix' or 'the eagle'. Legendary bird of which only one ever exists. A new bird rises from the ashes of the old *(Fenix)*

Pholma *see* Filma

Photina (GREEK) 'Light'

Phyllida *see* Phyllis

Phyllis (GREEK) 'A green bough' *(Filida, Filis, Fillida, Fillis, Philis, Phillis, Phylis, Phyllida* see also *Phillida)*

Pia (LATIN) 'Pious' *see also* Olympia

Pierette *see* Petrina

Pietra *see* Petrina

Pilar (SPANISH) 'A foundation or pillar'

Ping (CHINESE) 'Duckweed'

Pinon (GREEK) 'Pearl'

Piper (ENGLISH) 'Player of the pipes'

Pippa see **Philippa**

Placida (LATIN) 'Peaceful one' *(Placidia)*

Platona (GREEK) 'Broad shouldered'. Feminine of Plato. A woman of wisdom

Polly see **Mary**

Pomona (LATIN) 'Fruitful and fertile'

Poppaea see **Poppy**

Poppy (LATIN) 'Red flower' *(Poppaea)*

Portia (LATIN) 'An offering to God' *(Porcia)*

Poupée (FRENCH) 'Doll'

Prabha (HINDI) 'Light'

Precious (FRENCH) 'Precious', 'dear'

Preeti (HINDI) 'Love'

Prem see **Prema**

Prema (SANSKRIT) 'Love' *(Prem, Premala)*

Premala see **Prema**

Prima (LATIN) 'First born'

Primalia (LATIN) 'Like the springtime'

Primavera (SPANISH) 'Child of the spring'

Primmie see **Primrose**

Primrose (LATIN) 'The first flower of spring' *(Primmie, Primula, Rosa, Rose)*

Primula see **Primrose**

Prisca see **Priscilla**

Priscilla (LATIN) 'Of ancient lineage'. The descendant of princes *(Pris, Prisca, Prisilla, Prissie)* see also **Cilla**

Prissie see **Priscilla**

Proba (LATIN) 'Honest'

Prospera (LATIN) 'Favourable'

Prudence (LATIN) 'Cautious foresight' *(Prud, Prudentia, Prudie, Prudy, Prue)*

Prudentia see **Prudence**

Prue see **Prudence**

Prunella (FRENCH) 'Plum coloured' *(Prunelle)*

Psyche (GREEK) 'Of the soul or mind'

Pulcheria (LATIN) 'Very beautiful'

Purity (MIDDLE ENGLISH) 'Purity'

Pyrena (GREEK) 'Fiery one'. The warmth of home *(Pyrenia)*

Pyrenia *see* **Pyrena**

Pythea *see* **Pythia**

Pythia (GREEK) 'A prophet'. The oracle (Pythea)

GIRLS

Qadira (ARABIC) 'Powerful'

Qing (CHINESE) 'Blue'

Qiturah (ARABIC) 'Fragrance'

Queena (TEUTONIC) 'The queen'. The supreme woman *(Queenie)*

Queenie *see* **Queena**

Quenberga (LATIN) 'Queen's pledge'

Quenby (SCANDINAVIAN) 'Womanly', 'perfect wife'

Quendrida (LATIN) 'One who threatens the queen'

Querida (SPANISH) 'Beloved one' *(Cherida)*

Questa (FRENCH) 'Searcher'

Quinta (LATIN) 'The fifth child' *(Quintana, Quintella, Quintilla, Quintina)*

Quintana *see* **Quinta**

Quintella *see* **Quinta**

Quintessa (LATIN) 'Essence'

Quintilla *see* **Quinta**

Quintina *see* **Quinta**

Quisha (AFRICAN) 'Physical and spiritual beauty'

Quita (FRENCH) 'Tranquil'

R

Rabi (ARABIC) 'The harvest', 'breeze'

Rabiah (ARABIC) 'Garden'

Rachael *see* **Rachel**

Rachel (HEBREW) 'Innocent as a lamb'. One who suffers in silence *(Rachael, Rachele, Rachelle, Rae, Rahel, Raoghnailt, Raquel, Ray, Shelly) see also* **Rochelle** or **Shelley**

Rachida (ARABIC) 'Wise'

Radella (ANGLO-SAXON) 'Elf-like adviser'. A fairy-like creature whose advice is weighty

Radinka (SLAVIC) 'Alive and joyful'

Radmilla (SLAVIC) 'Worker for the people'

Rae (MIDDLE ENGLISH) 'A doe deer' *see also* **Rachel**

Rafa (ARABIC) 'Happy and prosperous'

Rafaela *see* **Raphaela**

Rafaella *see* **Raphaela**

Ragan *see* **Regina**

Ragini (SANSKRIT) 'A melody'

Rahel *see* **Rachel**

Rahima (ARABIC) 'Merciful'

Raina *see* **Regina**

Rainbow (ENGLISH) 'Bow of light'

Raine *see* **Regina**

Raissa (FRENCH) 'The believer' *(Raisse)*

Raja (ARABIC) 'Hopeful'

Rajani (SANSKRIT) 'Night'

Rama *see* **Ramona**

Ramona (TEUTONIC) 'Wise protector'. Feminine of Raymond *(Mona, Rama, Ramonda, Ramonde) see also* **Raymonda**

Ramonda *see* **Ramona**

Ramonde *see* **Ramona**

Ran (JAPANESE) 'Water lily'

Rana (SANSKRIT) 'Of royal birth', 'a queen' *(Ranee, Rani, Rania, Ranique, Rayna)*

Randa *see* **Miranda**

Ranee *see* **Rana** or **Rani**

Rani (SANSKRIT) 'Queen'

Ranee *see also* **Rana**

Rania *see* **Rana**

Ranique *see* **Rana**

Ranita (HEBREW) 'Joyful song' *(Ranite)*

Ranite *see* **Ranita**

Raoghnailt *see* **Rachel**

Raphaela (HEBREW) 'Blessed healer'. One who has a God-given healing touch *(Rafaela, Rafaella, Raphaella)*

Raquel *see* **Rachel**

Rasha (ARABIC) 'Young gazelle'

Rashida (AFRICAN) 'Righteous'

Rashmi (SANSKRIT) 'Sunlight'

Rasia *see* **Rose**

Raven (ENGLISH) 'Sleek, black bird'

Ray *see* **Rachel**

Raymonda (TEUTONIC) 'Wise protector'. Feminine of Raymond *(Raymonde) see also* **Ramona**

Rayna *see* **Rana** or **Regina**

Rea *see* **Rhea**

Reba *see* **Rebecca**

Rebecca (HEBREW) 'The captivator' *(Becca, Beckie, Becky, Bekky, Reba, Rebeca, Rebeka, Rebekah, Rebekka, Riba) see also* **Riva**

Rebeka *see* **Rebecca**

Rebekah *see* **Rebecca**

Rebekka *see* **Rebecca**

Rechaba (HEBREW) 'Horse woman'

Reena *see* **Rena**

Regan *see* **Regina**

Regina (LATIN) 'A queen, born to rule' *(Gina, Ragan, Raina, Raine, Rayna, Regan, Regine, Reina, Reine, Rina, Rioghnach)*

Regine *see* **Regina**

Rehka (SANSKRIT) 'Art'

Reiko (JAPANESE) 'Gratitude'

Reina *see* **Regina**

Reini *see* **Irene**

Rena (HEBREW) 'Song' *(Reena) see also* **Irene**

Renata (LATIN) 'Born again'. The spirit of reincarnation *(Renate, Rene, Renee, Rennie) see also* **Irene**

Renate *see* **Renata**

Rene *see* **Irene** or **Renata**

Renee (FRENCH) 'Born again' *see also* **Renata**

Renita (LATIN) 'A rebel'

Rennie *see* **Irene** or **Renata**

Renny *see* **Irene**

Reseda (LATIN) 'Mignonette flower'

Reshma (SANSKRIT) 'Silken' *(Reshmam, Reshmi)*

Reshmam *see* **Reshma**

Reshmi *see* **Reshma**

Retha *see* **Areta**

Reva (LATIN) 'Strength regained'

Rexana (LATIN) 'Regally graceful'. One whose bearing is regal *(Rexanna)*

Reyhan (TURKISH) 'Sweet-smelling flower'

Reynalda (TEUTONIC) 'King's advisor'

Rhea (GREEK) 'Mother', 'poppy'. The mother of the Greek gods *(Rea)*

Rhedyn (WELSH) 'Fern'

Rheta (GREEK) 'An orator'

Rhianna *see* **Rihana**

Rhiannon (WELSH) 'Nymph'

Rhianwen (WELSH) 'Blessed maiden'

Rhoda (GREEK) 'Garland of roses', 'girl from Rhodes' *(Rhodia, Rodina) see also* **Rose**

Rhodanthe (GREEK) 'The rose of roses'

Rhodia *see* **Rhoda** or **Rose**

Rhona *see* **Rona**

Rhonda (WELSH) 'Grand'

Rhonwen (WELSH) 'White lance'

Ria (SPANISH) 'The river'

Rianna *see* **Rihana**

Riba *see* **Rebecca**

Rica *see* **Roderica** or **Ulrica**

Ricadonna (ITALIAN) 'Ruling lady'. One who rules in her own right or on behalf of her son

Ricarda (TEUTONIC) 'Powerful ruler'. Feminine of Richard *(Dickie, Dicky, Richarda, Richarde, Rickie, Ricky)*

Richarda *see* **Ricarda**

Ricky *see* **Ricarda**

Rihana (ARABIC) 'Sweet basil herb' *(Rhiana, Rhianna, Riana, Rianna)*

Riju (SANSKRIT) 'Innocent' *(Rijuta)*

Rijuta *see* **Rijul**

Rika (SWEDISH) 'Ruler'

Rilla (TEUTONIC) 'A stream or brook' *(Rille, Rillette)*

Rille *see* **Rilla**

Rillette *see* **Rilla**

Rina *see* **Regina**

Rinah (HEBREW) 'Song', 'joy'

Rioghnach *see* **Regina**

Risa (LATIN) 'Laughter'

Risha (HINDI) 'Born under the constellation of Taurus'

Rita *see* **Margaret**

Riva (FRENCH) 'Riverbank' *see also* **Rebecca**

Ro *see* **Rolanda**

Roanna (LATIN) 'Sweet and gracious' *(Rohanna, Rohanne)*

Roberta (ANGLO-SAXON) 'Of shining fame'. Feminine of Robert *(Bertie, Bobbie, Bobby, Bobette, Bobina, Robertha, Roberthe, Robinette, Robina, Robinia, Ruberta, Ruperta)*

Robia (TEUTONIC) 'Famous'

Robin (OLD ENGLISH) 'Bright or shining with fame' *(Robina, Robyn)*

Robina *see* **Roberta** or **Robin**

Robinette *see* **Roberta**

Robinia *see* **Roberta**

Robyn *see* **Robin**

Rochalla *see* **Rochelle**

Rochana (PERSIAN) 'Sunrise'

Rochelle (FRENCH) 'From the small rock' *(Rochalla, Rochalle, Rochella, Rochette)* *see also* **Rachel**

Rochette *see* **Rochelle**

Roddie *see* **Roderica**

Roderica (TEUTONIC) 'Famous ruler'. Feminine of Roderick *(Rica, Roddie, Roddy, Rodericka, Rickie)*

Rodina *see* **Rhoda**

Rohana (HINDU) 'Sandalwood', 'sweet incense' *(Rohane, Rohanna)*

Rohesia *see* **Rose**

Rola *see* **Rolanda**

Rolanda (TEUTONIC) 'From the famed land'. Feminine of Roland *(Orlanda, Orlande, Ro, Rola, Rolande)*

Roma *see* **Romola**

Romella *see* **Romola**

Romelle *see* **Romola**

Romilda (TEUTONIC) 'Glorious warrior maiden' *(Romhilda, Romhilde, Romilde)*

Romola (LATIN) 'Lady of Rome' *(Roma, Romella, Romelle, Romula)*

Romy *see* **Rosemary**

Rona (SCANDINAVIAN) 'Mighty power' *(Rhona, Ronalda)*

Ronalda (TEUTONIC) 'All powerful'. Feminine of Ronald *(Ronalde, Ronnie, Ronny) see also* **Rona**

Ronnie *see* **Ronalda** or **Veronica**

Ros *see* **Rosalind**

Rosa *see* **Primrose** or **Rose**

Rosabel (LATIN) 'Beautiful rose' *(Rosabella, Rosabelle)*

Rosalee *see* **Rose**

Rosaleen *see* **Rose**

Rosalia *see* **Rose**

Rosalie *see* **Rose**

Rosalind (LATIN) 'Fair and beautiful rose' *(Ros, Rosalinda, Rosaline, Rosalyn, Rosalynd, Roseline, Roselyn, Roslyn, Roz, Rozalind, Rozaline, Rozeline)*

Rosalyn *see* **Rosalind**

Rosalynd *see* **Rosalind**

Rosamond (FRENCH) 'Rose of the world' *(Rosamonda, Rosamund, Rosamunda, Rosemond, Rosemonde, Rosemund, Rosmunda, Rozamond)*

Rosanna (ENGLISH) 'Graceful rose' *(Rosanne)*

Rosarana (CELTIC) 'Rose bush'

Rose (GREEK) 'The rose' *(Rasia, Rhoda, Rhodia, Rohesia, Rois, Rosa, Rosalee, Rosaleen, Rosalia, Rosalie, Rosel, Rosella, Roselle, Rosena, Rosene, Rosetta, Rosette, Rosia, Rosie, Rosina, Rosy, Rozalina, Rozella, Rozello) see also* **Primrose** or **Rhoda**

Roseline *see* **Rosalind**

Rosella *see* **Rose**

Roselle *see* **Rose**

Roselyn *see* **Rosalind**

Rosemary (LATIN) 'Dew of the sea' *(Romy, Rosie, Rosemarie, Rosy)*

Rosemund *see* **Rosamond**

Rosena *see* Rose

Rosetta *see* Rose

Rosgrana (CELTIC) 'Sunbeam'

Rosia *see* Rose

Rosie *see* Rose or Rosemary

Rosina *see* Rose

Roslyn *see* Rosalind

Rosmunda *see* Rosamond

Rosslyn (WELSH) 'Moorland lake'

Rosy *see* Rose or Rosemary

Roux *see* La Roux

Rowena (ANGLO-SAXON) 'Friend with white hair' *(Rowenna)*

Rox *see* Roxana

Roxana (PERSIAN) 'Brilliant dawn' *(Rox, Roxane, Roxanna, Roxanne, Roxie, Roxina, Roxine, Roxy)*

Roxanne *see* Roxana

Roxy *see* Roxana

Royale (FRENCH) 'Regal being'. Feminine of Roy

Roz *see* Rosalind

Rozalind *see* Rosalind

Rozamond *see* Rosamond

Rozeline *see* Rosalind

Rozella *see* Rose

Rozene (NATIVE AMERICAN) 'Rose'

Ruberta *see* Roberta

Rubetta *see* Ruby

Rubia *see* Ruby

Rubina *see* Ruby

Ruby (LATIN) 'Precious red jewel' *(Rubetta, Rubette, Rubia, Rubie, Rubina)*

Rucita (SANSKRIT) 'Shining'

Rudelle (TEUTONIC) 'Famous person' *(Rudella)*

Ruella (HEBREW) Combination of Ruth and Ella

Rufina (LATIN) 'Red-haired one'

Rugina (LATIN) 'Girl with bright red hair'

Rula (LATIN) 'A sovereign'. One who rules by right

Rupak (SANSKRIT) 'Beautiful' *(Rupali, Rupashi, Rupashri)*

Rupali *see* Rupak

Rupashi *see* Rupak

Rupashri *see* Rupak

Ruperta *see* Roberta

Ruri (JAPANESE) 'Emerald'

Ruth (HEBREW) 'Compassionate and beautiful' *(Ruthie)*

Ruthie *see* Ruth

Rutilia (LATIN) 'Fiery red'

Saba (GREEK) 'Woman of Sheba' *(Sheba)*

Sabella (LATIN) 'The wise' *(Sabelle)*

Sabelle *see* **Sabella**

Sabina (LATIN) 'Woman of Sabine' *(Bina, Binnie, Sabine, Saidhbhain, Savina) see also* **Bina**

Sabine *see* **Sabina**

Sabira (ARABIC) 'Patient'

Sabra (HEBREW) 'The restful one'

Sabrina (LATIN) 'A princess' *(Brina, Sabrine)*

Sabrine *see* **Sabrina**

Sacha (GREEK) 'Helpmate' *(Sasha)*

Sacharissa (GREEK) 'Sweet'

Sadella *see* **Sarah**

Sadhbh *see* **Sophia**

Sadhbha *see* **Sophia**

Sadie *see* **Sarah**

Sadira (PERSIAN) 'The lotus-eater'

Sadye *see* **Sarah**

Saffron *(English)* From the plant

Safia (ARABIC) 'Pure'

Sahlah (ARABIC) 'Smooth'

Sai (JAPANESE) 'Intelligence'

Saidhbhain *see* **Sabina**

Sajal *see* **Sajala**

Sajala (SANSKRIT) 'Clouds' *(Sajal)*

Sakhi (SANSKRIT) 'Friend' *(Sakina)*

Sakina *see* **Sakhi**

Sal *see* **Sarah**

Salaidh *see* **Sarah**

Salema (HEBREW) 'Girl of peace' *(Selemas, Selima) see also* **Selima**

Salene *see* **Selena**

Saliha (ARABIC) 'Goodness'

Salima (ARABIC) 'Safe', 'unharmed'

Salina (GREEK) 'From the salty place'

Sallie *see* **Sarah**

Sally *see* **Sarah**

Saloma *see* **Salome**

Salome (HEBREW) 'Peace'. 'Shalom' is the traditional Hebrew greeting, meaning 'peace' *(Saloma, Salomi)*

Salvia (LATIN) 'Sage herb' *(Salvina)*

Salvina *see* **Salvia**

Samala (HEBREW) 'Asked of God'

Samantha (ARAMAIC) 'A listener'

Samara (HEBREW) 'Watchful', 'cautious', 'guarded by God'

Samella *see* **Samuela**

Samelle *see* **Samuela**

Samira (ARABIC) 'Entertaining'

Samuela (HEBREW) 'His name is God'. Feminine of Samuel *(Samella, Samelle, Samuella, Samuelle)*

Samuelle *see* **Samuela**

Sancha *see* **Sancia**

Sanchia *see* **Sancia**

Sancia (LATIN) 'Sacred' *(Sancha, Sanchia)*

Sandeep (PUNJABI) 'Enlightened'

Sandip (SANSKRIT) 'Beautiful one'

Sandra *see* **Alexandra**

Sandy *see* **Alexandra**

Sanjay (SANSKRIT) 'Charioteer'

Santina (SPANISH) 'Little saint'

Sapphira (GREEK) 'Eyes of sapphire colour' *(Sapphire)*

Sapphire *see* **Sapphira**

Sara *see* **Sarah**

Sarah (HEBREW) 'Princess' *(Morag, Sadella, Sadie, Sadye, Sal, Salaidh, Sallie, Sally, Sara, Sarene, Sarette, Sari, Sarine, Sarita, Sharie, Sorcha, Zara, Zarah, Zaria* see also *Morag* and *Zara)*

Saree (ARABIC) 'Most noble'

Sarene *see* **Sarah**

Sarette *see* **Sarah**

Sarila (TURKISH) 'Waterfall'

Sarine *see* **Sarah**

Sarita *see* **Sarah**

Sasha *see* **Alexandra** or **Sacha**

Sashenka *see* **Alexandra**

Saskia (NORSE) 'Protector of humankind' *see also* **Alexandra**

Savanna (SPANISH) 'An open plain' *(Savannah)*

Savina *see* **Sabina**

Saxona (TEUTONIC) 'A sword bearer'

Scarlet *see* **Scarlett**

Scarlett (MIDDLE ENGLISH) 'Scarlet coloured' *(Scarlet, Scarletta)*

Scholastica (LATIN) 'Scholar'

Sean *see* **Jane**

Sebastiane (LATIN) 'Revered one' *(Sebastianan, Sebastianna, Sebastianne, Sebastienna, Sebastienne)*

Sebastianna *see* **Sebastiane**

Sebastianne *see* **Sebastiane**

Sebastienna *see* **Sebastiane**

Sebastienne *see* **Sebastiane**

Sebila (LATIN) 'Wise old woman'

Secunda (LATIN) 'Second born'

Seema (HEBREW) 'Treasure'

Seirian (WELSH) 'Sparkling'

Seiriol (WELSH) 'Bright' *(Siriol)*

Sela *see* **Selena**

Selam (SUDANESE) 'Peaceful'

Selda *see* **Griselda**

Selemas *see* **Salema**

Selena (GREEK) 'The Moon'
(*Celene, Celie, Celina,
Celinda, Lena, Salene, Sela,
Selene, Selia, Selie, Selina,
Selinda, Sena*)

Selene *see* **Selena**

Selia *see* **Selena** or **Sheila**

Selie *see* **Selena**

Selima (HEBREW) 'Peaceful' *see
also* **Salema**

Selina *see* **Selena**

Selinda *see* **Selena**

Selma (CELTIC) 'The fair' *see also*
Anselma

Semele (LATIN) 'The single one'
(*Semelia*)

Semelia *see* **Semele**

Semira (HEBREW) 'Height of the
heavens'

Sena *see* **Selena**

Senalda (SPANISH) 'A sign'

Seon *see* **Jane**

Seonaid *see* **Jane**

Septima (LATIN) 'Seventh born'

Sera *see* **Seraphina**

Serafina *see* **Seraphina**

Seraphina (HEBREW) 'The ardent
believer'. One with a
burning faith (*Sera,
Serafina, Serafine, Seraphine*)

Seraphine *see* **Seraphina**

Serena (LATIN) 'Bright tranquil
one'

Serhilda *see* **Serilda**

Serhilde *see* **Serilda**

Serica (LATIN) 'Silken'

Serilda (TEUTONIC) 'Armoured
battle maid' (*Serhilda,
Serhilde, Serilde*)

Shafira (ARABIC) 'Eminent',
'honourable'

Shahdi (PERSIAN) 'Happiness'

Shahla (AFRICAN) 'Beautiful
eyes'

Shaina (HEBREW) 'Beautiful'
(*Shayna, Shayne*)

Shaira (ARABIC) 'Thankful'
(*Shakira*)

Shakira *see* **Shaira**

Shakra *see* **Chakra**

Shama (SANSKRIT) 'A flame'

Shamara (ARABIC) 'Ready for battle' *(Shamari, Shamora)*

Shamari *see* **Shamara**

Shamita (SANSKRIT) 'Peace-maker'

Shamora *see* **Shamara**

Shani (AFRICAN) 'Marvellous'

Shanley (GAELIC) 'Child of the old hero'

Shannah *see* **Shannon**

Shannon (GAELIC) 'Small but wise' *(Shannah)*

Shari *see* **Sharon**

Sharie *see* **Sarah**

Sharleen *see* **Charlotte** or **Caroline**

Sharlene *see* **Caroline**

Sharline *see* **Caroline**

Sharon (HEBREW) 'A princess of exotic beauty' *(Shari, Sharri, Sharron, Sharry, Sherry, Sheryl)*

Sharri *see* **Sharon**

Sharron *see* **Sharon**

Sharry *see* **Sharon**

Shava *see* **Shelah**

Shayna *see* **Shaina**

Shayne *see* **Shaina**

Shea (GAELIC) 'From the fairy fort' *see also* **Shelah**

Sheba *see* **Saba**

Shedea (NATIVE AMERICAN) 'Wild geese'

Sheela *see* **Sheena** or **Sheila**

Sheelah *see* **Sheena** or **Sheila**

Sheena (GAELIC) 'Dim-sighted' *(Sheela, Sheelah, Sheilah) see also* **Jane**

Sheila (CELTIC) 'Musical' *(Selia, Sheela, Shelagh, Sheelah, Sheilah) see also* **Cecilia**

Sheilah *see* **Sheena** or **Sheila**

Shela *see* **Shelah**

Shelagh *see* **Sheila**

Shelah (HEBREW) 'Asked for' *(Shava, Shea, Shela, Sheva, Sheya)*

Shelby (OLD ENGLISH) 'From the estate'

Shelley (ENGLISH) 'From the edge of the meadow' *see also* **Rachel**

Shelly *see* **Rachel**

Shena *see* **Jane**

Sher *see* **Cher**

Shereen (ARABIC) 'Sweet'

Sheri *see* **Shirley**

Sherrie *see* **Cherie**

Sherry *see* **Charlotte, Cherie** or **Sharon**

Sheryl *see* **Charlotte, Cherie** or **Sharon**

Sheva *see* **Shelah**

Sheya *see* **Shelah**

Shifra (HEBREW) 'Beautiful'

Shina (JAPANESE) 'Good virtue'

Shiri (HEBREW) 'My song'

Shirlee *see* **Shirley**

Shirleen *see* **Shirley**

Shirlene *see* **Shirley**

Shirley (ANGLO-SAXON) 'From the white meadow' *(Sheri, Sherry, Sheryl, Shirlee, Shirleen, Shirlene, Shirlie)*

Shirlie *see* **Shirley**

Shoshana (HEBREW) 'Rose'

Shula (ARABIC) 'Flame', 'brightness'

Shulamith (HEBREW) 'Peace'

Siân *see* **Jane**

Sib *see* **Sybil**

Sibbie *see* **Sybil**

Sibby *see* **Sybil**

Sibel *see* **Sybil**

Sibell *see* **Sybil**

Sibella *see* **Sybil**

Sibie *see* **Sybil**

Sibil *see* **Sybil**

Sibilla *see* **Sybil**

Sibille *see* **Sybil**

Sibyl *see* **Sybil**

Sibylle *see* **Sybil**

Sida (GREEK) 'Water lily'

Sidney *see* Sydney

Sidonia *see* Sydney

Sidonie *see* Sydney

Sidra (LATIN) 'Glittering lady of the stars' *(Sidria)*

Sidria *see* Sidra

Sierna (GREEK) 'A sweetly singing mermaid'

Sierra (IRISH) 'Black'

Sigfreda (TEUTONIC) 'Victorious and peaceful' *(Sigfrieda, Sigfriede)*

Sigfrieda *see* Sigfreda

Sigfriede *see* Siegfreda

Signa (LATIN) 'Signed on the heart'

Sigourney (ENGLISH) 'Victorious'

Sigrath *see* Sigrid

Sigrid (NORSE) 'Victorious counsellor' *(Sigrath, Sigrud, Sigurd)*

Sigrud *see* Sigrid

Sigurd *see* Sigrid

Sile *see* Julia

Sileas *see* Cecilia or Julia

Silva *see* Sylvia

Silvana (LATIN) 'Wood-dweller' *see also* Sylvia

Silvie *see* Sylvia

Simona *see* Simone

Simone (HEBREW) 'Heard by the Lord'. Feminine of Simon or Simeon *(Simona, Simonetta, Simonette)*

Simonetta *see* Simone

Simonette *see* Simone

Sine *see* Jane

Sinead (WELSH) *see* Jane

Siobhan (GAELIC) 'Gift of God' *see also* Jane

Sireen *see* Sirena

Sirena (GREEK) 'Sweet-singing mermaid'. Originally from the sirens who lured mariners to their deaths on the rocks with their beautiful singing. Used sometimes in World War II for babies born during an air raid *(Sireen, Sirene)*

Sirene *see* Sirena

Siriol *see* **Seiriol**

Sisile *see* **Cecilia**

Sisle *see* **Cecilia**

Sisley *see* **Cecilia**

Sissie *see* **Cecilia**

Siuban *see* **Judith**

Skye *see* **Skylar**

Skylar (DUTCH) 'Sheltering' *(Skye)*

Smita (SANSKRIT) 'Smiling'

Snowdrop (ENGLISH) From the plant

Sofia *see* **Sophia**

Sofie *see* **Sophia**

Solah (LATIN) 'Alone' *(Solita)*

Solana (SPANISH) 'Sunshine'

Solange (LATIN) 'Good shepherdess'

Solita *see* **Solah**

Solvig (TEUTONIC) 'Victorious battle maid'

Sonia *see* **Sophia**

Sonja *see* **Sophia**

Sonya *see* **Sophia**

Sophia (GREEK) 'Wisdom' *(Beathag, Sadhbh, Sadhbha, Sofia, Sofie, Sonia, Sonja, Sonya, Sophie, Sophy)*

Sophie *see* **Sophia**

Sophronia (GREEK) 'Sensible one'

Sophy *see* **Sophia**

Sorcha (GAELIC) 'Bright one' *see also* **Sarah**

Sparkle (DUTCH) 'Gleaming'

Sperata (LATIN) 'Hoped for'

Spring (ENGLISH) 'Joyous season'

Stacey *see* **Anastasia** or **Eustacia**

Stacia *see* **Anastasia** or **Eustacia**

Stacie *see* **Anastasia** or **Eustacia**

Stacy *see* **Anastasia** or **Eustacia**

Star *see* **Starr**

Starr (ENGLISH) 'A star' *(Star)*

Stefa *see* **Stephanie**

Steffie *see* **Stephanie**

Stella *see* Estelle

Stelle *see* Estelle

Stepha *see* Stephanie

Stephanie (GREEK) 'A crown, garland'. Feminine of Stephen *(Stefa, Steffie, Stepha, Stephania, Stephena, Stephenia, Stephenie, Stevana, Stevania, Stevena, Stevenia, Stevie)*

Stephena *see* Stephanie

Stephenia *see* Stephanie

Stephenie *see* Stephanie

Stevana *see* Stephanie

Stevania *see* Stephanie

Stevena *see* Stephanie

Stevenia *see* Stephanie

Stevie *see* Stephanie

Storm (ANGLO-SAXON) 'A tempest'. One of turbulent nature

Sucheta (SANSKRIT) 'With a beautiful mind' *(Suchi, Suchira, Suchita, Suchitra)*

Suchi *see* Sucheta

Suchira *see* Sucheta

Suchita *see* Sucheta

Suchitra *see* Sucheta

Sue *see* Susan

Sukey *see* Susan

Suki (JAPANESE) 'Loved one' *see also* Susan

Suky *see* Susan

Sulia (LATIN) 'Downy, youthful' *(Suliana)*

Suliana *see* Sulia

Sulwyn (WELSH) 'Beautiful as the sun'

Sumalee (THAI) 'Beautiful flower'

Sumi (JAPANESE) 'Refined'

Sunita (HINDI) 'Good conduct and deeds'

Sunny (ANGLO-SAXON) 'Bright and cheerful'. The brightness of the sun after the storm

Supriti *see* Supriya

Supriya (SANSKRIT) 'Loved' *(Supriti)*

Susan (HEBREW) 'Graceful lily'
(Sue, Sukey, Suki, Suky,
Susana, Susanna, Susannah,
Susanne, Susette, Susi, Susie,
Susy, Suzanna, Suzanne,
Suzetta, Suzette, Suzie, Suzy,
Zsa, Zsa-Zsa)

Susana see **Susan**

Susanna see **Susan**

Susannah see **Susan**

Susanne see **Susan**

Susette see **Susan**

Sushila (SANSKRIT) 'Well-behaved'

Susi see **Susan**

Susie see **Susan**

Susy see **Susan**

Suzanna see **Susan**

Suzanne see **Susan**

Suzetta see **Susan**

Suzette see **Susan**

Suzie see **Susan**

Suzy see **Susan**

Swetlana (GERMAN) 'A star'

Sybella see **Sybil**

Sybil (GREEK) 'Prophetess'. The
female soothsayer of ancient
Greece (Cybil, Sib, Sibbie,
Sibby, Sibel, Sibell, Sibella,
Sibie, Sibil, Sibilla, Sibille,
Sibyl, Sibylle, Sybella,
Sybille, Sybyl)

Sybille see **Sybil**

Sybyl see **Sybil**

Syd see **Sydney**

Sydel (HEBREW) 'That
enchantress' (Sydelle)

Sydney (HEBREW) 'The enticer'
(FRENCH) 'From St. Denis'.
Feminine of Sidney (Sid,
Sidney, Sidonia, Sidonie,
Syd)

Syl see **Sylvia**

Sylgwyn (WELSH) 'Born on
Whit Sunday'

Sylvana (LATIN) 'From the woods'

Sylvia (LATIN) 'From the forest'
(Sil, Silva, Silvana, Silvia,
Silvie, Slyvana, Syl, Sylva,
Zilva, Zilvia)

Syna (GREEK) 'Together' (Syne)

Syne see **Syna**

Syntyche (GREEK) 'With good
fortune'

GIRLS

Tabbie *see* **Tabitha**

Tabby *see* **Tabitha**

Tabina (ARABIC) 'Muhammed's follower'

Tabitha (ARAMAIC) 'The gazelle'. One of gentle grace *(Tabbie, Tabby, Tabithe)*

Tabithe *see* **Tabitha**

Tacita *see* **Tacitah**

Tacitah (LATIN) 'Silence' *(Tacita)*

Tacy (LATIN) 'Peace'

Tahani (ARABIC) 'Congratulations'

Tahira (ARABIC) 'Pure'

Takara (JAPANESE) 'Treasure'

Talia (GREEK) 'Blooming'

Taliba (ARABIC) 'Student'

Talitha (ARAMAIC) 'The maiden'

Tallie *see* **Tallulah**

Tallu *see* **Tallulah**

Tallulah (NATIVE AMERICAN) 'Laughing water'. One who bubbles like a spring *(Tallie, Tallu, Tallula, Tally)*

Tally *see* **Tallulah**

Tama (JAPANESE) 'Jewel'

Tamali (SANSKRIT) 'Tree with the black bark' *(Tamalika)*

Tamalika *see* **Tamali**

Tamar *see* **Tamara**

Tamara (HEBREW) 'Palm tree'
(Tamar, Tammie, Tammy)

Tammie *see* **Tamara**

Tammy (HEBREW) 'Perfection'
see also **Tamara**

Tamsin *see* **Thomasina**

Tandi *see* **Tansy**

Tangerine (ANGLO-SAXON) 'Girl
from Tangiers'

Tangwystl (WELSH) 'Peace pledge'

Tani (JAPANESE) 'Valley'

Tania (RUSSIAN) *see* **Tatiana**

Tansy (LATIN) 'Tenacious'. A
woman of determination.
Also the name of a herb
(Tandi)

Tanuka (SANSKRIT) 'Slender'

Tanya *see* **Tatiana**

Tara (GAELIC) 'Towering rock'.
The home of the ancient
kings of Ireland *(Tarah,
Terra)*

Tarah *see* **Tara**

Tate (OLD ENGLISH) 'To be
cheerful' *(Tatum)*

Tatiana (RUSSIAN)
'Silver-haired one'

Tatum *see* **Tate**

Tavi *see* **Octavia**

Tavia *see* **Octavia**

Tavie *see* **Octavia**

Tavy *see* **Octavia**

Taylor (MIDDLE ENGLISH)
'A tailor'

Tecla *see* **Thecla**

Teddie *see* **Theodora**

Tegan (WELSH) 'Beautiful'

Tegwen (WELSH) 'Beautiful and
blessed'

Temira (HEBREW) 'Tall' *(Timora)*

Tempest (FRENCH) 'Stormy one'
(Tempesta, Tempeste)

Tempesta *see* **Tempest**

Tempeste *see* **Tempest**

Teodora *see* **Theodora**

Teodore *see* **Theodora**

Terencia *see* **Terentia**

Terentia (GREEK) 'Guardian'. Feminine of Terence *(Terencia, Teri, Terri, Terrie, Terry)*

Teresa (GREEK) 'The harvester' *(Terese, Teresina, Teresita, Teressa, Terri, Terrie, Terry, Tess, Tessa, Tessie, Tessy, Theresa, Therese, Toireasa, Tracie, Tracy, Trescha, Zita)* *see also* **Tessa** and **Tracy**

Terese *see* **Teresa**

Teresina *see* **Teresa**

Teresita *see* **Teresa**

Teressa *see* **Teresa**

Teri *see* **Terentia**

Terra *see* **Tara**

Terri *see* **Terentia**

Terrie *see* **Terentia** or **Teresa**

Terry *see* **Terentia** or **Teresa**

Tertia (LATIN) 'Third child'

Terza (GREEK) 'Girl from the farm'

Tess *see* **Teresa**

Tessa (GREEK) 'Fourth child' *see also* **Teresa**

Tessie *see* **Teresa**

Tessy *see* **Teresa**

Tewdews (WELSH) 'Divinely given'

Thada *see* **Thaddea**

Thadda *see* **Thaddea**

Thaddea (GREEK) 'Courageous being'. A girl of great bravery and endurance *(Thada, Thadda)*

Thalassa (GREEK) 'From the sea'

Thalia (GREEK) 'Luxurious blossom'

Thea (GREEK) 'Goddess' *see also* **Althea, Anthea, Dorothea** or **Theodora**

Theadora *see* **Theodora**

Theadosia *see* **Theodora**

Theafania *see* **Theophila**

Theana *see* **Theano**

Theano (GREEK) 'Divine name' *(Theana)*

Theaphania *see* **Theophila**

Thecla (GREEK) 'Divine follower'. A disciple of St Paul *(Tecla, Thekla)*

Theda see **Theodora**

Thekla see **Thecla**

Thelma (GREEK) 'The nursling'

Theo see **Theodora** or **Theola**

Theodora (GREEK) 'Gift of God'
*(Dora, Feadora, Feadore,
Fedora, Fedore, Feodora,
Feodore, Teddie, Teodora,
Teodore, Thea, Theadora,
Theadosia, Theda, Theo,
Theodosia) see also* **Dorothy**

Theodosia see **Theodora**

Theofanie see **Theophila**

Theofila see **Theophania**

Theofilia see **Theophania**

Theola (GREEK) 'Sent from God'
(Theo, Lola)

Theona see **Theone**

Theone (GREEK) 'In the name of
God' *(Theona)*

Theophania (GREEK) 'Beloved of
God' *(Theofila, Theofilia,
Theophilia) see also*
Theophila

Theophanie see **Theophila**

Theophila (GREEK) 'Appearance
of God' *(Theafania,
Theofanie, Theaphania,
Theophanie, Tiffanie, Tiffy)*

Theophilia see **Theophania**

Theora (GREEK) 'Watcher for
God'

Thera (GREEK) 'Wild, untamed
one'

Theresa see **Teresa**

Therese see **Teresa**

Thetis (GREEK) 'Positive one'.
One who knows her own
mind *(Thetys)*

Thetys see **Thetis**

Thia see **Anthea**

Thirza (HEBREW) 'Pleasantness'
(Thyrza, Tirza)

Thomasa see **Thomasina**

Thomase see **Thomasina**

Thomasina (HEBREW) 'The
twin'. Feminine of Thomas
*(Tamsin, Thomasa,
Thomase, Thomasine,
Tomasa, Tomase, Tomasina,
Tomasine)*

Thomasine see **Thomasina**

Thora (NORSE) 'Thunder'. From the Norse God of Thunder, Thor

Thorberta (NORSE) 'Brilliance of Thor' *(Thorberte, Thorbertha, Thorberthe)*

Thorberte *see* **Thorberta**

Thorbertha *see* **Thorberta**

Thorberthe *see* **Thorberta**

Thordia *see* **Thordis**

Thordie *see* **Thordis**

Thordis (NORSE) 'Spirit of Thor'. The sound of thunder *(Thordia, Thordie)*

Thyra (GREEK) 'Shield-bearer'

Thyrza *see* **Thirza**

Tia (GREEK) 'Princess'

Tiana (GREEK) 'Princess'

Tiara (LATIN) 'Crowned'

Tibelda (TEUTONIC) 'Boldest person'

Tiberia (LATIN) 'From the Tiber'. The river of ancient Rome

Tierney (GAELIC) 'Grandchild of the lordly'

Tiffanie *see* **Theophila**

Tiffany (GREEK) 'Manifestation of God' *(Tiphani)*

Tiffy *see* **Theophila**

Tilda *see* **Mathilda**

Tilly *see* **Mathilda**

Tim *see* **Timothea**

Timandra (GREEK) 'Honour' *(Tymandra)*

Timmie *see* **Timothea**

Timmy *see* **Timothea**

Timora *see* **Temira**

Timothea (GREEK) 'Honouring God' *(Tim, Timmie, Timmy)*

Tina *see* **Christine** or **Martina**

Tiphani *see* **Tiffany**

Tirza (SPANISH) 'Cypress' *see also* **Thirza**

Tish *see* **Letitia**

Tita (LATIN) 'Honoured title'

Titania (GREEK) 'Giantess'. Also the name of the Queen of the Fairies

Tizane (HUNGARIAN) 'A gypsy'
see also **Gitana**

Tobe see **Tobey**

Tobey (HEBREW) 'God is good'
(Tobe, Tobi, Toby)

Tobi see **Tobey**

Toby see **Tobey**

Toinette see **Antonia**

Toireasa see **Teresa**

Tomasa see **Thomasina**

Tomase see **Thomasina**

Tomasina see **Thomasina**

Tomasine see **Thomasina**

Tomi (JAPANESE) 'Riches'

Toni see **Antonia**

Tonia see **Antonia**

Topaz (LATIN) 'The topaz gem'

Tory see **Victoria**

Tourmalina see **Tourmaline**

Tourmaline (SRI LANKAN) 'A
Carnelian' (Tourmalina)

Tracey see **Tracy**

Tracie see **Teresa**

Tracy (GAELIC) 'Battler'

Tracey see also **Teresa**

Traviata (ITALIAN) 'The frail one'

Trescha see **Teresa**

Triantafilia (GREEK) 'Rose'

Trilby (ITALIAN) 'A singer who
trills'

Trina (GREEK) 'Girl of purity'

Triphena see **Tryphena**

Triphenia see **Tryphena**

Trista (LATIN) 'Melancholia',
'sorrow'

Trix see **Beatrice**

Trixie see **Beatrice**

Trixy see **Beatrice**

Trudey see **Trudy**

Trudi see **Trudy**

Trudie see **Gertrude** or **Trudy**

Trudy (TEUTONIC) 'Loved one'
(Trudey, Trudi, Trudie) see
also **Gertrude**

Tryphena (LATIN) 'The delicate one' *(Triphena, Triphenia, Tryphenia)*

Tryphenia *see* **Tryphena**

Tuesday (ANGLO-SAXON) 'Born on Tuesday'

Tullia (GAELIC) 'Peaceful one'

Turaya (ARABIC) 'Star'

Twyla (MIDDLE ENGLISH) 'Woven of double thread'

Tymandra *see* **Timandra**

Tyne (OLD ENGLISH) 'River'

Tyra (SCANDINAVIAN) 'Battler'

U

GIRLS

Uda (TEUTONIC) 'Prosperous'. A child of fortune *(Udella, Udelle)*

Udelle *see* **Uda**

Ula (CELTIC) 'Jewel of the sea' (TEUTONIC) 'The inheritor' *(Oola)*

Ulima (ARABIC) 'The learned one'. A woman who gives good advice

Ulrica (TEUTONIC) 'Ruler of all' *(Elrica, Rica, Ulrika)*

Ulrika *see* **Ulrica**

Ultima (LATIN) 'The most distant'

Ulva (TEUTONIC) 'The she-wolf'. A symbol of bravery

Umar (ARABIC) 'Flourishing'

Umeko (JAPANESE) 'Plum-blossom child'

Una (LATIN) 'One'. The one and only girl (IRISH) 'United' *(Ona, Oona, Oonagh)*

Undine *see* **Ondine**

Unity (MIDDLE ENGLISH) 'Unity'

Urania (GREEK) 'Heavenly'. The muse of astronomy

Urbana (LATIN) 'Born in the town'

Urith (OLD GERMAN) 'Deserving'

Ursa *see* **Ursula**

Ursel *see* **Ursula**

Ursie *see* **Ursula**

Ursola *see* **Ursula**

Ursula (LATIN) 'The she-bear'
(Ora, Orsa, Orsola, Ursa,
Ursel, Ursie, Ursola, Ursule,
Ursulette, Ursuline, Ursy)

Ursulette *see* **Ursula**

Ursuline *see* **Ursula**

Ursy *see* **Ursula**

Usha (SANSKRIT) 'Dawn'

Ushakiran (SANSKRIT) 'The first
rays of the sun'

Ushashi (SANSKRIT) 'Morning'

Uta (GERMAN) 'Rich'

Utano (JAPANESE) 'Field of song'

Utina (NATIVE AMERICAN)
'Woman from my country'

Utsa (SANSKRIT) 'Spring'

V

GIRLS

Vahsti (PERSIAN) 'Beautiful one'

Val *see* **Valentina** or **Valerie**

Vala (TEUTONIC) 'The chosen one'. Ideal name for an adopted daughter

Valborga (TEUTONIC) 'Protecting ruler' *(Valburga, Walborga, Walburga)*

Valburga *see* **Valborga**

Valda (TEUTONIC) 'Ruler' *(Walda, Welda)*

Valeda *see* **Valentina**

Valencia *see* **Valentina**

Valentia *see* **Valentina**

Valentina (LATIN) 'Strong and vigorous' *(Val, Valeda, Valencia, Valentia, Valentine, Valera, Valida, Vallie)*

Valentine *see* **Valentina**

Valera *see* **Valentina**

Valeria *see* **Valerie**

Valerie (FRENCH) 'Strong' *(Val, Valeria, Valery, Vallie, Valora, Valorey, Valorie, Valory)*

Valeska (SLAVIC) 'Glorious ruler' *(Waleska)*

Valida *see* **Velda** or **Valentina**

Vallie *see* **Valentina** or **Valerie**

Valma (WELSH) 'Mayflower' *(Valmai)*

Valmai *see* **Valma**

Valona *see* **Valonia**

Valonia (LATIN) 'From the vale' *(Valona)*

Valora *see* **Valerie**

Valory *see* **Valerie**

Van *see* **Vanessa**

Vancy *see* **Evangeline**

Vanda (TEUTONIC) 'Family'

Vanessa (GREEK) 'The butterfly' *(Van, Vania, Vanna, Vanni, Vannie, Vanny, Vanya)*

Vangie *see* **Evangeline**

Vania (HEBREW) 'God's precious gift' *(Vanina) see also* **Vanessa**

Vanina *see* **Vania**

Vanita (SANSKRIT) 'Desired'

Vanna *see* **Vanessa**

Vanni *see* **Vanessa**

Vanny *see* **Vanessa**

Vanora *see* **Genevieve**

Vanya *see* **Vanessa**

Varina (SLAVIC) 'Stranger'

Vashti (PERSIAN) 'The most beautiful'

Veda (SANSKRIT) 'Wisdom and knowledge' *(Vedis)*

Vedette (ITALIAN) 'The sentinel' *(Vedetta)*

Vedis *see* **Veda**

Vega (ARABIC) 'The great one'

Velda (TEUTONIC) 'Very wise' *(Valida)*

Velda (DUTCH) 'Field'

Velica *see* **Velika**

Velika (SLAVIC) 'The falling one' *(Velica)*

Velma *see* **Wilhelmina**

Velvet (ENGLISH) 'Soft as velvet'

Venetia (LATIN) 'Lady of Venice'

Venita *see* **Venus**

Ventura (SPANISH) 'Happiness and good luck'

Venus (LATIN) 'Loveliness', 'beauty'. The Roman goddess of beauty and love *(Venita, Vinita, Vinnie, Vinny)*

Vera (LATIN) 'Truth'. One who is honest and steadfast *(Vere, Verena, Verene, Veria, Verina, Verine)*

Verbena (LATIN) 'The sacred bough'

Verda (LATIN) 'Fresh youth'. Possessing the verdant qualities of spring *see also* **Verna**

Vere *see* **Vera**

Verena *see* **Vera** or **Verna**

Verene *see* **Vera**

Veria *see* **Vera**

Verina *see* **Vera**

Verine *see* **Vera** or **Verity**

Verity (LATIN) 'Truth' *(Verine)*

Verla *see* **Vera**

Vern *see* **Laverne**

Verna (LATIN) 'Spring-like' *(Verda, Verena, Verneta, Vernice, Vernis, Vernita, Virina, Virna) see also* **Laverne**

Verne *see* **Laverne**

Verneta *see* **Verna**

Vernice *see* **Verna**

Vernis *see* **Verna**

Vernita *see* **Verna**

Verona (LATIN) 'Lady of Verona'

Veronica (LATIN) 'True image' *(Ronnie, Ronny, Veronique, Vonnie, Vonny,* and all variations of **Bernice**) *see also* **Bernice**

Veronique *see* **Veronica**

Vesna (SLAVIC) 'Spring'

Vespera (LATIN) 'The evening star'

Vesta (LATIN) 'Guardian of the sacred flame', 'melodious one'. The vestal virgins tended the temples of ancient Greece

Veta *see* **Vita**

Vevila (GAELIC) 'Melodious one'

Vi *see* **Violet**

Vicenta *see* **Vincentia**

Vicki *see* **Victoria**

Vicky *see* **Victoria**

Victoria (LATIN) 'The victorious one'. Became very popular in Britain during the long reign of Queen Victoria *(Tory, Vicki, Vicky, Victorine, Victorie, Vitoria, Vittoria)*

Victorie *see* **Victoria**

Victorine *see* **Victoria**

Vida (HEBREW) 'Beloved one'. Feminine of David

Vidette (HEBREW) 'Beloved'

Vidonia (PORTUGUESE) 'Vine branch'

Vidula (SANSKRIT) 'The moon'

Vienna (LATIN) 'Geography'. The capital of Austria

Vigilia (LATIN) 'The alert', 'vigilant'

Vignette (FRENCH) 'The little vine'

Vijaya (SANSKRIT) 'Victory'

Villette (FRENCH) 'From the village'

Vina (SPANISH) 'From the vineyard' *see also* **Alviona** or **Lavinia**

Vinaya (SANSKRIT) 'Modest'

Vincencia *see* **Vincentia**

Vincentia (LATIN) 'The conqueror'. Feminine of Vincent *(Vicenta, Vincencia)*

Vinia *see* **Lavinia**

Vinita *see* **Venus**

Vinnie *see* **Venus**

Vinny *see* **Venus**

Viola *see* **Violet**

Violante *see* **Violet**

Violet (LATIN) 'Modest flower'. Shy and retiring, like the flower *(Eolande, Vi, Viola, Violante, Violetta, Violette, Yolanda, Yolande, Yolanthe)* *see also* **Iolanthe**

Violetta *see* **Violet**

Virdis (LATIN) 'Fresh', 'blooming'

Virgi *see* **Virginia**

Virgie *see* **Virginia**

Virgilia (LATIN) 'The staff-bearer'

Virginia (LATIN) 'The virgin, maidenly and pure' *(Ginger, Ginnie, Ginny, Jinny, Virgi, Virgie, Virginie, Virgy)*

Virginie *see* **Virginia**

Viridis (LATIN) 'The green bough'

Virina *see* **Verna**

Virna *see* **Verna**

Vita (LATIN) 'Life'. One who likes living *(Evita, Veta, Vitia)*

Vitia *see* **Vita**

Vittoria *see* **Victoria**

Viv *see* **Vivian**

Viveca (LATIN/SCANDINAVIAN) 'Living voice'

Vivi *see* **Vivian**

Vivia *see* **Vivian**

Vivian (LATIN) 'Alive'. Vivid and vibrant with life *(Bibiana, Viv, Vivi, Vivia, Viviana, Viviane, Vivie, Vivien, Viviene, Vivienna, Vivienne, Vivyan, Vyvyan)*

Vivie *see* **Vivian**

Vivien *see* **Vivian**

Vivienna *see* **Vivian**

Vivienne *see* **Vivian**

Volante (LATIN) 'The flying one'. One who steps so lightly that she seems to fly

Voleta (FRENCH) 'A floating veil' *(Voletta)*

Voletta *see* **Voleta**

Von *see* **Yvonne**

Vonnie *see* **Veronica** or **Yvonne**

Vonny *see* **Veronica**

Vyvyan *see* **Vivian**

W

Wahilda (ARABIC) 'Unique'

Wahkuna (NATIVE AMERICAN) 'Beautiful'

Walida (ARABIC) 'New-born girl'

Wallace *see* **Wallis**

Wallis (ANGLO-SAXON) 'The Welshwoman', 'the stranger' *(Wallace, Wallie, Wally)*

Wanda (TEUTONIC) 'The wanderer'. The restless roamer *(Wandie, Wandis, Wenda, Wendeline, Wendy)*

Wandis *see* **Wanda**

Wanetta (ANGLO-SAXON) 'The pale one' *(Wanette)*

Warda (TEUTONIC) 'The guardian'

Wasima (ARABIC) 'Pretty'

Welma *see* **Wilhelmina**

Wendeline *see* **Wanda**

Wendy (ENGLISH) Character created in Peter Pan by J.M. Barrie *see also* **Gwendoline** or **Wanda**

Wenona *see* **Winona**

Wesla (OLD ENGLISH) 'From the west meadow'

Whitney (OLD ENGLISH) 'From the white island'

Wilfreda (TEUTONIC) 'The peacemaker'. Feminine of **Wilfred** *(Freda, Freddie, Wilf, Wilfreida, Wilfrieda)*

Wilhelmina (TEUTONIC) 'The protectress'. One who guards resolutely her own *(Billie, Billy, Guilla, Helma, Mina, Minnie, Minny, Velma, Welma, Willa, Willie, Willy, Wilma) see also* **Helma**

Willa (ANGLO-SAXON) 'Desirable' *see also* **Billie** or **Wilhelmina**

Willow (ENGLISH) Plant name

Wilma *see* **Wilhelmina**

Wilona (OLD ENGLISH) 'Desired'

Win *see* **Edwina** or **Wynne**

Winema (NATIVE AMERICAN) 'Chief of the tribe'

Winifred (TEUTONIC) 'Peaceful friend'. A restful person to have around *(Winifreida, Winifrida, Winifrieda, Winnie, Winny, Wynn)*

Winna (AFRICAN) 'Friend' *(Winnah)*

Winnie *see* **Edwina** or **Winifred**

Winola (TEUTONIC) 'Gracious friend'

Winona (AMERICAN-INDIAN) 'First-born daughter' *(Wenona, Wenonah, Winonah)*

Winsome (ENGLISH) 'Pleasant', 'attractive'

Wren (OLD ENGLISH) From the bird

Wyanet (NATIVE AMERICAN) 'Very beautiful'

Wylda (TEUTONIC) 'Rebellious'

Wylma (TEUTONIC) 'Resolute'

Wynne (CELTIC) 'Fair, white maiden' *(Win, Wyne)*

Xanthe (GREEK) 'Golden blonde'

Xanthippe (GREEK) The wife of Socrates

Xaverie (ARAMAIC) 'Bright'

Xaviera (SPANISH) 'Owner of the home'

Xena (GREEK) 'Hospitality' *(Xene, Xenia, Zenia)*

Xiaoli (CHINESE) 'Small and beautiful'

Xiiaoying (CHINESE) 'Small flower'

Ximena (GREEK) 'Heroine'

Xylia (GREEK) 'From the woods' *(Xyline, Xylona)*

Xyline see **Xylia**

Xylona see **Xylia**

Y

GIRLS

Yaffa (HEBREW) 'Beautiful'

Yakira (HEBREW) 'Valuable'

Yasmeen (PERSIAN) 'Flower'

Yasmin *see* **Jasmin**

Yasmina *see* **Jasmin**

Yasmine *see* **Jasmin**

Yasu (JAPANESE) 'Tranquil'

Yedda (ANGLO-SAXON) 'One with a melodious voice'

Yeira (HEBREW) 'Light'

Yepa (NATIVE AMERICAN) 'Snow girl'

Yerusha *see* **Jerusha**

Yesima (HEBREW) 'Right hand', 'strength'

Yetta (ANGLO-SAXON) 'To give', 'the giver' *see also* **Henrietta**

Yevetta *see* **Yvonne**

Ynes *see* **Agnes**

Yoanna *see* **Jane**

Yolanda *see* **Iolanthe** or **Violet**

Yolanthe *see* **Violet**

Yona (KOREAN) 'Lotus blossom'

Yosepha *see* **Josephine**

Yoshe (JAPANESE) 'Beautiful'

Yoshiko (JAPANESE) 'Good'

Yovela (HEBREW) 'Rejoicing'

Ysabeau *see* **Isabel**

Ysabelle *see* Isabel

Ysobel *see* Isabel

Yseult *see* Isolde

Yusepha *see* Josephine

Yvette *see* Yvonne

Yvonne (FRENCH) 'Archer with the yew bow' *(Evette, Evonne, Ivonne, Von, Vonnie, Yevetta, Yevette, Yvetta, Yvette, Yvona)*

GIRLS

Zabrina (ANGLO-SAXON) 'Noble maiden'

Zada (ARABIC) 'Lucky one'. Fortune's favourite

Zahra (ARABIC) 'Blossom'

Zakira (ARABIC) 'Remembrance'

Zamira (HEBREW) 'Song'

Zana (PERSIAN) 'Woman'

Zandra *see* **Alexandra**

Zaneta *see* **Jane**

Zara (HEBREW) 'Brightness of dawn' *(Zarah, Zaria)* see also **Sarah**

Zarah *see* **Sarah** or **Zara**

Zaria *see* **Azaria, Sarah** or **Zara**

Zarifa (ARABIC) 'Graceful'

Zea (LATIN) 'Ripened grain'

Zebada (HEBREW) 'Gift of the Lord'

Zelda *see* **Griselda**

Zelia (GREEK) 'Devoted to duty' *(Zele, Zelie, Zelina)*

Zella (HEBREW) 'Shadow'

Zelma *see* **Anselma**

Zelosa (GREEK) 'Jealous one'

Zena (GREEK) 'The hospitable one' *see also* **Zenobia** or **Zian**

Zennie *see* **Zenorbia**

Zenobia (GREEK) 'Zeus gave life' (ARABIC) 'Ornament to her father' *(Zena, Zenaida, Zenda, Zenia, Zenina, Zenna, Zennie, Zenorbie)*

Zenorbie *see* **Zenobia**

Zephirah (HEBREW) 'Dawn'

Zera (HEBREW) 'Seeds'

Zerelda (OLD GERMAN) 'Armoured warrior maid'

Zerla *see* **Zerlina**

Zerlina (TEUTONIC) 'Serene beauty' *(Zerla, Zerline)*

Zerlinda (HEBREW) 'Beautiful as the dawn'

Zerline *see* **Zerlina**

Zetta (ANGLO-SAXON) 'Sixth born'. The sixth letter of the Greek alphabet *(Zita, Zitao)*

Zeva (GREEK) 'Sword'

Zia (SANSKRIT) 'Enlightened' (LATIN) 'Kind of grain'

Zian (HEBREW) 'Abundance' *(Zena, Zinah)*

Zila (SANSKRIT) 'A shady place'

Zilla (HEBREW) 'Shadow' *(Zillah)*

Zilpah (HEBREW) 'Dropping'

Zinnia (LATIN) 'The zinnia flower' *(Zinia)*

Zippora (HEBREW) 'Trumpet', 'sparrow' *(Zipporah)*

Zita *see* **Teresa** or **Zetta**

Zitao *see* **Zetta**

Ziva (HEBREW) 'Brightness'

Zoë (GREEK) 'Life'

Zofeyah (HEBREW) 'God sees'

Zohara (HEBREW) 'The bright child'

Zona (LATIN) 'A girdle'. The belt of Orion *(Zonie)*

Zora (LATIN) 'The dawn' *(Zorah, Zorana, Zorina, Zorin)*

Zorina *see* **Zora**

Zosima (GREEK) 'Wealthy woman'

Zsa-Zsa *see* **Susan**

Zuleika (ARABIC) 'Fair'

Zulema (ARABIC/HEBREW) 'Peace'

BOYS

Aadi (SANSKRIT) 'First, most important'

Aahmes (EGYPTIAN) 'Child of the moon'

Aaron (HEBREW) 'Exalted'. Brother of Moses *(Ari, Arnie, Aron, Erin, Haroun)*

Abba (HEBREW) 'Father'

Abbey *see* **Abbott, Abelard** or **Abner**

Abbott (ANGLO-SAXON) 'Father of the abbey' *(Abba, Abbe, Abbey, Abbot, Abott)*

Abdel *see* **Abdul**

Abdi (HEBREW) 'My servant'

Abdiel (HEBREW) 'Servant of God'

Abdon (HEBREW) 'Son of'

Abdul (ARABIC) 'Son of' *(Abdel)*

Abdullah (ARABIC) 'Servant of Allah'

Abe *see* **Abraham** or **Abelard**

Abel (HEBREW) 'Breath'. The first recorded murder victim, according to the Bible

Abelard (TEUTONIC) 'Nobly resolute' *(Abbey, Abe)*

Abiah (HEBREW) 'The Lord is my father' *(Abija, Abijah)*

Abir (HEBREW) 'Strong' *(Abiri)*

Abisha (HEBREW) 'God's gift'

Abner (HEBREW) 'Father of light' *(Abbey, Eb)*

Abraham (HEBREW) 'Father of multitudes'. The original patriarch *(Abe, Abie, Abram, Abran, Avram, Bram, Ibrahim*

Abram *see* **Abraham**

Abric (TEUTONIC) 'Above authority'

Abros (GREEK) 'Elegant'

Absalom (HEBREW) 'Father of peace' *(Absolom)*

Ace (LATIN) 'Unity' *(Acey)*

Acelin (FRENCH) 'Noble' *(Aceline, Acelot)*

Achates (GREEK) 'Faithful companion'

Achilles (GREEK) 'Swift'

Acima (HEBREW) 'The Lord's judgement'

Ackerley (ANGLO-SAXON) 'From the acre meadow' *(Ackley)*

Acton (OLD ENGLISH) 'Town near oak trees'

Adair (GAELIC) 'From the oak tree near the ford'

Adal (TEUTONIC) 'Regal', 'noble'

Adalard (TEUTONIC) 'Noble and brave' *(Adelard, Adhelard)*

Adalric (OLD GERMAN) 'Noble ruler' *(Adelric)*

Adam (HEBREW) 'Of the red earth'. The first man, according to the Bible *(Adamo, Adan, Adao, Adhamh)*

Adams *see* **Adamson**

Adamson (HEBREW) 'Son of Adam' *(Adams)*

Adan *see* **Adam, Adin** or **Aidan**

Adao *see* **Adam**

Adar (HEBREW) 'Fiery'

Addison (ANGLO-SAXON) 'Adam's son'

Addo (TEUTONIC) 'Happy', 'cheerful'

Addy (TEUTONIC) 'Awesome', 'noble'

Ade *see* **Adrian**

Adelbert *see* **Albert**

Adelgar (HEBREW) 'Bright spear'

Adelpho (GREEK) 'Brother'

Ademar (TEUTONIC) 'Fierce, noble, famous' *(Ademaro)*

Adesh (SANSKRIT) 'Command'

Adham (ARABIC) 'Black'

Adhar (ARABIC) 'Waiting'

Adiel (HEBREW) 'One who is favoured by God'

Adin (HEBREW) 'Sensual' *(Adan)*

Adlai (HEBREW) 'My witness', 'my ornament'

Adler (TEUTONIC) 'Eagle'. One of keen perception

Adley (HEBREW) 'Fair-minded'

Adney (ANGLO-SAXON) 'One who lives on the island

Adolph (TEUTONIC) 'Noble wolf' *(Ad, Adolf, Adolfus, Adolphe, Adolpho, Adolphus, Dolf, Dolph)*

Adon (HEBREW) 'Lord'. The sacred Hebrew word for God

Adonis (GREEK) 'Manly and handsome'

Adrian (LATIN) 'Dark one', 'man from the sea' *(Ade, Adriano, Adrien, Hadrian)*

Adriel (HEBREW) 'From God's congregation'

Aeldred *see* **Alfred**

Aelhaearn (WELSH) 'Iron brow'

Aeneas (GREEK) 'The much praised one'. The defender of Troy *(Eneas)*

Afdal (ARABIC) 'Excellent'

Afif (ARABIC) 'Virtuous'

Agamemnon (GREEK) 'Resolute'

Agilard (TEUTONIC) 'Formidably bright'

Agur (HEBREW) 'Gatherer'

Ahanu (NATIVE AMERICAN) 'Laughing one'

Ahern (GAELIC) 'Horse lord', 'horse owner' *(Ahearn, Aherin, Aherne, Hearn, Hearne)*

Ahmed (ARABIC) 'Most highly praised'

Ahren (TEUTONIC) 'The eagle'

Aidan (GAELIC) 'Little fiery one' *(Adan, Eden)*

Aijaz (SANSKRIT) 'Favour'

Aiken (ANGLO-SAXON) 'Little Adam' *(Aickin, Aokin)*

Aimery (TEUTONIC) 'Industrious ruler'

Aimon (FRENCH FROM TEUTONIC) 'House'

Ainsley (ANGLO-SAXON) 'Meadow of the respected one'

Airell (CELTIC) 'Free man'

Ajax (GREEK) 'Eagle'

Ajay (SANSKRIT) 'Invincible'

Akbar (ARABIC) 'Great'

Akira (JAPANESE) 'Intelligent one'

Akmal (ARABIC) 'Perfect'

Akram (ARABIC) 'Noble', 'generous'

Akule (NATIVE AMERICAN) 'One who looks to the sky'

Al *see* **Alfred, Algernon** or **Alison**

Alabhaois *see* **Aloysius**

Aladdin (ARABIC) 'Servant of Allah'

Alair (GAELIC) 'Cheerful' *see also* **Alan**

Alam (ARABIC/SANSKRIT) 'Universe' *(Alaam)*

Alan (GAELIC) 'Cheerful harmony' *(Ailean, Ailin, Alain, Alair, Aland, Alano, Alanson, Allan, Allen, Allie, Allyn)*

Alanus (LATIN) 'Cheerful one'

Alard (GERMAN) 'Noble ruler' *see also* **Allard**

Alaric (TEUTONIC) 'Ruler of all' *(Alarick, Alric, Rich, Richie, Rick, Rickie, Ricky, Ricy, Ulric, Ulrich, Ulrick)*

Alastair *see* **Alexander**

Alban (LATIN) 'White complexion'. A man of outstandingly fair colouring *(Alben, Albin, Aleb, Alva, Aubin)*

Albern (ANGLO-SAXON) 'Noble warrior'

Albert (TEUTONIC) 'Noble and illustrious'. Name which became popular in Britain after the marriage of Queen Victoria to Prince Albert of Saxe-Coborg-Gotha *(Adelbert, Ailbert, Aldabert, Aubert, Bert, Bertie, Berty, Delbert, Elbert)*

Albor (LATIN) 'Dawn'

Alburn (LATIN) 'Pale complexion'

Alcander (GREEK) 'Strong'

Alcott (ANGLO-SAXON) 'One who lives at the old cottage'

Alden (ANGLO-SAXON) 'Wise old friend'. One on whom friends can rely *(Aldin, Aldwin, Aldwyn, Elden, Eldin)*

Alder (ANGLO-SAXON) 'At the alder tree'

Aldis (ANGLO-SAXON) 'From the old house' *(Aldo, Aldous, Aldus)*

Aldo (TEUTONIC) 'Old, wise and rich' *see also* **Aldis**

Aldred (TEUTONIC) 'Wise advisor'

Aldrich (ANGLO-SAXON) 'Wise old ruler' *(Aldric, Aldridge, Alric, Eldric, Eldrich, Eldridge)*

Aldwin *see* **Alden**, **Alvin** or **Audwin**

Alec *see* **Alexander**

Aled (WELSH) Name of a Welsh river

Aleem (SANSKRIT) 'Knowledgeable'

Alejandro *see* **Alexander**

Alem (ARABIC) 'Wise man'

Aleron (LATIN) 'The eagle'

Alexander (GREEK) 'Protector of mankind' (*Alasdair, Alastair, Alasteir, Alaster, Alec, Aleck, Alejandro, Alejo, Aleksandr, Alessandro, Alex, Alexis, Alick, Alister, Allister, Alsandair, Iskander, Sander, Sandie, Sandy, Sasha, Saunders*)

Alexis *see* **Alexander**

Alfonse *see* **Alphonso**

Alford (ANGLO-SAXON) 'The old ford' *see also* **Alphonso**

Alfred (ANGLO-SAXON) 'The wise counsel of the elf' (*Aelfred, Ailfrid, Al, Alf, Alfie, Alfredo, Alfy, Avery, Fred, Freddie, Freddy*)

Alger (TEUTONIC) 'Noble spearman' (*Algar, Elgar*) *see also* **Algernon**

Algernon (FRENCH) 'The whiskered one'. A man with a moustache or beard (*Al, Alger, Algie, Algy*)

Algis (FRENCH FROM TEUTONIC) 'Spear'

Ali (SANSKRIT) 'Protected by god' (ARABIC) 'greatest, noble, sublime'

Alim (ARABIC) 'Scholar'

Alison (ANGLO-SAXON) 'Son of a nobleman', 'Alice's son' (*Al, Allie, Allison*)

Alister *see* **Alexander**

Allan *see* **Alan**

Allard (ANGLO-SAXON) 'Noble and brave' (*Aethelard, Aethelhard, Alard, Ethelard*) *see also* **Alard**

Almer (ARABIC) 'Prince', 'ruler'

Almerick (TEUTONIC) 'Working ruler'

Almo (ANGLO-SAXON) 'Noble and famous'

Almund (TEUTONIC) 'Protection'

Alonso *see* **Alphonso**

Aloysius (LATIN) 'Famous warrior' (*Alabhaois, Aloys, Lewis, Louis, Ludwig*)

Alpha (GREEK) 'First-born'

Alpheus (GREEK) 'God of the river'

Alphonso (TEUTONIC) 'Noble and ready' *(Alfons, Alfonse, Alfonso, Alford, Alonso, Alonzo, Alphonse, Alphonsus, Fonz)*

Alpin (EARLY SCOTTISH) 'Blond one'. Name borne by the descendants of the earliest Scottish clan McAlpin

Alroy (GAELIC) 'Red-haired boy'

Alston (ANGLO-SAXON) 'From the old village'

Altman (TEUTONIC) 'Old, wise man'

Alton (ANGLO-SAXON) 'One who lives in the old town'

Alvah (HEBREW) 'The exalted one' *(Alvar)*

Alvin (TEUTONIC) 'Friend of all', 'noble friend' *(Aldwin, Aloin, Aluin, Aluino, Alva, Alvan, Alwin, Alwyn)*

Alward (TEUTONIC) 'Everyone's protector'

Alworth (TEUTONIC) 'Respected by everyone'

Amadeo (SPANISH) 'Beloved of God' *(Amadeus, Amando)*

Amadour (FRENCH FROM LATIN) 'Lovable' *(Amadeus)*

Amal (SANSKRIT) 'Pure' (ARABIC) 'hope' (HEBREW) 'work'

Amandus (LATIN) 'Worthy of love' *(Amand, Amando)*

Amaro (PORTUGUESE) 'Dark, moor'

Amasa (HEBREW) 'Burden bearer'

Ambar (HINDI) 'Sky'

Ambert (TEUTONIC) 'Shining, bright light'

Ambler (ENGLISH) 'Stable-keeper'

Ambrose (LATIN) 'Belonging to the divine immortals' *(Ambroise, Ambros, Ambrosi, Ambrosio, Ambrosius, Amby, Brose, Emrys, Gino)*

Amerigo *see* **Emery**

Amiel (HEBREW) 'Lord of my people'

Amijad (ARABIC) 'Glorious'

Amil (ARABIC/SANSKRIT)
'Industrious, invaluable'

Amin (ARABIC/HEBREW)
'Trustworthy, honest',
(SANSKRIT) 'divine grace'
(Ameen, Aman)

Amirov (HEBREW) 'My people
are great'

Amitan (HEBREW) 'True,
faithful'

Amiya (SANSKRIT) 'Nectar'

Amlan (SANSKRIT) 'Unfading'

Ammon (EGYPTIAN)
'The hidden'

Amnon (HEBREW) 'Faithful'

Amol (SANSKRIT) 'Priceless'
(Anmol)

Amory (TEUTONIC) 'Famous
ruler' *(Amery)*

Amos (HEBREW) 'A burden'. One
used to tackling difficult
problems

Amram (ARABIC) 'Life'

Amrit (SANSKRIT) 'Water of life'

Amund (SCANDINAVIAN) 'Divine
protection'

Amyot (FRENCH) 'Beloved'

Anand (HINDI) 'Peaceful'

Ananias (HEBREW) 'Grace of
the Lord'

Anarawd (WELSH) 'Eloquent'

Anastasius (GREEK) 'One who
shall rise again'

Anatole (GREEK) 'From the East'
(Anatol, Anatolio)

Ancel (GERMAN) 'God-like'
(Ancell)

Andreas *see* **Andrew**

Andrew (GREEK) 'Strong and
manly'. The patron saint of
Scotland *(Aindreas, Anders,
Anderson, Andie, Andonis,
Andre, Andreas, Andrej,
Andrien, Andris, Andy,
Drew)*

Andrias (GREEK) 'Courageous
one'

Androcles (GREEK) 'Male glory'

Aneurin (CELTIC) 'Truly golden'
(Nye)

Angelo (ITALIAN) 'Saintly
messenger' *(Ange, Angel)*

Angus (CELTIC) 'Outstanding and exceptional man'. One of unparalleled strength *(Ennis, Gus)*

Angwyn (WELSH) 'Very handsome'

Anil (SANSKRIT) 'God of the wind'

Annan (CELTIC) 'From the stream'

Anniss (ARABIC) 'Charming'

Ansari (ARABIC) 'Helper'

Anscom (ANGLO-SAXON) 'One who lives in the secret valley'. An awe-inspiring, solitary man *(Anscomb)*

Ansel (FRENCH) 'Nobleman's follower' *(Ancell, Ansell) see also* **Anselm**

Anselm (TEUTONIC) 'Divine helmet' *(Anse, Ansel, Anselme, Anshelm, Elmo)*

Anshar (TEUTONIC) 'Divine spear'

Ansley (ANGLO-SAXON) 'From Ann's meadow'

Anson (ANGLO-SAXON) 'Ann's son'

Anstice (GREEK) 'The resurrected'. One who returns to life after death *(Anstiss)*

Anthony (LATIN) 'Of inestimable worth'. A man without peer *(Anntoin, Antin, Antoine, Anton, Antonino, Antonio, Antons, Antony, Tony)*

Antin *see* **Anthony**

Antinous (GREEK) 'Contradictory'

Antoine *see* **Anthony**

Antol (HUNGARIAN) 'Estimable one'

Antony *see* **Anthony**

Anwell (CELTIC) 'Beloved one' *(Anwyl, Anwyll)*

Anyon (CELTIC) 'The anvil'. One on whom all the finest characteristics have been forged

Aodh (CELTIC) 'Fire' *see also* **Hubert**

Apollo (GREEK) 'Beautiful man'

Aquila (LATIN) 'Eagle'

Archard (TEUTONIC) 'Sacred and powerful' *(Archerd)*

Archer (ANGLO-SAXON) 'The bowman' *see also* **Archibald**

Archerd *see* **Archard**

Archibald (TEUTONIC) 'Noble and truly bold'. A brave and sacred warrior *(Arch, Archaimbaud, Archambault, Archer, Archibaldo, Archie, Archimbald, Archy, Arkady, Gilleasbuig)*

Archimedes (GREEK) 'Master mind'

Arden (LATIN) 'Ardent, fiery, fervent, sincere'. One of intensely loyal nature *(Ardin)*

Ardley (ANGLO-SAXON) 'From the domestic meadow'

Ardolph (ANGLO-SAXON) 'The home-loving wolf'. The roamer who longs only for home *(Ardolf)*

Aretino (GREEK) 'Victorious'

Argus (GREEK) 'The watchful one'. The giant with one hundred eyes, who saw everything at once

Argyle (GAELIC) 'From the land of the Gaels'

Ari (TEUTONIC) 'Eagle' *see also* **Aaron**

Aric (ANGLO-SAXON) 'Sacred ruler' *(Rick, Rickie, Ricky)*

Ariel (HEBREW) 'Lion of God' *(Arel)*

Aries (LATIN) 'A ram'. One born in April, from the sign of the Zodiac – Aries

Aristo (GREEK) 'The best'

Aristol (GREEK) 'Excellence'

Aristotle (GREEK) 'Best thinker'

Arjit (SANSKRIT) 'Earned'

Arka (SANSKRIT) 'The sun'

Arlen (GAELIC) 'Pledge' *(Airleas, Arlin)*

Arlie (ANGLO-SAXON) 'From the rabbit meadow' *(Arley, Arly, Harley, Harly) see also* **Harley**

Arlo (SPANISH) 'The barberry'

Arlyn (GREEK) 'Swift one'

Armand (TEUTONIC) 'Man of the army'. The military man personified *(Armando, Armin, Armond)* see also **Herman**

Armin *see* **Armand** or **Herman**

Armon (HEBREW) 'Castle'

Armstrong (ANGLO-SAXON) 'Strong arm'. The tough warrior who could wield a battle axe

Armyn *see* **Herman**

Arnall (TEUTONIC) 'Gracious eagle'. The nobleman who is also a gentleman

Arnaud *see* **Arnold**

Arnett (FRENCH) 'Little eagle' *(Arnatt, Arnott)*

Arney (TEUTONIC) 'The eagle' *(Arne, Arnie)*

Arnold (TEUTONIC) 'Strong as an eagle' *(Arnald, Arnaldo, Arnaud, Arne, Arnie, Arno)*

Arrio (SPANISH) 'War-like' *(Ario)*

Art *see* **Arthur**

Artemis (GREEK) 'Gift of Artemis' *(Artemas)*

Arthfael (WELSH) 'Strong as a bear'

Arthur (CELTIC) 'The noble bear man', 'strong as a rock'. The semi-legendary King of Britain, who founded the Round Table *(Art, Artair, Artie, Artur, Arturo, Artus, Aurthur)*

Arundel (ANGLO-SAXON) 'One who lives with eagles'. Man who shares their keen sight

Arvad (HEBREW) 'The wanderer' *(Arpad)*

Arval (LATIN) 'Much lamented' *(Arvel)*

Arvin (TEUTONIC) 'Friend of the people'. The first true socialist

Asa (HEBREW) 'The healer'

Asaph (HEBREW) 'Gatherer'

Ascelin (GERMAN) 'Of the moon' *(Aceline)*

Ascot (ANGLO-SAXON) 'Owner of the east cottage' *(Ascott)*

Aseem *see* **Ashim**

Ashburn (ANGLO-SAXON) 'The brook by the ash tree'

Ashby (ANGLO-SAXON) 'Ash tree farm' *(Ashbey, Ashton)*

Asher (HEBREW) 'Laughing one'

Ashford (ANGLO-SAXON) 'One who lives in the ford by the ash tree'

Ashim (SANSKRIT) 'Without limit' *(Aseem)*

Ashley (ANGLO-SAXON) 'One who lives in the ash tree meadow' *(Ashlin) see also* **Lee**

Ashlin (ANGLO-SAXON) 'One who lives by the ash tree pool' *see also* **Ashley**

Ashok (HINDI) 'Without sadness'

Ashraf (ARABIC) 'More noble', 'more honourable'

Ashton (ANGLO-SAXON) 'One who lives at the ash tree farm' *see also* **Ashby**

Ashur (SEMITIC) 'The martial one'. One of war-like tendencies

Ashwani (HINDI) 'First of 27 galaxies revolving round the moon'

Aslam (SANSKRIT) 'Greeting' (ARABIC) 'safe'

Astrophel (GREEK) 'Star-lover'

Aswin (ANGLO-SAXON) 'Spear comrade' *(Aswine)*

Athanasius (GREEK) 'Immortal'

Atherton (ANGLO-SAXON) 'One who lives at the spring farm'

Athol (SCOTTISH) Place name

Atley (ANGLO-SAXON) 'One who lives in the meadow'

Atwater (ANGLO-SAXON) 'One who lives by the water'

Atwell (ANGLO-SAXON) 'From the spring'. One who built his home by a natural well

Atwood (ANGLO-SAXON) 'From the forest' *(Attwood, Atwoode)*

Atworth (ANGLO-SAXON) 'From the farm'

Auberon (TEUTONIC) 'Noble' *(Oberon) see also* **Aubrey**

Aubert *see* **Albert**

Aubrey (TEUTONIC) 'Elf ruler'. The golden-haired king of the spirit world *(Alberik, Aube, Auberon, Avery)*

Audley (OLD ENGLISH) 'Prospering'

Audric (TEUTONIC) 'Noble ruler'

Audun (SCANDINAVIAN) 'Deserted, desolate'

Audwin (TEUTONIC) 'Noble friend' *(Adalwine, Aldwin, Aldwyn)*

August (Latin) 'Exalted one' *(Agosto, Aguistin, Augie, Auguste, Augustin, Augustine, Augustus, Austen, Austin, Gus, Gussy)*

Aurelius (LATIN) 'Golden friend'

Auryn (WELSH) 'Gold'

Austen *see* **August**

Avan (HEBREW) 'Proud' *(Evan)*

Avenall (FRENCH) 'One who lives in the oak field' *(Avenel, Avenell)*

Averia (TEUTONIC) 'One who is assertive'

Averill (ANGLO-SAXON) 'Boar-like', 'born in April' *(Averel, Averell, Averil, Everild)*

Avery (ANGLO-SAXON) 'Ruler of the elves' *see also* **Alfred** or **Aubrey**

Avidor (HEBREW) 'Father of a generation'

Avila (SPANISH) 'Brave and reckless'

Aviv (HEBREW) 'Spring'

Avram *see* **Abraham**

Axel (TEUTONIC) 'Father of peace'

Axton (ANGLO-SAXON) 'Stone of the sword fighter'. The whetstone of the warrior's sword

Aylmer (ANGLO-SAXON) 'Noble and famous' *see also* **Elmer**

Aylward (ANGLO-SAXON) 'Awe-inspiring guardian'

Aylwin (TEUTONIC) 'Devoted friend'

Aylworth (ANGLO-SAXON) 'Farm belonging to the awe-inspiring one'

Aymon (OLD FRENCH) 'Home'

Ayward (OLD ENGLISH) 'Noble guardian'

Azal (HEBREW) 'The heart of the mountain'

Azarias (HEBREW) 'One whom the Lord helps'

Azriel (HEBREW) 'Angel of the Lord'

B

Bachir (ARABIC) 'Welcome'

Bahar (ARABIC) 'Sailor'

Bahram (PERSIAN) 'Ancient king'

Bailey (FRENCH) 'Steward'. The trusted guardian of other men's properties *(Baillie, Baily, Bayley)*

Bainbridge (ANGLO-SAXON) 'Bridge over the white water'

Baird (CELTIC) 'The minstrel'. The ancient bard *(Bard, Barde, Barr)*

Balbo (LATIN) 'The mutterer'

Baldemar (TEUTONIC) 'Bold', 'famous prince'

Balder (NORSE) 'Prince'. The god of peace *(Baldhere, Baldur)*

Baldric (TEUTONIC) 'Princely ruler'

Baldwin (TEUTONIC) 'Bold, noble protector' *(Balduin, Baudouin, Baudowin)*

Balfour (GAELIC) 'From the pasture'

Ballard (TEUTONIC) 'Strong and bold'

Balraj (HINDI) 'Strongest'

Balthasar (GREEK) 'May the Lord protect the King' *(Belshazzar)*

Bancroft (ANGLO-SAXON) 'From the bean field'

Banning (GAELIC) 'The little golden-haired one'

Banquo (GAELIC) 'White'

Barak (HEBREW) 'Flash of lightning'

Baram (HEBREW) 'Son of the nation'

Barclay (ANGLO-SAXON) 'One who lives by the birch tree meadow' *(Berk, Berkeley, Berkley)*

Barden (OLD ENGLISH) 'One who lives near the boar's den'

Bardolf (ANGLO-SAXON) 'Axe wolf' *(Bardolph, Bardolphe, Bardulf, Bardulph)*

Bardon (ANGLO-SAXON) 'Barley valley'

Bardrick (ANGLO-SAXON) 'Axe ruler'. One who lived by the battle axe *(Baldric, Baldrick)*

Barend (DUTCH) 'Firm bear'

Bari (ARABIC) 'The maker'

Barker (OLD ENGLISH) 'Birch tree'

Barlow (ANGLO-SAXON) 'One who lives on the barren hills'

Barnaby (HEBREW) 'Son of consolation' *(Barnaba, Barnabe, Barnabus, Barney, Barny, Burnaby)*

Barnes (OLD ENGLISH) 'Bear'

Barnett (ANGLO-SAXON) 'Noble leader' *(Barnet, Barney, Barron, Barry) see also* **Bernard**

Barney *see* **Barnaby, Barnett** or **Bernard**

Barnum (ANGLO-SAXON) 'Nobleman's house'

Baron (ANGLO-SAXON) 'Noble warrior'. The lowest rank of the peerage *(Barron) see also* **Barnett**

Barr (ANGLO-SAXON) 'A gateway' *see also* **Baird**

Barret (TEUTONIC) 'As mighty as the bear' *(Barrett)*

Barris (CELTIC) 'Barry's son' *see also* **Barry**

Barry (GAELIC) 'Spear-like'. One whose intellect is sword sharp *(Barrie) see also* **Barris, Barnett, Baruch**

Bartholomew (HEBREW) 'Son of the furrows, ploughman'. One of the 12 apostles *(Bardo, Bart, Bartel, Barth, Barthel, Barthelmey, Barthol, Bartholomeo, Bartholomeus, Bartlett, Bartley, Bartolome, Bat, Parlan)*

Bartley (ANGLO-SAXON) 'Bartholomew's meadow' *see also* **Bartholomew**

Barton (ANGLO-SAXON) 'Barley farmer' *(Bart, Bartie)*

Bartram (OLD GERMAN) 'Bright raven' *see also* **Bertram**

Baruch (HEBREW) 'Blessed' *(Barrie, Barry)*

Barulai (HEBREW) 'Man of iron'

Bashir (SANSKRIT) 'Bringer of good news'

Basil (GREEK) 'Kingly'. St Basil was the founder of the Greek Orthodox Church *(Base, Basile, Basilio, Basilius, Vassily)*

Basir (TURKISH) 'Intelligent', 'discerning'

Basum (ARABIC) 'Smiling'

Baudric *see* **Baldric**

Baxter (TEUTONIC) 'The baker of bread' *(Bax)*

Bayard (ANGLO-SAXON) 'Red-haired and strong'. The personification of knightly courtesy *(Bay)*

Baylor (ANGLO-SAXON) 'Horse-trainer'

Beacher (ANGLO-SAXON) 'One who lives by the oak tree' *(Beach, Beech, Beecher)*

Beagan (GAELIC) 'Little one' *(Beagen)*

Beal (FRENCH) 'Handsome'. In the form 'Beau' used to identify the smart, well-dressed, personable men of the 17th and early 18th centuries *(Beale, Beall, Beau, Beaufort)*

Beaman (ANGLO-SAXON) 'The bee-keeper'

Beasley (OLD ENGLISH) 'Field of peas'

Beattie (GAELIC) 'Public provider'. One who supplies food and drink for the inhabitants of a town *(Beatie, Beatty, Beaty)*

Beaufort (FRENCH) 'Beautiful stronghold'. The name adopted by the descendants of the union of John of Gaunt and Katharine Swynford *see also* **Beal**

Beaumont (FRENCH) 'Beautiful mountain'

Beauregard (OLD FRENCH) 'Beautiful in expression' *(Beau, Bo)*

Beck (ANGLO-SAXON) 'A brook' *(Bec)*

Bede (OLD ENGLISH) 'A prayer'

Bedell (OLD ENGLISH) 'Messenger'

Behram (PERSIAN) 'Mythological figure'

Belden (ANGLO-SAXON) 'One who lives in the beautiful glen' *(Beldon)*

Bellamy (FRENCH) 'Handsome friend'

Belton (OLD FRENCH) 'Beautiful town'

Beltran (GERMAN) 'Brilliant' *see also* **Bertram**

Bemus (GREEK) 'Platform'

Ben *see* **Benedict** or **Benjamin**

Benedict (LATIN) 'Blessed'. One blessed by God *(Ben, Bendick, Bendix, Benedetto, Benedic, Benedick, Benedicto, Benedikt, Benedix, Bengt, Benito, Bennet, Bennett, Bennie, Benny, Benoit, Benot)* *see also* **Dixon**

Beniah (HEBREW) 'Son of the Lord'

Benito *see* **Benedict**

Benjamin (HEBREW) 'Son of my right hand'. The beloved youngest son *(Beathan, Ben, Beniamino, Benjie, Benjy, Bennie, Benny, Benson, Benyamin)*

Benoit *see* **Benedict**

Benoni (HEBREW) 'Son of my sorrow'. The former name of the Biblical Benjamin

Benroy (HEBREW) 'Son of a lion'

Benson (HEBREW) 'Son of Benjamin' *see also* **Benjamin**

Bently (ANGLO-SAXON) 'From the farm where the grass sways' *(Bentley)*

Benton (ANGLO-SAXON) 'From the town on the moors'

Berard *see* **Bernard**

Béraud (FRENCH) 'Strong leader' *(Beraut)*

Berenger (TEUTONIC) 'Bear spear'

Beresford (ANGLO-SAXON) 'From the barley ford'

Berg (TEUTONIC) 'The mountain' *see also* **Bergren, Burgess**

Berger (FRENCH) 'The shepherd' *see also* **Burgess**

Bergren (SCANDINAVIAN) 'Mountain stream' *(Berg)*

Berkeley *see* **Barclay**

Berman (TEUTONIC) 'Man like a bear'

Bernado *see* **Bernard**

Bernard (TEUTONIC) 'As brave as a bear'. A courageous warrior *(Barnard, Barnet, Barnett, Barney, Barny, Bearnard, Berard, Bern, Bernado, Bernhard, Bernie, Berny, Burnard)*

Bert *see* **Albert, Berthold, Bertram, Burton, Egbert, Gilbert, Herbert, Hubert, Humbert** or **Osbert**

Berthold (TEUTONIC) 'Brilliant ruler' *(Bert, Berthoud, Bertie, Bertold, Berty)*

Berton (ANGLO-SAXON) 'Brilliant one's estate' *(Bertie, Burt, Burton) see also* **Burton** or **Bertram**

Bertram (ANGLO-SAXON) 'Bright raven' *(Bart, Bartram, Beltran, Bert, Bertran, Bertrand, Bertrando, Berty)*

Bertwin (TEUTONIC) 'Bright friend'

Berwick (OLD ENGLISH) 'Barley grange'

Berwin (TEUTONIC) 'Warrior friend'

Bevan (WELSH) 'Son of a noble man' *(Beavan, Beaven, Beven)*

Beverley (ANGLO-SAXON) 'From the beaver meadow' *(Beverly)*

Bevis (FRENCH) 'Fair view' *(Beavais)*

Bhagat (ARABIC) 'Joy'

Bibiano (SPANISH) Spanish variation of **Vyvyan**

Bickford (ANGLO-SAXON) 'Hewer's ford'

Bienvenido (SPANISH) 'Welcome'

Bildad (HEBREW) 'Beloved'

Bill *see* **William**

Bing (TEUTONIC) 'Kettle-shaped hollow'

Bion (GREEK) 'Life'

Birch (ANGLO-SAXON) 'At the birch tree' *(Birk, Burch)*

Birkett (ANGLO-SAXON) 'One who lives by the birch headland' *(Birket)*

Birley (ANGLO-SAXON) 'Cattle shed in the field'

Birney (ANGLO-SAXON) 'One who lives on the island in the brook'

Birtle (ANGLO-SAXON) 'From the bird hill'

Bishop (ANGLO-SAXON) 'The bishop'

Bjorn (SCANDINAVIAN) 'Bear'

Black (ANGLO-SAXON) 'Of dark complexion'

Blade (ANGLO-SAXON) 'Prosperity, glory'

Blagden (ANGLO-SAXON) 'From the dark valley'

Blagoslav (POLISH) 'Good glory'

Blaine (GAELIC) 'Thin, hungry-looking' *(Blane, Blain, Blayn, Blayne)*

Blair (GAELIC) 'A place', 'from the plain'

Blaise (LATIN) 'Stammerer', 'firebrand' *(Blase, Blayze, Blaze)*

Blake (ANGLO-SAXON) 'Of fair complexion'

Blakeley (ANGLO-SAXON) 'From the black meadow'

Blakey (ANGLO-SAXON) 'Little fair one'

Bland (LATIN) 'Mild and gentle'

Blanford (ANGLO-SAXON) 'River crossing belonging to one with grey hair' *(Blandford)*

Bliss (ANGLO-SAXON) 'Joyful one'. One who always sees the cheerful side

Blythe (ANGLO-SAXON) 'The merry person' *(Blyth)*

Boaz (HEBREW) 'Strength is in the Lord' *(Boas, Boase)*

Bob *see* **Robert**

Boden (FRENCH) 'The herald'. The bringer of news

Bogart (TEUTONIC) 'Strong bow' *(Bo)*

Bogdan (POLISH) 'God's gift'

Bolton (FRENCH) 'Manor farm'

Bonamy (FRENCH) 'Good friend'

Bonar (FRENCH) 'Good, gentle and kind'

Bonaro (ITALIAN/SPANISH) 'Friend'

Bond (ANGLO-SAXON) 'Tiller of the soil' *(Bondie, Bondon)*

Boniface (LATIN) 'One who does good'

Booker (ANGLO-SAXON) 'Beech tree'

Boone (NORSE) 'The good one' *(Boonie)*

Booth (TEUTONIC) 'From a market', 'herald' *(Both, Boot, Boote, Boothe)*

Borden (ANGLO-SAXON) 'From the valley of the boar' *(Bord)*

Borg (NORSE) 'One who lives in the castle'

Boris (SLAVIC) 'A fighter'. A born warrior

Bosley (OLD ENGLISH) 'Grove of trees'

Boswell (FRENCH) 'Forest town'

Bosworth (ANGLO-SAXON) 'At the cattle enclosure'

Botolf (ANGLO-SAXON) 'Herald wolf' *(Botolph, Botolphe)*

Boucard (FRENCH/TEUTONIC) 'Beech tree' *(Bouchard)*

Bourne (ANGLO-SAXON) 'From the brook' *(Bourn, Burn, Burne, Byrne)*

Bow *see* **Bowie**

Bowen (CELTIC) 'Descendant of Owen'. A proud Welsh name borne by descendants of the almost legendary Owen *see also* **Bowie**

Bowie (GAELIC) 'Yellow-haired' *(Bow, Bowen, Boyd)*

Bowman (OLD ENGLISH) 'Archer'

Boyce (FRENCH) 'From the woods'. A forester *(Boycie)*

Boyd (GAELIC) 'Light haired'. The blond Adonis *see also* **Bowie**

Boydell (CELTIC) 'Wise and fair'

Boyden (CELTIC) 'Herald'

Boyle (TEUTONIC) 'Spirited', 'nervous'

Boyne (GAELIC) 'White cow'. A very rare person

Brad *see* **Bradford** or **Bradley**

Bradburn (ANGLO-SAXON) 'Broad brook'

Braden (ANGLO-SAXON) 'From the wide valley' *(Bradan, Brade)*

Bradford (ANGLO-SAXON) 'From the broad crossing' *(Brad, Ford)*

Bradley (ANGLO-SAXON) 'From the broad meadow' *(Brad, Bradly, Bradney, Lee, Leigh)*

Bradshaw (OLD ENGLISH) 'Large virginal forest'

Brady (GAELIC) 'Spirited one', 'from the broad island'

Brage (NORDIC) Norse god of poetry

Braham (HINDI) 'Creator'

Brainard (ANGLO-SAXON) 'Bold as a raven'. One who knows no fear *(Brainerd)*

Bram *see* **Abraham, Bramwell** or **Bran**

Bramwell (ANGLO-SAXON) 'From the bramble bush spring' *(Bram)*

Bran (CELTIC) 'Raven'. The spirit of eternal youth *(Bram) see also* **Brand**

Branch (LATIN) 'Paw, claw', 'branch of a tree'

Brand (ANGLO-SAXON) 'Firebrand'. The grandson of the god Woden *(Bran, Brander, Brandt, Brandyn, Brannon, Brantley)*

Brander (NORSE) 'Sword of fire' *see also* **Brand**

Brandon (ANGLO-SAXON) 'From the beacon on the hill' *(Brandyn, Brannon)*

Brannon *see* **Brandon** or **Brand**

Brant (ANGLO-SAXON) 'Fiery or proud one'

Brantley *see* **Brand**

Brawley (ANGLO-SAXON) 'From the meadow on the hillside'

Braxton (ANGLO-SAXON) 'Brock's town'

Brendan (GAELIC) 'Little raven', 'from the fiery hill' *(Bren, Brendis, Brendon, Brennan, Bryn)*

Brent (ANGLO-SAXON) 'Steep hill' *(Brenton)*

Brenton (OLD ENGLISH) 'From the steep hill' *(Brent)*

Brett (CELTIC) 'Native of Brittany', 'from the island of Britain'. One of the original Celts *(Bret, Britt)*

Brevis (LATIN) 'Short', 'thrifty'

Brewster (ANGLO-SAXON) 'The brewer' *(Brew, Bruce)*

Brian (CELTIC) 'Powerful strength with virtue and honour'. Brian Boru, the great Irish king *(Briano, Briant, Brien, Brion, Bryan, Bryant, Bryon)*

Briand (FRENCH) 'Castle'

Brice (CELTIC) 'Quick, ambitious and alert' *(Bryce)*

Bridger (ANGLO-SAXON) 'One who lives by the bridge'

Brien *see* **Brian**

Brigham (ANGLO-SAXON) 'One who lives where the bridge is enclosed' *(Brigg)*

Brinsley (ANGLO-SAXON) 'Brin's meadow'

Brisbane (GAELIC) 'Noble or royal mount'

Brock (ANGLO-SAXON) 'The badger' *(Broc, Brockie, Brok)*

Brockley (ANGLO-SAXON) 'From the badger meadow'

Broderick (ANGLO-SAXON) 'From the broad ridge', 'son of Roderick' *(Broderic) see also* **Roderick**

Brodie (GAELIC) 'A ditch' *(Brody)*

Bromley (ANGLO-SAXON) 'One who lives in the broom meadow'

Bromwell (TEUTONIC) 'One who lives by the spring where the wild broom grows'

Bronislav (SLAVONIC) 'Weapon of glory'

Bronson (ANGLO-SAXON) 'The brown-haired one's son' *(Bronnie, Sonny)*

Brook (ANGLO-SAXON) 'One who lives by the brook' *(Brooke, Brooks)*

Brougher (ANGLO-SAXON) 'The fortified residence' *(Brough)*

Broughton (ANGLO-SAXON) 'From a fortified town'

Bruce (FRENCH) 'From the thicket'. From Robert the Bruce, Scotland's hero king *see also* **Brewster**

Bruno (TEUTONIC) 'Brown-haired man'

Brutus (LATIN) 'Coarse', 'stupid'

Bryan *see* **Brian**

Bryant *see* **Brian**

Bryce *see* **Brice**

Brychan (WELSH) 'Freckled'

Brymer (ANGLO-SAXON) 'Bright one'

Bryn (WELSH) 'Hill' *see also* **Brendan**

Buck (ANGLO-SAXON) 'The buck deer'. A fast-running youth

Buckley (ANGLO-SAXON) 'One who dwells by the buck deer meadow'

Budd (ANGLO-SAXON) 'Herald'. The welcome messenger *(Buddy)*

Bundy (ANGLO-SAXON) 'Free man'. An enfranchised serf

Burbank (ANGLO-SAXON) 'One who lives on the hill by the castle'

Burchard (ANGLO-SAXON) 'Strong as a castle' *(Burckhard, Burgard, Burkhart)*

Burdett (FRENCH) 'Little shield'

Burdon (ANGLO-SAXON) 'One who lives by the castle on the hill'

Burford (ANGLO-SAXON) 'One who lives at the river crossing by the castle'

Burgess (ANGLO-SAXON) 'One who lives in a fortified town' *(Berg, Berger, Bergess, Burg, Burr)*

Burke (FRENCH) 'From the stronghold' *(Berk, Berke, Birk, Birke, Bourke, Burk)*

Burkett (FRENCH) 'From the little fortress'

Burl (ANGLO-SAXON) 'The cup-bearer'. The wine server *(Byrle)*

Burley (ANGLO-SAXON) 'One who lives in the castle by the meadow' *(Burleigh)*

Burnaby (NORSE) 'Warrior's estate' *see also* **Barnaby**

Burnard *see* **Bernard**

Burne *see* **Bourne**

Burnell (FRENCH) 'Little one with brown hair'

Burnett (ANGLO-SAXON) 'Little one with brown complexion'

Burney (ANGLO-SAXON) 'One who lives on the island in the brook'

Burr (NORSE) 'Youth' *see also* **Burgess**

Burrell (FRENCH) 'One of light brown complexion'

Burris (OLD ENGLISH) 'Of the town'

Burt *see* **Berton** or **Burton**

Burton (ANGLO-SAXON) 'Of bright and glorious fame', 'one who lives at the fortified town' *(Bert, Berton, Burt) see also* **Berton**

Busby (NORSE) 'One who lives in the thicket'

Butch Familiar form of **Bert** or **Burt**

Byford (ANGLO-SAXON) 'One who lives by the ford'

Byram (ANGLO-SAXON) 'One who lives at the cattle pen'

Byrd (ANGLO-SAXON) 'Like a bird'

Byrle *see* **Burl**

Byrne *see* **Bourne**

Byron (FRENCH) 'From the cottage', 'the bear' *(Byram, Byran)*

BOYS

Cadby (NORSE)
'Warrior's settlement'

Caddaric *see* **Cedric**

Caddock (CELTIC) 'Keenness in battle'

Cadell (CELTIC) 'Battle spirit'

Cadeyrn (WELSH) 'Battle king'

Cadfael (WELSH) 'Battle metal'

Cadfan (WELSH) 'Battle peak'

Cadman (CELTIC) 'Battle man'

Cadmus (GREEK) 'Man from the east'. The legendary scholar who devised the Greek alphabet

Cadogan (CELTIC) 'War'

Cadwallader (CELTIC)
'Battle leader'

Caedmon (CELTIC)
'Wise warrior'

Caesar (LATIN) 'Emperor'. Source of all names meaning Emperor – Tsar, Kaiser, Shah, etc *(Cesar, Cesare)*

Cailean *see* **Colin**

Cain (HEBREW) 'The possessed'. The original Biblical murderer

Cal *see* **Caleb** or **Calvin**

Calder (ANGLO-SAXON)
'The brook'

Caldwell (ANGLO-SAXON) 'The cold spring'

Caleb (HEBREW) 'The bold one'.
Impetuous *(Cal, Cale)*

Caley (GAELIC) 'Thin, slender'

Calhoun (GAELIC) 'From the
forest strip'

Callum (CELTIC) 'Dove' *see also*
Columba

Calvert (ANGLO-SAXON) 'One
who looks after the calves'
see also **Calvin**

Calvin (LATIN) 'Bald' *(Cal,
Calvino) see also* **Calvert**

Cam *see* **Cameron** or
Campbell

Camden (GAELIC) 'From the
valley which winds'

Cameron (CELTIC) 'Crooked
nose'. The founder of the
Scottish clan *(Cam, Camey,
Camm)*

Camilo (SPANISH) 'Free born'

Campbell (CELTIC) 'Crooked
mouth'. Founder of
Campbell clan *(Cam)*

Candan (TURKISH) 'Sincerely,
heartily'

Cannon *see* **Channing**

Canute (NORSE) 'The knot'. King
who tried to hold back the
waves *(Knut, Knute)*

Caradoc (CELTIC) 'Beloved' *see
also* **Craddock**

Carey (CELTIC) 'One who lives in
a castle' *(Care, Cary) see
also* **Charles**

Carl *see* **Carleton, Carlin**
or **Charles**

Carleton (ANGLO-SAXON)
'Farmers' meeting place'
(Carl, Carlton, Charlton)

Carlin (GAELIC) 'Little
champion' *(Carl, Carling,
Carlyle)*

Carlisle (ANGLO-SAXON) 'Tower
of the castle' *(Carlile,
Carlyle, Carlysle)*

Carlo *see* **Charles**

Carlos *see* **Charles**

Carlton *see* **Carleton**

Carmichael (CELTIC) 'From St
Michael's castle'

Carmine (LATIN) 'Song'

Carney (GAELIC) 'Victorious'. The warrior who never lost a battle *(Carny, Kearney)*

Carol (GAELIC) 'The champion' *(Carolus, Carrol, Carroll, Caryl) see also* **Charles**

Carollan (GAELIC) 'Little champion'

Carr (NORSE) 'One who dwells beside a marsh' *(Karr, Kerr)*

Carrick (GAELIC) 'The rocky cape'

Carroll *see* **Carol**

Carson (ANGLO-SAXON) 'Son of the man who lives by the marsh'

Carswell (ANGLO-SAXON) 'The watercress grower'

Carter (ANGLO-SAXON) 'The cart driver'. One who transports cattle and goods

Cartland (CELTIC) 'The land between the rivers'

Carvell (FRENCH) 'Estate in the marshes' *(Carvel)*

Carver (OLD ENGLISH) 'Woodcarver'

Carvey (GAELIC) 'The athlete' *(Carvy)*

Cary *see* **Carey** or **Charles**

Casey (GAELIC) 'Brave and watchful'. The warrior who never slept *(Case)*

Casimir (SLAVIC) 'The proclaimer of peace' *(Cass, Cassie, Cassy, Kasimir, Kazimir)*

Caspar (PERSIAN) 'Master of the treasure'. Guard of the most precious possessions *(Casper, Gaspar, Gasper) see also* **Gaspar**

Cass *see* **Casimir**, **Cassidy** or **Cassius**

Cassidy (GAELIC) 'Ingenuity', 'curly haired' *(Cass, Cassy)*

Cassius (LATIN) 'Vain and conceited' *(Cash, Cass, Cassie, Cassy)*

Castor (GREEK) 'The beaver'. An industrious person

Cathmor (GAELIC) 'Great warrior'

Cato (LATIN) 'The wise one'. With worldly knowledge

Cavan (GAELIC) 'Handsome'. The Irish Adonis *(Kavan)*

Cavell (FRENCH) 'Little lively one'. Always active

Cawley (NORSE) 'Ancestral relic'

Cecil (LATIN) 'The unseeing one' *(Cece, Cecilio, Cecilius, Celio, Sissil)*

Cedric (CELTIC) 'Chieftain' *(Caddaric, Rick, Rickie, Ricky)*

Cedron (LATIN) 'Cedar tree'

Cephas (ARAMAIC) 'Rock'

Cerwyn (WELSH) 'Fair love'

Chad (ANGLO-SAXON) 'War-like, bellicose' *(Cadda, Chadda, Chaddie) see also* **Chadwick** or **Charles**

Chadwick (ANGLO-SAXON) 'Town of the warrior' *(Chad)*

Chaim (HEBREW) 'Life' *(Hy, Hyman, Mannie, Manny)*

Chalmer (CELTIC) 'The chamberlain's son', 'king of the household' *(Chalmers)*

Chan *see* **Chandler, Channing** or **Chauncey**

Chance (ANGLO-SAXON) 'Good fortune' *see also* **Chauncey**

Chancellor (ANGLO-SAXON) 'King's counsellor'. A man trusted with the highest state secrets *(Chanceller, Chaunceler, Chaunceller)*

Chander (SANSKRIT) 'The moon who outshines the stars'

Chandler (FRENCH) 'The candle-maker' *(Chan, Chane)*

Channing (FRENCH) 'The canon' *(Cannon, Chan, Chane)*

Chapman (ANGLO-SAXON) 'The merchant'. The travelling salesman of medieval times *(Mannie, Manny)*

Charles (Teutonic) 'The strong man'. The personification of all that is masculine *(Carey, Carl, Carlo, Carlos, Carol, Carrol, Cary, Charlie, Charley, Charlton, Chas, Chic, Chick, Chuck, Karl, Karlan, Karlens, Karol, Tearlach) see also* **Carol**

Charlie *see* **Charles**

Charlton (ANGLO-SAXON)
'Charles's farm' *(Charleton)*
see also **Carlton** or **Charles**

Chas *see* Charles

Chase (FRENCH) 'The hunter'.
One who enjoys the chase

Chatham (ANGLO-SAXON) 'Land
of the soldier'

Chauncey (FRENCH) 'Chancellor,
record-keeper' *(Chancey,
Chaunce) see also* **Chance** or
Chancellor

Cheiro (GREEK) 'Hand'

Chelton *see* **Chilton**

Chen (CHINESE) 'Great'

Cheney (FRENCH) 'One who lives
in the oak wood'. A
woodman *(Chaney, Cheyney)*

Chester (LATIN) 'The fortified
camp' *(Ches, Cheston) see
also* **Chet**

Chet (THAI) 'Brother' *see also*
Chester

Chetwin (ANGLO-SAXON) 'Cottage
dweller by the winding
path' *(Chetwyn)*

Cheung (CHINESE) 'Good luck'

Chevalier (FRENCH) 'Knight'
(Chevy)

Chick *see* **Charles**

Chico (SPANISH) Familiar form of
Francis, from Francisco

Chilton (ANGLO-SAXON) 'From
the farm by the spring'
(Chelton, Chilt)

Chris *see* **Christian** or
Christopher

Christian (LATIN) 'Believer in
Christ, a Christian'
*(Chretien, Chris, Christiano,
Christie, Christy, Kit,
Kristian, Kristin)*

Christopher (GREEK) 'The Christ
carrier'. The man who
carried the infant Christ
across the river *(Chris,
Christoforo, Christoper,
Christoph, Christophe,
Christophorus, Cristobal,
Gillecirosd, Kit, Kester, Kris,
Kriss)*

Christophorus *see* **Christopher**

Chrysander (GREEK) 'Golden man'

Chuck *see* **Charles**

Chung (CHINESE) 'Intelligent'

Churchill (ANGLO-SAXON) 'One who lives by the church on the hill'

Cian (GAELIC) 'The ancient one'. Long-living

Ciaran (IRISH) 'Dark-haired' *(Keiran)*

Cicero *(Latin)* 'The chick-pea'

Cid *(Spanish)* 'A lord'. El Cid was an 11th-century Spanish hero and soldier of fortune *(Cyd)*

Clare (LATIN) 'Famous one', (ANGLO-SAXON) 'bright, illustrious' *(Clair) see also* **Clarence**

Clarence (LATIN/ANGLO-SAXON) 'Famous, illustrious one' *(Clare, Clavance)*

Clark (FRENCH) 'Wise and learned scholar' *(Clarke, Clerk)*

Claud (LATIN) 'The lame one' *(Chlaudio, Claude, Claudian, Claudianus, Claus)*

Claus *see* **Claude** or **Nicholas**

Clay (ANGLO-SAXON) 'From the clay pit' *see also* **Clayborne**

Clayborne (ANGLO-SAXON) 'From the brook by the clay pit' *(Claiborn, Clay, Claybourne)*

Clayton (ANGLO-SAXON) 'From the clay town', 'mortal man' *(Clayson)*

Cleary (GAELIC) 'The scholar'

Cleavon (OLD ENGLISH) 'Cliff'

Cledwyn (WELSH) 'Blessed sword'

Clement (LATIN) 'Kind and merciful' *(Clem, Clemence, Clemens, Clementius, Clemmy, Clim)*

Cleon (GREEK) 'Famous'

Clerk *see* **Clark**

Cletus (GREEK) 'Summoned' *(Cletis)*

Cleveland (ANGLO-SAXON) 'From the cliff land' *(Cleve, Clevey)*

Clifford (ANGLO-SAXON) 'From the ford by the cliff' *(Clif, Cliff)*

Clifton (ANGLO-SAXON) 'From the farm by the cliff' *(Clift)*

Clint *see* **Clinton**

Clinton (ANGLO-SAXON) 'From the farm on the headland' *(Clint)*

Clive (ANGLO-SAXON) 'Cliff' *(Cleeve, Cleve, Clyve)*

Clovis (TEUTONIC) 'Famous warrior'. An early form of **Lewis**

Cluny (GAELIC) 'From the meadow'

Clydai (WELSH) 'Fame'

Clyde (WELSH CELTIC) 'Warm' (SCOTS CELTIC) 'heard from the distance' *(Cly, Clywd)*

Clydias (GREEK) 'Glorious'

Cobb *see* **Jacob**

Coburn (OLD ENGLISH) 'Small stream'

Cody (OLD ENGLISH) 'A cushion'

Coel (WELSH) 'Trust' *(Cole)*

Colbert (ANGLO-SAXON) 'Brilliant seafarer', 'cool and calm' *(Cole, Colvert, Culbert)*

Colby (NORSE) 'From the dark country' *(Cole)*

Coleman (CELTIC) 'Keeper of the doves' (ANGLO-SAXON) 'follower of Nicholas' *(Col, Cole, Colman)*

Colin (GAELIC) 'Strong and virile', 'the young child', 'victorious army' *(Colan, Cailean, Collin and all derivatives of **Nicholas**)*

Colley (OLD ENGLISH) 'Swarthy' *see also* **Nicholas**

Collier (ANGLO-SAXON) 'Charcoal merchant' *(Colier, Colis, Collyer, Colton, Colyer)*

Colter (ANGLO-SAXON) 'The colt herder'

Colton (ANGLO-SAXON) 'From the dark town' *see also* **Collier**

Columba (LATIN) 'Dove' *(Colm, Colum) see also* **Callum**

Conan (CELTIC) 'High and mighty', 'wisely intelligent' *(Con, Conal, Conant, Conn, Connall, Connel, Kynan, Quinn)*

Conlan (GAELIC) 'The hero' *(Conlin, Conlon)*

Connor (OLD ENGLISH) 'Wise aid'

Conrad (TEUTONIC) 'Brave counsellor' *(Con, Conn, Connie, Conrade, Conrado, Cort, Curt, Konrad, Kort, Kurt)*

Conroy (GAELIC) 'The wise one' *(Con, Conn, Connie, Roy)*

Constantine (LATIN) 'Firm and unwavering'. Always constant *(Conn, Connie, Constant, Constantin, Constantino, Costa, Konstantin, Konstantine)*

Constantino *see* **Constantine**

Cooper (ANGLO-SAXON) 'Barrel-maker' *(Coop)*

Corbett (FRENCH) 'The raven'. From the raven device worn by the ancient Vikings *(Corbet, Corbie, Corbin, Corby)*

Corcoran (GAELIC) 'Reddish complexion' *(Corquoran)*

Cordell (FRENCH) 'Rope-maker' *(Cord, Cory)*

Corey (GAELIC) 'One who lives in a ravine' *(Cory)*

Cormick (GAELIC) 'The charioteer' *(Cormac, Cormack)*

Cornelius (LATIN) 'Battle horn' *(Connie, Cornal, Cornall, Cornel, Cornell, Neal, Neel, Neil)*

Corquoran *see* **Corcoran**

Corwin (FRENCH) 'Friend of the heart' *(Corwen)*

Cory *see* **Cordell, Corey, Cornelius** or **Corydon**

Corydon (GREEK) 'The helmeted man' *(Cory)*

Cosmo (GREEK) 'The perfect order of the universe' *(Cosimo, Cosme)*

Court *see* **Courtenay** or **Courtland**

Courtenay (FRENCH) 'A place' *(Cort, Cortie, Corty, Court, Courtney, Curt)*

Courtland (Anglo-Saxon) 'One who dwelt on the court land' *(Court)*

Courtney *see* **Courtenay**

Covell (ANGLO-SAXON) 'One who lives in the cave on the hill' *(Covill)*

Cowan (GAELIC) 'Hollow in the hillside'

Coyle (GAELIC) 'Battle flower' *(Coile)*

Craddock (CELTIC) 'Abundance of love' *(Caradoc, Caradock)*

Craig (CELTIC) 'From the stony hill' *(Craggie)*

Crandell (ANGLO-SAXON) 'One who lives in the valley of the crane' *(Crandall)*

Crane (OLD ENGLISH) 'Cry'

Cranley (ANGLO-SAXON) 'From the crane meadow'

Cranog (WELSH) 'Heron'

Cranston (ANGLO-SAXON) 'From the farmstead where the cranes gather'

Crawford (ANGLO-SAXON) 'From the crow ford' *(Crowford)*

Creighton (ANGLO-SAXON) 'From the farm by the creek' *(Crayton, Creigh, Creight, Crichton)*

Crichton *see* **Creighton**

Crispin (LATIN) 'Curly haired'. Patron saint of shoemakers *(Crepin, Crisp, Crispen)*

Cristobal *see* **Christopher**

Cromwell (ANGLO-SAXON) 'One who lives by a winding spring'. The small rivulet that winds through the countryside

Crosby (ANGLO-SAXON/ NORSE) 'One who lives at the crossroads' *(Crosbey, Crosbie)*

Crosley (ANGLO-SAXON) 'From the meadow with the cross'

Cullen (GAELIC) 'Handsome one' *(Cullan, Cullin, Cully)*

Culley (GAELIC) 'From the woodland' *(Cully)*

Culver (ANGLO-SAXON) 'Gentle as the dove', peaceful'. The symbol of peace *(Colver, Cully)*

Curran (GAELIC) 'The resolute hero' *(Curren, Currey, Currie, Curry)*

Curt *see* **Conrad, Courtney** or **Curtis**

Curtis (FRENCH) 'The courteous one'. A gentleman with perfect manners *(Curelo, Curt, Kurt)*

Cuthbert (ANGLO-SAXON) 'Famous and brilliant'

Cutler (OLD ENGLISH) 'Knife-maker' *(Cuttie)*

Cybard (FRENCH) 'Ruler'

Cyndeyrn (WELSH) 'Chief lord'

Cynfael (WELSH) 'Chief metal'

Cynfor (WELSH) 'Great chief'

Cyngen (WELSH) 'Chief son'

Cynric (ANGLO-SAXON) 'From the royal line of kings'

Cynyr (WELSH) 'Chief hero'

Cyprian (GREEK) 'Man from Cyprus' *(Ciprian, Cyprien)*

Cyrano (GREEK) 'From Cyrene' *(Cyrenaica)*

Cyril (GREEK) 'The lord' *(Cirilo, Cy, Cyrill, Cyrille, Cyrillus)*

Cyrus (PERSIAN) 'The sun god'. The founder of the Persian Empire *(Ciro, Cy, Russ)*

D'Arcy *see* **Darcy**

Dabert (FRENCH) 'Bright action'

Dacey (GAELIC) 'The southerner'
(Dacy)

Daegal (SCANDINAVIAN) 'Boy
born at dawn'

Dag *(Norse)* 'Day of brightness'
(Dagny)

Dagan (SEMITIC) 'The earth',
'the small fish' *(Dagon)*

Dagny (TEUTONIC) 'Fresh as day'
(Dagobert) see also **Dag**

Dagwood (ANGLO-SAXON) 'Forest
of the shining one'

Dahab (ARABIC) 'Gold'

Daimon (LATIN) 'Guardian
angel'

Dakota (NATIVE AMERICAN)
'Friend, partner'. Tribal
name

Dalbert (ANGLO-SAXON) 'From
the shining valley' *(Delbert)*

Dale (TEUTONIC) 'One who lives
in the valley' *(Dael, Dal)*

Dallas (CELTIC) 'Skilled', 'from
the water field' *(Dal,
Dallia)*

Dalston (OLD ENGLISH) 'From
Daegal's place' *(Dallon)*

Dalton (ANGLO-SAXON) 'From the
farm in the valley' *(Dal,
Dalt, Tony)*

Daly (GAELIC) 'The counsellor'

Dalziel (CELTIC) 'From the little field' *(Dalziell)*

Daman (SANSKRIT) 'One in control' *(Damian)*

Damek (SLAVIC) 'Man of the earth'

Damian *see* **Daman** or **Damon**

Damon (GREEK) 'Tame and domesticated'. The true friend *(Damian, Damiano, Damien)*

Dana (ANGLO-SAXON) 'Man from Denmark' *(Dane)*

Danby (NORSE) 'From the settlement of the Danish'

Dane *see* **Dana** or **Daniel**

Daniel (HEBREW) 'The lord is my judge' *(Dan, Dane, Daniell, Danielle, Danny) see also* **Darnell**

Dante *see* **Durant**

Darby (GAELIC) 'Freeman' *(Derby)*

Darcy (FRENCH) 'From the fortress' *(Darcie, D'Arcy, Darsey, Darsy)*

Darien (SPANISH) A place name

Darius (PERSIAN) 'The wealthy man' *(Dare, Dario) see also* **Derek** or **Derry**

Darnell (FRENCH) 'From the hidden nook' *(Darnall) see also* **Daniel**

Darrell (FRENCH) 'Beloved one' *(Darryl, Daryl, Derril)*

Darren (GAELIC) 'Little great one' *(Daren, Darin, Daron, Derron)*

Darton (ANGLO-SAXON) 'From the deer forest'

Darwin (OLD ENGLISH) 'Beloved friend' *(Derwin)*

David (HEBREW) 'The beloved one'. The patron saint of Wales *(Dave, Daven, Davidson, Davie, Davin, Davon, Davy, Dewey, Taffy, Tay) see also* **Davis** or **Dov**

Davin (SCANDINAVIAN) 'Brightness of the Finns' *see also* **David**

Davis (ANGLO-SAXON) David's son
see also **David**

Davorin (SLAVONIC) 'God of war'

De Witt (FLEMISH) 'Fair-haired one' *(Dwight)*

Dean (ANGLO-SAXON) 'From the valley' *(Deane, Dene, Dino)*

Dearborn (ANGLO-SAXON) 'Beloved child', 'from the deer brook'

Deck *see* **Dexter**

Declan (IRISH) 'Man of prayer'

Dedrick (TEUTONIC) 'Ruler of the people'

Deems (ANGLO-SAXON) 'The judge's son'

Dekkel (ARABIC) 'Palm tree'

Delaney (GAELIC) 'Descendant of the challenger'

Delano (FRENCH) 'From the nut tree woods'

Delbert *see* **Albert** or **Dalbert**

Delling (NORSE) 'Very shining one'

Delmar (LATIN) 'From the sea' *(Delmer, Delmor, Delmore)*

Delwyn (ANGLO-SAXON) 'Bright friend from the valley' *(Delwin)*

Demas (GREEK) 'The popular person'

Demetrius (GREEK) 'Belonging to Demeter' *(Demetri, Demetris, Demmy, Dimitri, Dmitri)*

Demos (GREEK) 'The spokesman of the people'

Demosthenes (GREEK) 'Strength of the people'

Dempsey (GAELIC) 'The proud one'

Dempster (ANGLO-SAXON) 'The judge'

Denby (NORSE) 'From the Danish settlement' *(Den)*

Denholm (SCOTTISH) 'Island valley'

Denison *see* **Dennison**

Denley (ANGLO-SAXON) 'One who lives in the meadow in the valley'

Denman (ANGLO-SAXON) 'Resident in the valley'

Dennis (GREEK) 'Wine lover'. From Dionysus, the god of wine *(Den, Denis, Dennie, Dennison, Denny, Deny, Denys, Denzil, Dion, Dionisio, Dionysus, Ennis)* *see also* **Denzil**

Dennison (ANGLO-SAXON) 'Son of Dennis' *(Denison) see also* **Dennis**

Denny *see* **Dennis**

Denton (ANGLO-SAXON) 'From the farm in the valley' *(Den, Dennie, Denny)*

Denver (ANGLO-SAXON) 'From the edge of the valley'

Denzil (CORNISH) 'High stronghold' *(Dennis)*

Deodatus (LATIN) 'God-given'

Derby *see* **Darby**

Derek (TEUTONIC) 'Ruler of the people' *(Darrick, Derk, Derrick, Derry, Dirk) see also* **Derry** or **Theodoric**

Derk *see* **Derek** or **Theodoric**

Dermot (GAELIC) 'Free man' *(Diarmid) see also* **Kermit**

Derry (GAELIC) 'The red one' *see also* **Darius, Derek** or **Kermit**

Derward (ANGLO-SAXON) 'Guardian of the deer'

Desmond (GAELIC) 'Man of the world, sophisticated' *(Desmund)*

Deverell (CELTIC) 'From the river bank'

Devin (CELTIC) 'A poet'

Devland *see* **Devlin**

Devlin (GAELIC) 'Fierce bravery' *(Devland)*

Devon (ENGLISH) 'From Devon'. Someone born in that county, the name of which means 'people of the deep valley'

Dewain *see* **Dwayne**

Dewar (CELTIC) 'Hero'

Dewey (CELTIC) 'The beloved one'. The Celtic form of David *(Dew)*

Dexter (LATIN) 'The right-handed man, dextrous' *(Decca, Deck, Dex)*

Diamond (ANGLO-SAXON) 'The shining protector'

Diarmid *see* **Dermot**

Dick *see* **Richard**

Dickon *see* **Richard**

Dickson *see* **Dixon**

Diego *see* **Jacob**

Dieter (GERMAN) 'From strong people' *(Dietrich) see also* **Theodoric**

Digby (NORSE) 'From the settlement by the dyke'

Diggory (FRENCH) 'Strayed, lost'

Dillon (GAELIC) 'Faithful'. A true and loyal man

Dilwin (TEUTONIC) 'Serene friend'

Dimitri *see* **Demetrius**

Dinar (SANSKRIT) 'Golden coin'

Dino *see* **Dean**

Dinsdale (ENGLISH) 'Settlement surrounded by a moat'

Dinsmore (GAELIC) 'From the fortified hill'

Diomede (GREEK) 'Divine ruler'

Dion *see* **Dennis**

Dionysus *see* **Dennis**

Dirk *see* **Derek** or **Theodoric**

Dixon (ANGLO-SAXON) 'Son of Richard' (Dick's son) *(Dickson) see also* **Benedict**

Dmitri *see* **Demetrius**

Doane (CELTIC) 'From the sand dune'

Dodd (TEUTONIC) 'Of the people'

Dolan (GAELIC) 'Black haired'

Dolph *see* **Adolph** or **Rudolph**

Dominic (LATIN) 'Belonging to the Lord, born on the Lord's day' *(Dom, Domenico, Domingo, Dominic, Dominik, Dominy, Nic, Nick, Nickie, Nicky)*

Donaghan (CELTIC) 'Dark skinned'

Donahue (GAELIC) 'Warrior dressed in brown' *(Don, Donn, Donnie, Donny)*

Donal *see* **Donald**

Donald (CELTIC) 'Ruler of the world'. The founder of the MacDonald clan *(Don, Donal, Donn, Donnall, Donalt, Donaugh, Donnell, Donnie, Donny)*

Donato (LATIN) 'A gift'

Donnelly (GAELIC) 'Brave, dark man' *(Don, Donn, Donnell, Donaugh, Donny)*

Donovan (IRISH) 'Dark brown' *(Don, Donn, Donnie, Donny)*

Doran (CELTIC) 'The stranger' *(Dore)*

Dorcas (HEBREW) 'From the forest'

Dorian (GREEK) 'Man from Doria'

Dory (FRENCH) 'The golden-haired boy'

Douglas (CELTIC) 'From the dark stream'. One of the largest Scottish clans *(Doug, Dougal, Douggie, Douggy, Dugal, Dugald, Duggie, Duggy, Duglass)*

Dovev (HEBREW) 'To whisper' *(Dov)*

Dow (GAELIC) 'Black haired'

Doyle (GAELIC) 'The dark-haired stranger'

Drake (ANGLO-SAXON) 'The dragon'

Drew (CELTIC) 'The wise one' *(Drud) see also* **Andrew**

Driscoll (CELTIC) 'The interpreter' *(Driscol)*

Drostan *see* **Tristan**

Druce (CELTIC) 'Son of Drew'

Drummond (CELTIC) 'One who lives on the hill'

Drury (FRENCH) 'The dear one'

Dryden (ANGLO-SAXON) 'From the dry valley'

Duane *see* **Dwayne**

Dubert (TEUTONIC) 'Bright knight'

Dudley (ANGLO-SAXON) 'From the people's meadow' *(Dud, Duddie, Duddy, Dudly)*

Duff (GAELIC) 'Dark complexion'

Dugal *see* **Douglas**

Dugan (GAELIC) 'Dark skinned'. The sun-tanned man *(Doogan, Dougan)*

Duke (FRENCH) 'The leader' *see also* **Marmaduke**

Dulal (SANSKRIT) 'Precious one'

Dunbar (CELTIC) 'Dark branch'

Duncan (CELTIC) 'Brown warrior' *(Dunc, Dunn)*

Dunham (CELTIC) 'Dark man'

Dunlea (TEUTONIC) 'From the dark field'

Dunley (ANGLO-SAXON) 'From the meadow on the hill'

Dunmore (CELTIC) 'From the fortress on the hill'

Dunn (ANGLO-SAXON) 'Dark skinned' *see also* **Duncan**

Dunstan (ANGLO-SAXON) 'From the brown stone hill'

Durant (LATIN) 'Enduring'. One whose friendship is lasting *(Dante, Durand)*

Durward (ANGLO-SAXON) 'The gate-keeper'. The guardian of the drawbridge *(Ward)*

Durwin (ANGLO-SAXON) 'Dear friend' *(Durwyn)*

Dustin (OLD GERMAN) 'Valiant fighter' *(Dustan, Dusty)*

Dusty *see* **Dustin**

Dwayne (CELTIC) 'The singer', (GAELIC) 'the small, dark man' *(Dewain, Duane, Dwain)*

Dwight (TEUTONIC) 'The light-haired one' *see also* **De Witt**

Dyfan (WELSH) 'Ruler of the tribe'

Dyfrig (WELSH) 'Princely hero'

Dylan (WELSH) 'Man from the sea' *(Dilan, Dilly)*

Dynami (NATIVE AMERICAN) 'Eagle'

Dynawd (WELSH) 'Given'

BOYS

Eachan (GAELIC) 'Little horse' *(Eacheann) see also* **Hector**

Eachann *see* **Hector**

Eamonn *see* **Edmund**

Eanruig *see* **Henry**

Earl (ANGLO-SAXON) 'Nobleman', 'chief' *(Erle, Earle, Erl, Errol, Early, Rollo)*

Earn (TEUTONIC) 'One who is like the eagle'

Eaton (ANGLO-SAXON) 'From the estate by the river'

Eb *see* **Aber**, **Ebenezer** or **Everard**

Ebenezer (HEBREW) 'Stone of help' *(Eb, Eben)*

Eberard (TEUTONIC) 'Strong and steadfast' *see also* **Everard**

Ed *see* **Edgar**, **Edmund** or **Edward**

Edan (CELTIC) 'Flame'

Edbert (ANGLO-SAXON) 'Prosperous', 'brilliant'

Eddie *see* **Edgar**, **Edmund**, **Edward** or **Edwin**

Edel (TEUTONIC) 'The noble one'

Edelmar (ANGLO-SAXON) 'Noble and famous'

Eden (HEBREW) 'Place of delight and pleasure'. The original paradise *see also* **Aidan**

Edgar (ANGLO-SAXON) 'Lucky spear warrior' *(Ed, Eddie, Eddy, Edgard, Ned, Neddie, Neddy, Ted, Teddie, Teddy)*

Edison *see* **Edson**

Edlin (ANGLO-SAXON) 'Prosperous friend' *see also* **Edwin**

Edmund (ANGLO-SAXON) 'Rich guardian' *(Eamon, Eamonn, Ed, Eddie, Eddy, Edmon, Edmond, Edmondo, Edmonn, Ned, Neddie, Ted, Teddie, Teddy)*

Edolf (ANGLO-SAXON) 'Prosperous wolf'

Edouard *see* **Edward**

Edred (TEUTONIC) 'Wise adviser'

Edric (ANGLO-SAXON) 'Fortunate ruler'

Edryd (WELSH) 'Restoration'

Edsel (ANGLO-SAXON) 'A prosperous man's house', 'profound thinker'

Edson (ANGLO-SAXON) 'Edward's son' *(Edison)*

Edwald (ANGLO-SAXON) 'Prosperous ruler'

Edward (ANGLO-SAXON) 'Prosperous guardian' *(Ed, Eddie, Eddy, Edouard, Eduard, Ewart, Ned, Neddie, Neddy, Ted, Teddy)*

Edwin (ANGLO-SAXON) 'Prosperous friend' *(Edd, Eddie, Eddy, Edlin, Eduino)*

Edwy (OLD ENGLISH) 'Richly beloved'

Efrem *see* **Ephraim**

Egan (GAELIC) 'Formidable, fiery' *(Egon)*

Egbert (ANGLO-SAXON) 'Bright, shining sword'. The name of the first king of all England *(Bert)*

Egerton (OLD ENGLISH) 'Town on ridge'

Egmont (ANGLO-SAXON) 'Protected by a sword'

Egon *see* **Egan**

Ehren (TEUTONIC) 'Honourable one'

Einar (NORSE) 'Warrior leader'

Eiros (WELSH) 'Bright'

Elan (HEBREW) 'Tree'

Elazar (HEBREW) 'God helps'

Elbert see **Albert**

Elden (ANGLO-SAXON) 'Elf valley' *(Eldon) see also* **Alden**

Elder (ANGLO-SAXON) 'One who lives by an elder tree'

Eldin see **Alden**

Eldo (GREEK) 'A wish'

Eldon (TEUTONIC) 'Respected elder' (ANGLO-SAXON) 'from the holy hill' *see also* **Elden**

Eldoris (TEUTONIC) 'The point of a spear'

Eldridge (ANGLO-SAXON) 'Wise adviser' *(Eldred, Eldredge, Eldrid, Eldwin, Eldwyn) see also* **Aldrich**

Eldwin (OLD ENGLISH) 'Old friend' *see also* **Eldridge**

Eleazar (HEBREW) 'Helped by God' *(Elizer, Lazar, Lazarus)*

Elery see **Ellery**

Eleutherios (GREEK) 'A free man'

Elfed (WELSH) 'Autumn'

Elford (TEUTONIC) 'One who lives by the ford'

Elgar see **Alger**

Elgin (GAELIC) 'Earldom of the Bruces of Scotland'

Elhanan (HEBREW) 'God is gracious'

Eli (HEBREW) 'The highest' *(Ely)*

Elia (HEBREW) 'God's own man'

Elian (HEBREW) 'Bright'

Elias (HEBREW) 'The Lord is God' *(Elihu, Elijah, Eliot, Elliott, Ellis, Ilia)*

Elidr (WELSH) 'Brass'

Elika (HEBREW) 'Sanctified by God'

Elim (HEBREW) 'Oak tree'

Elisha (HEBREW) 'God is my salvation'

Elkan (HEBREW) 'Created by God'

Elkanah (HEBREW) 'God has created'

Elki (NATIVE AMERICAN) 'Bear'

Ellard (ANGLO-SAXON) 'Noble', 'brave'

Ellery (TEUTONIC) 'From the elder tree' *(Elery, Ellerey)*

Elliot *see* **Elias**

Ellis *see* **Elias**

Ellison (ANGLO-SAXON) 'Son of Elias' *(Elson)*

Ellsworth (ANGLO-SAXON) 'A farmer' or 'lover of the land'

Elmen (TEUTONIC) 'Sturdy', 'built like an oak tree'

Elmer (ANGLO-SAXON) 'Noble', 'famous' *(Aylmer)*

Elmo (GREEK/ITALIAN) 'Friendly protector' *see also* **Anselm**

Elmore (ANGLO-SAXON) 'One who lives by the elm tree on the moor'

Elnathan (HEBREW) 'God gives'

Elner (TEUTONIC) 'Famous'

Elon (TEUTONIC) 'The strong oak tree'

Elrad (HEBREW) 'God is my ruler'

Elred (ANGLO-SAXON) 'Wise advice'

Elrod (TEUTONIC) 'Famous'

Elroy (FRENCH) 'The king'. The name is supposed to be an anagram of 'le roi' or it may be from the Spanish 'el rey', both meaning 'the king'

Elsdon (ANGLO-SAXON) 'Hill belonging to the noble one'

Elston (ANGLO-SAXON) 'Estate of the noble one'

Elsworth (ANGLO-SAXON) 'Estate of the noble one'

Elton (ANGLO-SAXON) 'From the old farm'

Elvan (TEUTONIC) 'Strong willed'

Elvis (NORSE) 'All wise'. The prince of wisdom

Elvy (ANGLO-SAXON) 'Elfin warrior'. Though small in stature he had the heart of a lion

Elwell (ANGLO-SAXON) 'From the old well'

Elwin (ANGLO-SAXON) 'Friend of the elves'

Elwood (ANGLO-SAXON) 'From an ancient forest'

Ely *see* Eli

Emanuel *see* Emmanuel

Emeria (TEUTONIC) 'One who works hard'

Emelen *see* Emil

Emerson *see* Emery

Emery (TEUTONIC) 'Industrious ruler', 'joint ruler' *(Amerigo, Emerson, Emmerich, Emmery, Emory, Merrick)*

Emil (TEUTONIC) 'Industrious' *(Emelen, Emile, Emilio, Emlen, Emlyn)*

Emlyn (Welsh) 'One who lives on the border' *see also* Emil

Emmanuel (HEBREW) 'God is with us' *(Emanuel, Immanuel, Mannie, Manny, Mano, Manolo, Manuel)*

Emmet (ANGLO-SAXON) 'The industrious ant' *(Emmett, Emmit, Emmot, Emmott, Emmy)*

Emry (WELSH) 'Honorable'

Emry (WELSH) 'Honour'

Emrys *see* Ambrose

Emyr (WELSH) 'Honour'

Enan (WELSH) 'Firm and unyielding'

Endemon (GREEK) 'Fortunate'

Endimion (GREEK) Mythological figure, son of Jupiter and Calyce (nymph), so beautiful, honest and just, Jupiter made him immortal

Eneas *see* Aeneas

Engelbert (OLD GERMAN) 'Bright as an angel' *see also* Inglebert

Ennis (GAELIC) 'The only choice' *see also* Angus or Dennis

Enoch (HEBREW) 'Consecrated', 'dedicated', 'devoted'

Enos (HEBREW) 'The mortal'

Enrico *see* Henry

Ensley (CELTIC) 'Watchword'

Enzio *see* **Ezio**

Eoghan (CELTIC) 'Young warrior'

Eoin *see* **John**

Ephraim (HEBREW) 'Abounding in fruitfulness' *(Efrem, Eph)*

Erasmus (GREEK) 'Worthy of being loved' *(Erasme, Ras, Rasmus)*

Erastus (GREEK) 'The beloved' *(Ras)*

Erdogan (TURKISH) 'Son is born'

Erhard (OLD GERMAN) 'Honour' *(Erhart)*

Eric (NORSE) 'All-powerful ruler', 'kingly' *(Erich, Erick, Erik, Rick, Ricky)*

Erin (GAELIC) 'Peace' *see also* **Aaron**

Erland (ANGLO-SAXON) 'Land of the nobleman'

Erling (ANGLO-SAXON) 'Son of the nobleman'

Erlon (TEUTONIC) 'Like an elf'

Ermos (TEUTONIC) 'Popular one'

Ernest (ANGLO-SAXON) 'Sincere and earnest' *(Ernesto, Ernestus, Ernie, Ernst, Erny)*

Errol *see* **Earl**

Erskine (CELTIC) 'From the cliff's height'

Ervand (SCANDINAVIAN) 'Sea warrior'

Erwin (OLD ENGLISH) 'Army friend' *see also* **Ervin, Irving**

Esau (HEBREW) 'The one who finishes the job', 'the hairy one'

Esbern (TEUTONIC) 'Divine ruler'

Esdras (HEBREW) 'Rising light'

Esmond (ANGLO-SAXON) 'Gracious protector'

Este (ITALIAN) 'Man from the East' *(Estes)*

Estevan (GREEK) 'Crown'

Ethan (HEBREW) 'Steadfast and firm' *(Etan)*

Ethelard *see* **Allard**

Ethelbert (TEUTONIC) 'Noble, bright'

Ethelred (TEUTONIC) 'Noble counsel'

Etienne *see* **Stephen**

Euclid (GREEK) 'True glory'

Eudon (GREEK) 'Rich ruler'

Eugene (GREEK) 'Nobly born' *(Eugenio, Eugenius, Gene)*

Eurwyn (WELSH) 'Golden and fair'

Eusebius (GREEK) 'Honourable'

Eustace (GREEK) 'Stable', 'tranquil', 'fruitful' *(Eustazio, Eustis)*

Evan (GAELIC) 'Well-born young warrior'. Also Welsh form of **John** *(Evyn, Ewan, Ewen, Owen) see also* **Avan, John** or **Owen**

Evaristus (GREEK) 'Most excellent'

Evelyn (ENGLISH) From a surname *(Evelin)*

Everard (ANGLO-SAXON) 'Strong as a boar' *(Eb, Eberhard, Eberhart, Ev, Evelin, Evered, Everett, Ewart)*

Everild *see* **Averill**

Everley (ANGLO-SAXON) 'Field of the wild boar'

Evner (TURKISH) 'House'

Ewald (ANGLO-SAXON) 'The power of the law'

Ewan *see* **Evan**

Ewart *see* **Edward** or **Everard**

Ewert (ANGLO-SAXON) 'Ewe herder'. One who tended the ewes in lamb

Ewing (ANGLO-SAXON) 'Friend of the law'

Eymer (TEUTONIC) 'Royal worker'

Ezekiel (HEBREW) 'Strength of God' *(Zeke)*

Ezio (ITALIAN) 'Aquiline nose' *(Enzio)*

Ezra (HEBREW) 'The one who helps' *(Esra, Ez)*

BOYS

Fabian (LATIN) 'The bean-grower', 'prosperous farmer' *(Fabe, Faber, Fabiano, Fabien, Fabio)*

Fabio *see* **Fabian**

Fabron (FRENCH) 'The little blacksmith' *(Faber, Fabre)*

Fadoul (ARABIC) 'Honest'

Fagan (GAELIC) 'Little, fiery one' *(Fagin)*

Fagin *see* **Fagan**

Fai (CHINESE) 'Beginning'

Fairburn (TEUTONIC) 'Handsome boy'

Fairchild (TEUTONIC) 'Blond or fair-haired boy'

Fairfax (ANGLO-SAXON) 'Fair-haired one'

Fairhold (TEUTONIC) 'Powerful one'

Fairley (ANGLO-SAXON) 'From the far meadow' *(Fairly, Fairlie, Farl, Farley)*

Faisal (ARABIC) 'Wise judge'

Falah (ARABIC) 'Success'

Falkner (ANGLO-SAXON) 'Falcon trainer'. One who trained the birds used in the hunt *(Faulkener, Faulkner, Fowler)*

Fane (ANGLO-SAXON) 'Glad, joyful'

Faramond (TEUTONIC) 'Journey protection'

Farand (TEUTONIC) 'Pleasant and attractive' *(Farant, Farrand, Ferrand)*

Farland (OLD ENGLISH) 'Land near road'

Farley (OLD ENGLISH) 'From the bull meadow' *(Fairleigh, Farleigh) see also* **Fairley**

Farnell (ANGLO-SAXON) 'From the fern slope' *(Farnall, Fernald, Fernall)*

Farnham (TEUTONIC) 'Village among the ferns'

Farnley (ANGLO-SAXON) 'From the fern meadow' *(Fernley)*

Farold (ANGLO-SAXON) 'Mighty traveller'

Farquhar (CELTIC) 'Man', 'friendly'

Farr (ANGLO-SAXON) 'The traveller'

Farrell (CELTIC) 'The valorous one' *(Farrel, Ferrell)*

Faulkner *see* **Falkner**

Faust (LATIN) 'Lucky, auspicious'

Favian (LATIN) 'A man of understanding'

Fawaz (ARABIC) 'Victorious'

Faxon (TEUTONIC) 'Thick haired'

Fay (GAELIC) 'The raven'. Symbol of great wisdom *(Fayette)*

Fayad (ARABIC) 'Generous'

Faysal (ARABIC) 'Decision-maker'

Fayza (ARABIC) 'Victorious'

Feargus *see* **Fergus**

Felicio *see* **Felix**

Felix (LATIN) 'Fortunate' *(Felice, Felicio, Felizio)*

Felton (ANGLO-SAXON) 'From the town estate'

Fenton (ANGLO-SAXON) 'One who lives of the marshland'

Fenwick (TEUTONIC) 'From the marshlands'

Fenwood (TEUTONIC) 'From the low-lying forest'

Feodore *see* **Theodore**

Ferdinand (TEUTONIC) 'Bold,
daring adventurer' *(Ferd,
Ferdie, Ferdy, Fernand,
Fernando, Hernando)*

Ferdusi (PERSIAN) 'Paradisical'

Fergus (GAELIC) 'The best
choice' *(Feargus, Fergie,
Ferguson)*

Fermin (LATIN/SPANISH) 'Firm,
steadfast'

Fernando *see* **Ferdinand**

Ferner (TEUTONIC) 'Far away'

Fernley *see* **Farnley**

Ferrand (FRENCH) 'One with
iron grey hair' *(Ferand,
Ferant, Ferrant) see also*
Farand

Ferris (GAELIC) 'The rock'
(LATIN) 'man of iron' *(Farris)*

Festus (LATIN) 'Happy and
joyful'

Fidel (LATIN) 'Advocate of the
poor' *(Fidele, Fidelio)*

Fielding (ANGLO-SAXON) 'One
who lives near the field'

Filbert (ANGLO-SAXON) 'Very
brilliant one' *(Filberto,
Philbert)*

Filmer (ANGLO-SAXON) 'Very
famous one'

Findal (TEUTONIC)
'Inventive one'

Fingal (SCOTTISH)
'Blond stranger'

Finlay (GAELIC) 'Fair soldier'
*(Fin, Findlay, Findley,
Finley, Lee)*

Finn (GAELIC) 'Fair haired'

Finnegan (CELTIC) 'Fair one'

Firman (ANGLO-SAXON)
'Long-distance traveller'
(Farman)

Firmin (FRENCH) 'The firm,
strong one'

Fiske (ANGLO-SAXON) 'Fish'

Fitch (ANGLO-SAXON)
'The marten'

Fitz (ANGLO-FRENCH) 'Son'. Originally in the form of 'fils' (French for son), the present form was introduced into Britain by the Normans *see also* names beginning with 'Fitz'

Fitzgerald (ANGLO-SAXON) 'Son of Gerald' *(Fitz)*

Fitzhugh (ANGLO-SAXON) 'Son of Hugh' *(Fitz)*

Fitzpatrick (OLD ENGLISH) 'Son of a nobleman' *(Fitz, Pat, Patrick)*

Fitzroy (FRENCH) 'King's son'

Flann (GAELIC) 'Lad with red hair'

Flavius (LATIN) 'Yellow-haired one' *(Flavian)*

Fleming (ANGLO-SAXON) 'The Dutchman' *(Flem)*

Fletcher (FRENCH) 'The arrow maker' *(Fletch)*

Flinn (GAELIC) 'Son of the red-haired one' *(Flynn)*

Flint (ANGLO-SAXON) 'A stream'

Florean (LATIN) 'Beautiful as a flower'

Florian (LATIN) 'Flowering', 'blooming' *(Flory)*

Floyd *see* **Lloyd**

Forbes (GAELIC) 'Man of prosperity, owner of many fields'. A great landowner

Ford (ANGLO-SAXON) 'The river crossing' *see also* **Bradford** or **Crawford**

Forrest (TEUTONIC) 'Guardian of the forest' *(Forest, Forester, Forrester, Forrie, Forster, Foss, Foster)*

Fortescue (TEUTONIC) 'Sturdy shield'

Fortune (FRENCH) 'The lucky one'. Child of many blessings

Fowler *see* **Falkner**

Francis (LATIN) 'Free man' *(Chico, Fran, Franchot, Frank, Frankie, Franz)*

Frank *see* **Francis** or **Franklin**

Franklin (ANGLO-SAXON) 'Free-holder of property'. One who owns his own land to use as he wished *(Francklin, Francklyn, Frank, Frankie, Franklyn)*

Fraser (FRENCH) 'Strawberry', 'curly-haired one' *(Frasier, Frazer, Frazier)*

Frayne (ANGLO-SAXON) 'Stranger' *(Fraine, Frean, Freen, Freyne)*

Fred *see* **Alfred, Frederick** or **Wilfred**

Frederick (TEUTONIC) 'Peaceful ruler'. One who uses diplomacy not war *(Fred, Freddie, Freddy, Frederic, Frederik, Fredric, Fredrick, Friedrich, Fritz)*

Freeborn (OLD ENGLISH) 'Child of freedom'

Freeland (OLD ENGLISH) 'From free land'

Freeman (ANGLO-SAXON) 'Born a free man' *(Freedman)*

Fremont (TEUTONIC) 'Free and noble protector'

Frewin (ANGLO-SAXON) 'Free, noble friend' *(Frewen)*

Frey (ANGLO-SAXON) 'The lord of peace and prosperity'. From the ancient Norse god

Frick (ANGLO-SAXON) 'Bold man'

Friedrich *see* **Frederick**

Frith (ANGLO-SAXON) 'One who lives in the woods'

Fritz *see* **Frederick**

Frysa (ANGLO-SAXON) 'One with curly hair'

Fulbright (OLD GERMAN) 'Very bright' *(Fulbert)*

Fuller (ANGLO-SAXON) 'One who works with cloth' *(Tucker)*

Fulton (ANGLO-SAXON) 'From the field', 'living by the chicken pen'

Fyfe (SCOTTISH) 'Man from Fife' *(Fife, Fyffe)*

G

BOYS

Gable (FRENCH)
'The small Gabriel'

Gabriel (HEBREW) 'Messenger of God'. The archangel who announced the birth of Christ *(Gabbie, Gabby, Gabe, Gabie, Gabriello)*

Gadiel (HEBREW) 'God is my fortune'

Gadman (HEBREW) 'The lucky one' *(Gadmann)*

Gage (FRENCH) 'A pledge'. The glove that was given as an earnest pledge of good faith

Gair (GAELIC) 'Short one'

Gaius (LATIN) 'Rejoiced'

Galahad (HEBREW) 'Gilead'

Galdemar (FRENCH/OLD GERMAN) 'Famous ruler'

Gale (CELTIC) 'The lively one' *(Gail, Gayle)*

Galen (GAELIC/GREEK) 'Little bright one', 'helper' *(Gaelen)*

Gallagher (GAELIC) 'Eager helper from overseas'

Galloway (CELTIC) 'Man from the stranger lands' *(Gallway, Galway)*

Galpin (FRENCH) 'Swift runner'

Galt (OLD ENGLISH) 'High land'

Galton (ANGLO-SAXON) 'Lease holder of an estate'

Galvin (GAELIC) 'Bright, shining white', 'the sparrow' *(Galvan, Galven)*

Gamal (ARABIC) 'Camel' *(Gammali, Jamaal, Jammal)*

Gamalat (ARABIC) 'Beautiful one'

Gamaliel (HEBREW) 'The recompense of the Lord'

Gannon (GAELIC) 'Little blond one'

Ganymede (GREEK) 'Rejoicing in mankind'

Gardiner (TEUTONIC) 'A gardener, a flower-lover' *(Gardener, Gardner)*

Gareth (WELSH) 'Gentle'

Garfield (ANGLO-SAXON) 'War or battlefield'

Garland (ANGLO-SAXON) 'From the land of the spears'

Garman (ANGLO-SAXON) 'The spearman'

Garmon *see* **Garmond**

Garmond (ANGLO-SAXON) 'Spear protector' *(Garmon, Garmund)*

Garner (TEUTONIC) 'Army guard, noble defender'

Garnet (LATIN) 'A red seed', 'pomegranate seed'

Garnett (ANGLO-SAXON) 'Compulsive spear man'. He struck first and challenged afterwards

Garnock (CELTIC) 'One who dwells by the river alder'

Garrard *see* **Garrett**

Garrett (ANGLO-SAXON) 'Mighty spear warrior' *(Garett, Garrard, Garret, Garritt, Gerard, Jarrett)*

Garrick (ANGLO-SAXON) 'Spear ruler' *(Garek, Garrek)*

Garroway (ANGLO-SAXON) 'Spear warrior' *(Garraway)*

Garson (FRENCH) 'Young man', 'garrison'

Garth (NORSE) 'From the garden'

Garton (ANGLO-SAXON) 'The one who lives by the triangular-shaped farm'

Garvey (GAELIC) 'Rough peace'. Peace obtained after victory *(Garvie)*

Garvin (TEUTONIC) 'Spear friend' *(Garwin)*

Garwood (ANGLO-SAXON) 'From the fir trees'

Gary (ANGLO-SAXON) 'Spearman' *(Gare, Garey, Gari, Garry)*

Gaspar (PERSIAN) 'Master of the treasure'. One of the Magi *(Caspar, Casper, Gasper, Jasper, Kaspar, Kasper) see also* **Caspar**

Gaston (FRENCH) 'Man from Gascony'

Gaubert (OLD GERMAN) 'Brilliant ruler'

Gauderic (OLD GERMAN) 'Ruler, king'

Gawain (CELTIC) 'The battle hawk' *(Gavan, Gaven, Gavin, Gawaine, Gawen)*

Gaylord (FRENCH) 'The happy noble man' *(Gallard, Galor, Gayler)*

Gaynell (TEUTONIC) 'One who makes a profit'

Gaynor (GAELIC) 'Son of the blond-haired one'

Geary (ANGLO-SAXON) 'Changeable' *(Gearey, Gery)*

Gemmel (SCANDINAVIAN) 'Old'

Gene *see* **Eugene**

Genesius (LATIN) 'Welcome newcomer'

Geno *see* **John**

Gentilis (LATIN) 'Kind man'

Geoffrey (TEUTONIC) 'God's divine peace' *(Geof, Geoff, Godfrey, Jeff, Jeffers, Jeffery, Jeffrey, Jeffry)*

George (GREEK) 'The farmer'. The patron saint of England *(Geordie, Georg, Georges, Georgie, Georgy, Giorgio, Gordie, Gordy, Jorge, Jorgen, Jorin, Joris, Jurgen, Yorick)*

Geraint (WELSH) 'Old'

Gerald (TEUTONIC) 'Mighty spear ruler' *(Garold, Gearalt, Ger, Geraud, Gereld, Gerrald, Gerry, Gery, Giraldo, Giraud, Jer, Jerald, Jereld, Jerold, Jerrold, Jerry)*

Gerard (ANGLO-SAXON) 'Spear strong, spear brave' *(Gearard, Gerardo, Gerhard, Gerhardt, Gerrard, Gerry)* see also **Garrett**

Gerius (LATIN) 'Reliable'

Germain (MIDDLE ENGLISH) 'Sprout', 'bud'

Gerome see **Jerome**

Gerry see **Gerald** or **Gerard**

Gershom (HEBREW) 'Exile *(Gersham)*

Gervase (TEUTONIC) 'Spear vassal' *(Ger, Gervais, Jarv, Jarvey, Jarvis, Jervis, Jervoise)*

Gerwyn (WELSH) 'Fair love'

Gethin (WELSH) 'Dark skinned'

Ghislaine (FRENCH) 'A pledge'

Giacomo see **Jacob**

Gianni see **John**

Gibson (ANGLO-SAXON) 'Son of Gilbert'

Gideon (HEBREW) 'Brave indomitable spirit', 'the destroyer'

Gifford (TEUTONIC) 'The gift' *(Giffard, Gifferd)*

Gilbert (ANGLO-SAXON) 'Bright pledge', 'a hostage' *(Bert, Gib, Gibb, Gil, Gilibeirt, Gill, Gilleabart, Gillie)* see also **Gilby**

Gilby (NORSE) 'The pledge', 'a hostage' *(Gilbey)* see also **Gilbert**

Gilchrist (GAELIC) 'The servant of Christ' *(Gilecriosd)*

Gildas (LATIN) 'Servant of the Lord'

Gilecriosd see **Gilchrist**

Giles (LATIN/FRENCH) 'Shield-bearer' *(Gil, Gilles)*

Gilford (TEUTONIC) 'One who lives by the big ford'

Gilibeirt see **Gilbert**

Gilland (TEUTONIC) 'Bold young man'

Gilles see **Giles**

Gillet (FRENCH) 'Little Gilbert'

Gilman (TEUTONIC) 'Tall man'

Gilmer (ANGLO-SAXON) 'Famous hostage'. An eminent knight taken captive in battle

Gilmore (GAELIC) 'Mary's servant' *(Gillmore, Gilmour)*

Gilroy (LATIN/GAELIC) 'The king's servant'

Gino see **Ambrose**

Giorgio see **George**

Giovanni see **John**

Girvin (GAELIC) 'Little rough one' *(Girvan, Girven)*

Giuseppe see **Joseph**

Gladwin (ANGLO-SAXON) 'Kind friend'

Glanmor (WELSH) 'Seashore'

Glanville (FRENCH) 'One who lives on the oak tree estate' *(Glanvil)*

Glen (CELTIC) 'From the valley' *(Glenn, Glyn, Glynn)*

Glendon (CELTIC) 'From the fortress in the glen' *(Glenden)*

Gleve (TEUTONIC) 'The point of a spear'

Glynn see **Glen**

Goddard (TEUTONIC) 'Divinely firm'. Firm in belief and trust in God *(Godard, Godart, Goddart)*

Godfrey see **Geoffrey**

Godwin see **Goodwin**

Golding (ANGLO-SAXON) 'Son of the golden one'

Goldwin (ANGLO-SAXON) 'Golden friend' *(Goldwyn)*

Goldwyn see **Goldwin**

Gomez (SPANISH) 'Man'

Gonzalo (SPANISH) 'Wolf'

Goodman (ANGLO-SAXON) 'Good man'

Goodwin (ANGLO-SAXON) 'Good friend', 'God's friend' *(Godewyn, Godwin, Godwine)*

Gordon (ANGLO-SAXON) 'From the cornered hill' *(Gordan, Gorden, Gordie, Gordy)*

Gorhan (OLD ENGLISH) 'One who lives in the mud hut'

Gorman (GAELIC) 'Small, blue-eyed boy'

Gouveneur (FRENCH) 'The governor, the ruler'

Gower (CELTIC) 'The pure one'

Grady (GAELIC) 'Illustrious and noble'

Graeme *see* **Graham**

Graham (TEUTONIC) 'From the grey lands'. One from the country beyond the mists *(Graeme)*

Granger (ANGLO-SAXON) 'The farmer' *(Grange)*

Grant (FRENCH) 'The great one' *(Grantley, Grenville)*

Grantham (OLD ENGLISH) 'From the big meadow'

Grantland (ANGLO-SAXON) 'From the great lands'

Granville (FRENCH) 'One who lives in the large town' *(Grandvil, Grandville, Granvil, Greville)*

Grayson (ANGLO-SAXON) 'The bailiff's son'

Greeley (ANGLO-SAXON) 'From the grey meadow'

Gregory (GREEK) 'The watchful one'. Someone ever vigilant *(Greagoir, Greg, Gregg, Gregor, Gregorio, Gregorius, Greiogair)*

Grenville *see* **Grant**

Gresham (ANGLO-SAXON) 'From the grazing meadow'

Greville *see* **Granville**

Griff *see* **Rufus**

Griffith (CELTIC) 'Fierce red-haired warrior' *(Griffin, Gruffydd, Rufus) see also* **Rufus**

Grimbald (TEUTONIC) 'Fierce power'

Griswold (TEUTONIC) 'From the grey forest'

Grosvenor (OLD FRENCH) 'Great hunter'

Grover (ANGLO-SAXON) 'One who comes from the grove'

Gruffydd *see* **Griffith**

Guido *see* **Guy**

Guillermo *see* **William**

Gunther (TEUTONIC) 'Bold warrior' *(Gunar, Gunnar, Gunner, Guntar, Gunter, Gunthar)*

Gurion (HEBREW) 'Dwelling place of God'

Guru (SANSKRIT) 'Teacher'

Gus *see* **Angus, August** or **Gustave**

Gustave (SCANDINAVIAN) 'Staff of the Goths' *(Gus, Gustaf, Gustav, Gustavo, Gustavus)*

Guthrie (CELTIC) 'War serpent', 'war hero', 'from the windy country' *(Guthry)*

Guy (LATIN) 'Life', (FRENCH) 'guide' (TEUTONIC) 'warrior' *(Guido, Guyon, Wiatt, Wyatt)*

Gwion (WELSH) 'Elf'

Gwylim *see* **William**

Gwynfor (WELSH) 'Fair place'

Gwynllyw (WELSH) 'Blessed leader'

Gwynn (CELTIC) 'The blond one' *(Guin)*

Haakon (SCANDINAVIAN) 'Noble kin' *see also* **Hakon**

Haaris (ARABIC) 'Vigilant'

Haarwyn *see* **Hardwin**

Habakkuk (HEBREW) 'Embrace'

Habib (SANSKRIT/ARABIC) 'Beloved'

Habor (TEUTONIC) 'Dexterous'

Hachmann (HEBREW) 'Wise or learned one'

Hackett (TEUTONIC) 'The small woodsman'. The apprentice forester *(Hacket)*

Hacon (OLD NORSE) 'Useful'

Hadar (HEBREW) 'Ornament'

Hadden (ANGLO-SAXON) 'From the heath valley' *(Haddan, Haddon)*

Hadi (ARABIC) 'Guide'

Hadley (ANGLO-SAXON) 'From the hot meadow' *(Had, Hadlee, Hadleigh)*

Hadrian *see* **Adrian**

Hadwin (ANGLO-SAXON) 'Battle companion'

Hafiz (ARABIC) 'He who remembers'

Hagen (GAELIC) 'The young one' *(Hagan, Haggan, Haggen)*

Haggai (HEBREW) 'Festive'

Hagley (ANGLO-SAXON) 'From the hedged meadow'

Hagos (ETHIOPIAN) 'Happy'

Haig (ANGLO-SAXON) 'One who lives in an enclosure'. Popular name for boys during early part of 20th century in compliment to the Field Marshal Lord Haig

Haines (OLD GERMAN) 'From a vined cottage'

Hakan (NATIVE AMERICAN) 'Fiery'

Hakeem (ARABIC) 'Wise' *(Hakim)*

Hakon (NORSE) 'From an exalted race' *(Haakon, Hako) see also* **Haakon**

Hal *see* **Harold** or **Henry**

Halbert (ANGLO-SAXON) 'Brilliant hero'

Halden (NORSE) 'Half Danish' *(Haldan, Haldane, Halfdan)*

Hale (ANGLO-SAXON) 'From the hall'

Haley (GAELIC) 'The ingenious one'. One with a scientific intelligence

Halford (ANGLO-SAXON) 'From the ford by the manor house'

Halim (ARABIC) 'Patient'

Hall (ANGLO-SAXON) 'One who lives at the manor house'

Hallam (ANGLO-SAXON) 'One who lives on the hill slopes'

Halley (ANGLO-SAXON) 'From the manor house meadow', 'holy'

Halliwell (ANGLO-SAXON) 'The one who lives by the holy well'

Hallward (ANGLO-SAXON) 'Guardian of the manor house' *(Halward)*

Halsey (ANGLO-SAXON) 'From Hal's island' *(Halsy)*

Halstead (ANGLO-SAXON) 'From the manor house' *(Halsted)*

Halton (ANGLO-SAXON) 'From the estate on the hill slope'

Ham (HEBREW) 'South'

Hamal (ARABIC) 'The lamb'. A very gentle person

Hamar (NORSE) 'Symbol of ingenuity'. A great gift for invention *(Hammar)*

Hamdan (ARABIC) 'Thankful'

Hamed (ARABIC) 'One who receives praise'

Hamford (TEUTONIC) 'From the old ford'

Hamid (SANSKRIT) 'Friend', (ARABIC) 'thanking God

Hamilton (FRENCH/ANGLO-SAXON) 'From the mountain village' *(Hamil)*

Hamish *see* **Jacob**

Hamlet (TEUTONIC) 'Little village'

Hamlin (TEUTONIC) 'Small home-lover' *(Hamelin, Hamelyn, Hamlyn) see also* **Henry**

Hamon (GREEK) 'Faithful'

Hanafi (ARABIC) 'Orthodox'

Hanan (HEBREW) 'Grace'

Hananel (HEBREW) 'God is gracious'

Hanford (ANGLO-SAXON) 'From the high ford'

Hanif (ARABIC) 'Orthodox, true'

Hank *see* **Henry**

Hanley (ANGLO-SAXON) 'From the high meadow' *(Handley, Henleigh, Henley)*

Hannibal (GREEK) The hero of Carthage

Hans *see* **John**

Hansel (SCANDINAVIAN) 'Gift from the Lord'

Harbert *see* **Herbert**

Harbin *see* **Herbert**

Harcourt (FRENCH) 'From a fortified court'

Harden (ANGLO-SAXON) 'From the valley of the hare' *see also* **Harley**

Hardik (SANSKRIT) 'Heartfelt'

Harding (ANGLO-SAXON) 'Son of the hero'

Hardwin (ANGLO-SAXON) 'Brave friend' *(Haarwyn, Hardwyn, Harwin)*

Hardwyn *see* **Hardwin**

Hardy (TEUTONIC) 'Bold and daring' *(Hardey, Hardi, Hardie)*

Hareford *see* **Harford**

Harem (HEBREW) 'One who climbs mountains'

Harford (ANGLO-SAXON) 'From the hare ford' *(Hareford, Hereford, Herford)*

Hargrove (ANGLO-SAXON) 'From the hare grove' *(Hargrave, Hargreave, Hargreaves)*

Harim (HEBREW) 'Boy with a flat nose'

Harley (ANGLO-SAXON) 'From the hare meadow' *(Arley, Arlie, Harden, Harl, Harleigh, Hart, Hartleigh, Hartley) see also* **Arlie** *or* **Hartwell**

Harlon (TEUTONIC) 'From the battle land' *(Harlan, Harland)*

Harlow (ANGLO-SAXON) 'The fortified hill'. An army camp on the hillside

Harly *see* **Arlie**

Harmon *see* **Herman**

Harold (ANGLO-SAXON) 'Army commander'. A mighty general *(Araldo, Hal, Harailt, Harald, Harry, Herald, Hereld, Herold, Herrick)*

Haroun *see* **Aaron**

Harper (ANGLO-SAXON) 'The harp player'. The wandering minstrel

Harris (ANGLO-SAXON) 'Harold's son' *(Harrison)*

Harshad (SANSKRIT) 'Joy bringer'

Harshit (SANSKRIT) 'Joyful', 'happy' *(Harshil)*

Hart (ANGLO-SAXON) 'The hart' *see also* **Harley** *or* **Hartwell**

Hartford (ANGLO-SAXON) 'The river crossing of the deer' *(Hertford)*

Hartley (ANGLO-SAXON) 'Meadow of the hart deer' *(Hartleigh) see also* **Harley**

Hartman (ANGLO-SAXON) 'Keeper of the stags' (TEUTONIC) 'strong and austere' *(Hartmann)*

Hartwell (ANGLO-SAXON) 'Well where the deer drink' *(Harwell, Hart, Hartwill, Harwill)*

Hartwood (ANGLO-SAXON) 'Forest of the hart deer' *(Harwood)*

Harvey (TEUTONIC/FRENCH) 'Army warrior' *(Harv, Harve, Herv, Herve, Hervey)*

Harwood *see* **Hartwood**

Hasaka (SANSKRIT) 'Jester'

Hashim (ARABIC) 'Destroyer of evil' *(Hasheem)*

Hasin (SANSKRIT) 'Laughing one'

Haskel (HEBREW) 'Understanding' *(Haskell)*

Haslett (ANGLO-SAXON) 'Hazel tree grove on the headland' *(Haslitt, Hazlett, Hazlitt)*

Hassan (ARABIC) 'Handsome'

Hastings (ANGLO-SAXON) 'Son of violence'

Havelock (NORSE) 'Sea battle' *(Havlock)*

Haven (ANGLO-SAXON) 'A place of safety'

Hawley (ANGLO-SAXON) 'From the hedged meadow'

Hayden (TEUTONIC) 'From the hedged valley' *(Haydon)*

Hayes (OLD ENGLISH) 'From the hedged forest'

Hayward (ANGLO-SAXON) 'Keeper of the hedged field' *(Haywood, Heyward, Heywood)*

Hazlett *see* **Haslett**

Hearne *see* **Ahern**

Hearst *see* **Hurst**

Heath (ANGLO-SAXON) 'Heathland'

Heathcliff (ANGLO-SAXON) 'From the heather cliff' *(Heathcliffe)*

Hector (GREEK) 'Steadfast, unswerving, holds fast' *(Eachan, Eachann, Eachunn, Heck)*

Heddwyn (WELSH) 'Blessed peace' *see also* **Hedley**

Hedley (OLD ENGLISH) 'Blessed peace' *see also* **Heddwyn**

Heer (SANSKRIT) 'Diamond'

Heilyn (WELSH) 'Cup-bearer'

Heinrich *see* **Henry**

Henderson (OLD ENGLISH) 'Son of Henry'

Hendry (TEUTONIC) 'Manly'

Hendy (TEUTONIC) 'Skilful one'

Henleigh *see* **Hanley**

Henry (TEUTONIC) 'Ruler of the estate'. Lord of the manor *(Eanruig, Hal, Hamlin, Hank, Hanraoi, Hark, Harry, Heinrich, Heinrick Hendrick, Henri, Henrik)*

Herbert (TEUTONIC) 'Brilliant warrior' *(Bert, Harbert, Harbin, Hebert, Herb, Herbie, Heriberto, Hoireabard)*

Hercules (LATIN) 'Glory of Hera'

Herman (TEUTONIC) 'Army warrior' *(Armand, Armin, Armond, Armyn, Ermin, Harman, Harmon, Herm, Hermann, Hermie, Hermon)*

Hernando *see* **Ferdinand**

Herrick (TEUTONIC) 'Army ruler' *see also* **Harold**

Herschel (HEBREW) 'Deer'

Herwin (TEUTONIC) 'Lover of war', 'battle companion'

Hewett (ANGLO-SAXON) 'Little Hugh'

Hezekiah (HEBREW) 'God is strength'. Belief in God arms this man against all adversity

Hilary (LATIN) 'Cheerful and merry' *(Hilaire, Hillary, Hillery)*

Hildebrand (TEUTONIC) 'Sword of war'

Hillel (HEBREW)
'Greatly praised'

Hilliard (TEUTONIC) 'War guardian', 'brave in battle' *(Hillard, Hillier, Hillyer)*

Hilton (ANGLO-SAXON) 'From the hill farm' *(Hylton)*

Himmet (TURKISH) 'Support', 'help'

Hiram (HEBREW) 'Most noble and exalted one' *(Hi, Hy, Hyram)*

Hiroshi (JAPANESE) 'Generous man'

Hisham (ARABIC) 'Generosity'

Hobart *see* **Hubert**

Hogan (CELTIC) 'Youth'

Holbrook (ANGLO-SAXON) 'From the brook in the valley'

Holcomb (ANGLO-SAXON) 'Deep valley' *(Holcombe, Holecomb, Holecombe)*

Holden (ANGLO-SAXON/TEUTONIC) 'From the valley', 'kind'

Holgate (ANGLO-SAXON) 'Gatekeeper'

Holger (SCANDINAVIAN) 'Faithful warrior'

Hollis (ANGLO-SAXON) 'One who lives in the holly grove'

Holman (DUTCH) 'Man from the hollow'

Holmes (ANGLO-SAXON) 'From the island in the river'

Holt (ANGLO-SAXON) 'From the forest'

Homer (GREEK) 'A pledge'

Horace (LATIN) 'Time keeper', 'hours of the sun' *(Horatio, Horatius, Race)*

Horst (GERMAN) 'From the thicket'

Horton (ANGLO-SAXON) 'From the grey farm'

Hosea (HEBREW) 'Salvation'

Houghton (ANGLO-SAXON) 'From the estate on the cliff'

Houston (ANGLO-SAXON) 'From the town in the mountains'

Howard (ANGLO-SAXON) 'Chief guardian' *(Howie)*

Howe (TEUTONIC*)* 'The eminent one'. A person of high birth

Howell (CELTIC) 'Little, alert one' *(Hywel, Hywell)*

Howie *see* **Howard**

Howland (ANGLO-SAXON) 'One who lives on the hill'

Hubert (TEUTONIC) 'Brilliant, shining mind' *(Aodh, Aoidh, Bert, Hobart, Hobbard, Hoibeard, Hoireabard, Hoyt, Hubbard, Hube, Huey, Hughes, Hugo)*

Hudson (ANGLO-SAXON) 'Son of the hoodsman'

Hugh (TEUTONIC) 'Brilliant mind' *(Hewe, Hughie, Hughy)*

Hulbert (TEUTONIC) 'Graceful' *(Hulbard, Hulburd, Hulburt)*

Humbert (TEUTONIC) 'Brilliant Hun', 'bright home' *(Bert, Bertie, Berty, Humbie, Umberto)*

Humphrey *(Teutonic)* 'Protector of the peace' *(Humfrey, Humfry, Hump, Humph)*

Hunter (ANGLO-SAXON) 'A hunter' *(Hunt)*

Huntingdon (ANGLO-SAXON) 'Hill of the hunter'

Huntly (ANGLO-SAXON) 'From the hunter's meadow' *(Huntley)*

Hurlbert (TEUTONIC) 'Brilliant army leader'

Hurley (GAELIC) 'Sea tide'

Hurst (ANGLO-SAXON) 'One who lives in the forest' *(Hearst)*

Hussain (SANSKRIT) Islamic saint

Hussein (ARABIC) 'Small and handsome'

Hutton (ANGLO-SAXON) 'From the farm on the ridge'

Huxford (ANGLO-SAXON) 'Hugh's ford'

Huxley (ANGLO-SAXON) 'Hugh's meadow'

Hy *see* **Chaim, Hiram** or **Hyman**

Hyatt (ANGLO-SAXON) 'From the high gate' *(Hiatt)*

Hyde (ANGLO-SAXON) 'From the hide of land'. An old unit of measurement of land

Hylton *see* **Hilton**

Hyman (HEBREW) 'Life'. The divine spark *(Hy, Hymen, Hymie) see also* **Chaim**

Hywell *see* **Howell**

I

BOYS

Iago (HEBREW) 'Supplanter'

Iaian *see* **Ian** or **John**

Iain *see* **Ian** or **John**

Ian (CELTIC) 'God is gracious' *(Iaian, Iain) see also* **John**

Ibald (TEUTONIC) 'Noble archer'

Ibrahim *see* **Abraham**

Icabod (HEBREW) 'Departed glory'

Icarus (GREEK) 'Dedicated to the moon'

Ichabod (HEBREW) 'The glory has departed'

Iddo (HEBREW) 'Loving and kind'

Iden (ANGLO-SAXON) 'Prosperous'

Idris (WELSH) 'Fiery lord'

Idwal (WELSH) 'Wall lord'

Iestin *see* **Iestyn** or **Justin**

Iestyn (WELSH) 'Just man' *(Iestin)*

Ieuan (WELSH) Form of **John**

Ifor *see* **Ivar**

Ignatius (LATIN) 'The ardent one'. A fiery patriot *(Ignace, Ignacio, Ignate, Ignazio, Inigo)*

Igor (SCANDINAVIAN) 'The hero'

Ikar (RUSSIAN) 'Ancient legendary hero'

Ike *see* Isaac

Ilia (RUSSIAN) Equivalent
of Elias

Illan (BASQUE) Equivalent
of Julian

Illaris (GREEK) 'Happy one'

Illtyd (WELSH) 'Ruler of
a district'

Imala (NATIVE AMERICAN) 'The
one who imposes discipline'

Immanuel *see* Emmanuel

Imo (GREEK) 'Beloved one'

Imran (ARABIC) 'Host'
(SANSKRIT) 'strong'

Indra (HINDI) 'Raindrop',
'god-like'

Ingeborg (SCANDINAVIAN)
'Protection'

Ingemar (NORSE) 'Famous son'
(Ingmar)

Inger (NORSE) 'A son's army'
(Ingar, Ingvar)

Inglebert (TEUTONIC) 'Brilliant
angel' *(Engelbert, Englebert)*

Ingram (TEUTONIC) 'The raven',
'the raven's son' *(Ingraham)*

Inir (WELSH) 'Honour'

Inness (CELTIC) 'From the island
in the river' *(Iniss, Innes,
Innis)*

Ionwyn (WELSH) 'Fair-skinned
ruler'

Iorweth (WELSH) 'Lord Worth'

Iorwyn (WELSH) 'Fair lord'

Iqbal (SANSKRIT) 'Prosperity'

Ira (HEBREW) 'The watcher',
(ARABIC) 'the stallion'

Iram (ARABIC) 'Mountain peak',
'crown of the head'

Irfon (WELSH) 'Annointed one'

Irving (ANGLO-SAXON) 'Friend of
the sea' (CELTIC) 'white river'
*(Ervin, Erwin, Irvin, Irvine,
Irwin)*

Isa (GREEK) 'Equal'

Isaac (HEBREW) 'The laughing
one' *(Ike, Ikey, Ikie, Isaak,
Izaak)*

Isaam (ARABIC) 'Noble'

Isaiah (HEBREW) 'God is my helper'

Isas (JAPANESE) 'Worthy of praise'

Isham (ANGLO-SAXON) 'From the estate of the iron man'

Ishi (HEBREW) 'Husband'

Ishmael (HEBREW) 'The wanderer'

Isidore (GREEK) 'The gift of Isis' (*Isador, Isidor, Issy, Iz, Izzie, Izzy*)

Iskander (ETHIOPIAN) Equivalent of **Alexander**

Isman (HEBREW) 'Faithful husband'

Isoep *see* **Joseph**

Israel (HEBREW) 'The Lord's soldier'. The warrior of God (*Issie, Izzie*)

Istvan (HUNGARIAN) Equivalent of **Stephen**

Ithel (WELSH) 'Generous ruler'

Ithnan (HEBREW) 'Strong seafarer'

Ivan *see* **John**

Ivander (HEBREW) 'Divine'

Ivar (NORSE) 'Battle archer'. The warrior with the long bow (*Iven, Iver, Ives, Ivo, Ivon, Ivor*)

Ives (ANGLO-SAXON) 'Son of the archer' (*Yves*) *see also* **Ivar**

Ivor *see* **Ivar**

Ixara (SANSKRIT) 'Master', 'prince'

Izaak *see* **Isaac**

Izod (CELTIC) 'Fair-haired one'

J

Jabez (HEBREW) 'Cause of sorrow'

Jabin (HEBREW) 'Born of god'

Jacinto (SPANISH) 'Purple flower'

Jack see **John**

Jackson (OLD ENGLISH) 'Son of Jack'

Jacob (HEBREW) 'The supplanter' *(Cobb, Diego, Giacomo, Hamish, Jacobus, Jacques, Jake, James, Jamie, Jas, Jem, Jemmie, Jemmy, Jim, Jimmie, Jimmy, Jock, Jocko, Koby)*

Jacques see **Jacob**

Jadda (HEBREW) 'Wise man'

Jael (HEBREW) 'To ascend'

Jagger (OLD ENGLISH) 'A carter'

Jaime see **James**

Jairus (HEBREW) 'Enlightened by God' *(Jair)*

Jake see **Jacob**

Jakeh (HEBREW) 'Pious one'

Jalaad (ARABIC) 'Glory'

Jalal (SANSKRIT) 'Glory'

Jaleel (ARABIC) 'Majestic'

Jamaal see **Gamal** and **Jamal**

Jamal (ARABIC) 'Beauty' *(Jamaal)*

James (HEBREW) 'The supplanter'. Derivative of Jacob *(Hamish, Jaime, Jamie, Jim, Jock, Seamus, Seumas, Shamus)*

Jamie *see* **Benjamin, Jacob** or **James**

Jamil (ARABIC) 'Handsome'

Jan *see* **John**

Janitra (SANSKRIT) 'Of noble origin'

Janos *see* **John**

Janus (LATIN) 'One who opens doors'

Japhet (HEBREW) 'Youthful, beautiful'

Jareb (HEBREW) 'He will contend' *(Jarib)*

Jared (HEBREW) 'The descendant' *(Jarid, Jarrad, Jarrod)*

Jarek (SLAVIC) 'January' *(Janiuszck, Januarius, Januisz)*

Jarlath (LATIN) 'Man of control' *(Jarlen)*

Jarman (TEUTONIC) 'The German' *(Jerman, Jermyn)*

Jaron (HEBREW) 'Sing out', 'cry out'

Jaroslav (SLAVIC) 'Praise of spring'

Jarratt (TEUTONIC) 'Strong spear'

Jarvis *see* **Gervase**

Jashan (SANSKRIT) 'Celebration'

Jason (GREEK) 'The healer' *(Jasun)*

Jasper *see* **Gaspar**

Javas (SANSKRIT) 'Swift'

Javier *see* **Xavier**

Jawahar (SANSKRIT) 'Jewel'

Jay (ANGLO-SAXON) 'Jay or crow'. Diminutive for any name beginning with J

Jean *see* **John**

Jedediah (HEBREW) 'Beloved by the Lord' *(Jed, Jeddy, Jedidiah)*

Jefferson (ANGLO-SAXON) 'Jeffrey's son'

Jeffrey *see* **Geoffrey**

Jehiel (HEBREW) 'May God live'

Jehoshaphat (HEBREW) 'The Lord judges'

Jem *see* **Jacob**

Jerald *see* **Gerald**

Jeremy (HEBREW) 'Exalted by the Lord' *(Jeramey, Jere, Jeremiah, Jeremias, Jerry)*

Jermyn *see* **Jarman**

Jerome (LATIN) 'Sacred, holy'. A man of God *(Gerome, Jerry)*

Jerry *see* **Gerald, Jeremy** or **Jerome**

Jervis *see* **Gervase**

Jesse (HEBREW) 'God's gift' *(Jess)*

Jesus (HEBREW) 'God will help'

Jethro (HEBREW) 'Excellent', 'without equal'

Jim *see* **Jacob** or **James**

Jivin (SANSKRIT) 'Life-giving'

Joab (HEBREW) 'Praise the lord' *(Jacob)*

Joachim (HEBREW) 'Judgement of the Lord' *(Akim, Joaquin)*

Joan (HEBREW) 'Praise the lord'

Job (HEBREW) 'The persecuted'

Jock *see* **Jacob** or **John**

Jodel (LATIN) 'Sportive'

Joe *see* **Joel** or **Joseph**

Joel (HEBREW) 'The Lord is God' *(Joe, Joey)*

John (HEBREW) 'God's gracious gift' *(Eoin, Evan, Geno, Gian, Gianni, Giovanni, Hans, Iaian, Iain, Ian, Ieuan, Ivan, Jack, Jackie, Jan, Janos, Jean, Jevon, Jock, Johan, Johann, Johnnie, Johnny, Jon, Juan, Seain, Sean, Seann, Shane, Shawn, Sian, Siân, Zane)*

Jolyon *see* **Julius**

Jon *see* **John** or **Jonathan**

Jonah (HEBREW) 'Peace'

Jonas (HEBREW) 'Dove'. A man of tranquillity

Jonathan (HEBREW) 'Gift of the Lord' *(Jon, Jonathon)*

Jordan (HEBREW) 'The descending river' *(Jordon, Jourdain)*

Jorens (NORSE) 'Laurel'

Jorgen *see* **George**

Jorin (SPANISH FROM HEBREW) 'Child of freedom' *see also* **George**

Joris *see* **George**

Joseph (HEBREW) 'He shall add' *(Guiseppe, Isoep, Jodi, Jodu, Joe, Joey, Jose, Josiah, Jozef, Seosaidh)*

Josh *see* **Joshua**

Joshua (HEBREW) 'God's salvation' *(Josh)*

Josiah *see* **Joseph**

Jotham (HEBREW) 'God is perfect'

Jozef *see* **Joseph**

Juan *see* **John**

Juaud (ARABIC) 'Generous'

Judd (HEBREW) 'Praised, extolled' *(Judah, Jude)*

Jude *see* **Judd**

Julian *see* **Julius**

Julius (LATIN) 'Youthful shaveling' *(Joliet, Jolyon, Jule, Jules, Julian, Julie)*

Junayd (ARABIC) 'Warrior'

Junius (LATIN) 'Born in June'

Jurgen *see* **George**

Jurisa (SCANDINAVIAN) 'Storm'

Justin (LATIN) 'The just one'. One of upright principles and morals *(Iestin, Just, Justinian, Justino, Justus)*

Justis (FRENCH) 'Justice'. Upholder of moral laws

BOYS

Kabir (SANSKRIT)
Name of a saint

Kadmiel (HEBREW) 'God is the ancient one'

Kadrri (ARABIC) 'My destiny'

Kaleva (SCANDINAVIAN) 'Hero'

Kalil (ARABIC) 'Good friend' *(Kahaleel)*

Kalo (GREEK) 'Royal, noble' *(Kalon)*

Kalon *see* **Kalo**

Kamal (ARABIC) 'Perfect'

Kamper (TEUTONIC) 'Fighter'

Kamran (SANSKRIT) 'Successful'

Kane (CELTIC) 'Little, war-like one', 'radiant brightness' *(Kayne)*

Kaniel (ARABIC) 'Spear'

Kano (JAPANESE) 'God of waters'

Kareem (ARABIC) 'Noble' *(Karim)*

Karl *see* **Charles**

Karr *see* **Carr**

Karsten (SLAVONIC) 'Christian'

Kasimir *see* **Casimir**

Kaspar *see* **Gaspar**

Kavan *see* **Cavan**

Kay (CELTIC) 'Rejoiced in'. Also diminutive for any name beginning with K

Kayne *see* **Kane**

Kazimir *see* **Casimir**

Kean (IRISH) 'Fast'

Keane (ANGLO-SAXON) 'Bold and handsome'. A sharp-witted man *(Kearney)*

Kedar (ARABIC) 'Powerful'

Keefe (CELTIC) 'Handsome, noble and admirable'

Keegan (CELTIC) 'Little fiery one'

Keelan (CELTIC) 'Little slender one'

Keeley (CELTIC) 'Little handsome one'

Keenan (CELTIC) 'Little ancient one' *(Keen, Kienan)*

Keir (TEUTONIC) 'Ever king'

Keira (SCANDINAVIAN) 'Regal'

Keiran *see* **Ciaran**

Keith (CELTIC) 'A place', 'from the forest'

Kelby (OLD GERMAN) 'From the farm by the spring' *(Keelby, Kelbee)*

Kell (NORSE) 'From the well'

Keller (GAELIC) 'Little companion'

Kelly (GAELIC) 'The warrior' *(Kellen, Kelley)*

Kelsey (NORSE/TEUTONIC) 'One who lives on the island'

Kelton (CELTIC) 'Celtic town'

Kelvin (GAELIC) 'From the narrow stream' *(Kelvan, Kelven, Kelwin)*

Kemp (ANGLO-SAXON) 'The warrior champion'

Ken *see* **Kendall, Kenn** or **Kenneth**

Kenaz (HEBREW) 'The hunter'

Kendall (CELTIC) 'Chief of the valley' *(Ken, Kendal, Kendell)*

Kendrick (ANGLO-SAXON/GAELIC) 'Royal ruler, son of Henry'

Kenelm (ANGLO-SAXON) 'Brave helmet'. A courageous protector

Kenley (ANGLO-SAXON) 'Owner of a royal meadow'

Kenn (CELTIC) 'Clear as bright water' *(Ken, Kennan, Kenon)*

Kennard (ANGLO-SAXON) 'Bold and vigorous'

Kennedy (GAELIC) 'The helmeted chief'

Kenneth (CELTIC) 'The handsome', 'royal oath' *(Ken, Keneth, Kennet, Kennith, Kenny, Kent)*

Kenrick (ANGLO-SAXON) 'Bold ruler'

Kensell (TEUTONIC) 'Royal and brave'

Kent (CELTIC) 'Bright and white' *see also* **Kenneth**

Kenton (ANGLO-SAXON) 'From the royal estate'

Kenward (ANGLO-SAXON) 'Bold guardian'

Kenway (ANGLO-SAXON) 'Bold or royal warrior'

Kenyon (CELTIC) 'White haired'

Kermit (CELTIC) 'A free man' *(Dermot, Derry, Kerry)*

Kern (GAELIC) 'Little dark one'

Kerry (GAELIC) 'Son of the dark one' *see also* **Kermit** or **Kieran**

Kerwin (GAELIC) 'Small black-haired one' *(Kirwin)*

Kester (ANGLO-SAXON/LATIN) 'From the army camp' *see also* **Christopher**

Keung (CHINESE) 'Universe'

Kevin (GAELIC) 'Gentle, kind and lovable' *(Kev, Kevan, Keven, Kevon)*

Key (GAELIC) 'Son of the fiery one'

Khalid (ARABIC) 'Immortal'

Khalil (ARABIC) 'Friend'

Khalipha (ARABIC) 'Successor'

Khayam (ARABIC) 'Tent-maker'

Kieran (GAELIC) 'Small and dark skinned' *(Kerrin, Kerry, Kiernan, Kieron)*

Kilby (TEUTONIC) 'Farm by the spring'

Kilian (CELTIC) 'Innocent'

Killian (GAELIC) 'Little war-like one' *(Killie)*

Kimball (CELTIC) 'Royally brave', 'warrior chief' *(Kembell, Kemble, Kim, Kimbell, Kimble)*

Kincaid (CELTIC) 'Battle chief'

King (ANGLO-SAXON) 'The sovereign'. The ruler of his people

Kingdom (OLD ENGLISH) 'King's hill'

Kingsley (ANGLO-SAXON) 'From the king's meadow' *(Kinsley)*

Kingston (ANGLO-SAXON) 'From the king's farm'

Kingswell (ANGLO-SAXON) 'From the king's well'

Kinnard (GAELIC) 'From the high mountain' *(Kinnaird)*

Kinnell (GAELIC) 'One who lives on the top of the cliff'

Kinsey (ANGLO-SAXON) 'Royal victor'

Kipp (ANGLO-SAXON) 'One who lives on the pointed hill' *(Kippar, Kippie)*

Kirby (TEUTONIC) 'From the church village' *(Kerby, Kerr)*

Kirin (LATIN) 'Spearman'

Kirk (NORSE) 'One who lives at the church'

Kirkley (ANGLO-SAXON) 'From the church meadow'

Kirkwood (ANGLO-SAXON) 'From the church wood'

Kit *see* **Christian** or **Christopher**

Kitron (HEBREW) 'Crown'

Klaus *see* **Nicholas**

Knight (ANGLO-SAXON) 'Mounted soldier'

Knox (ANGLO-SAXON) 'From the hills'

Knute *see* **Canute**

Koby *see* **Jacob**

Kong (CHINESE) 'Glorious', 'sky'

Konrad *see* **Conrad**

Konstantine *see* **Constantine**

Kosey (AFRICAN) 'Son' *(Kosse)*

Kris *see* **Christopher**

Krishna (HINDI) 'Delightful' *(Krisha)*

Kriss *see* **Christopher**

Kristian *see* **Christian**

Kurt *see* **Conrad** or **Curtis**

Kwasi (AFRICAN) 'Born on Sunday'

Kyle (GAELIC) 'From the strait' *(Kiel)*

Kyne (ANGLO-SAXON) 'Royal one'

BOYS

Laban (HEBREW) 'White'

Labid (ARABIC) 'Intelligent'

Lach (CELTIC) 'One who lives by the water' *(Lache)*

Lachlan (CELTIC) 'War-like'

Lacy (LATIN) 'From the Roman manor house'

Ladd (ANGLO-SAXON) 'Attendant, page' *(Laddie)*

Ladislas (SLAVIC) 'A glory of power'

Laibrook (ANGLO-SAXON) 'Path by the brook'

Laidley (ANGLO-SAXON) 'From the water meadow'

Laird (CELTIC) 'The land owner'. The lord of the manor

Lakshman (HINDI) 'Younger brother of Ram'

Lamar (TEUTONIC) 'Famous throughout the land'

Lambert (TEUTONIC) 'Rich in land'. An owner of vast estates

Lamech (HEBREW) 'Strong young man'

Lamont (NORSE) 'A lawyer' *(Lamond, Lammond, Lammont)*

Lancelot (FRENCH) 'Spear attendant' *(Lance, Lancey, Launce, Launcelot)*

Lander (ANGLO-SAXON) 'Owner of a grassy plain' *(Landers, Landor, Launder)*

Landon (ANGLO-SAXON) 'One who lives on the long hill' *(Langdon, Langston)*

Landric (OLD GERMAN) 'Land ruler'

Lane (ANGLO-SAXON) 'From the narrow road' *(Laina, Layne)*

Lanfrance (ITALIAN FROM TEUTONIC) 'Free country'

Lang (TEUTONIC) 'Tall or long-limbed man'

Langford (ANGLO-SAXON) 'One who lives by the long ford'

Langley (ANGLO-SAXON) 'One who lives by the long meadow'

Langston (ANGLO-SAXON) 'The farm belonging to the tall man' *(Langsdon) see also* **Landon**

Langworth (ANGLO-SAXON) 'From the long enclosure'

Lann (CELTIC) 'Sword'

Lanny *see* **Roland**

Laris (LATIN) 'Cheerful'

Larkin (LATIN) 'Laurel bush'

Larry *see* **Lawrence**

Larson (NORSE) 'Son of Lars'

Latham (NORSE) 'From the barns'

Lathrop (ANGLO-SAXON) 'From the barn farmstead'

Latimer (ANGLO-SAXON) 'The interpreter', 'the language teacher'

Laughton *see* **Lawton**

Laurence *see* **Lawrence**

Laurent *see* **Lawrence**

Lawford (ANGLO-SAXON) 'One who lives at the ford by the hill'

Lawler (GAELIC) 'The mumbler'

Lawley (ANGLO-SAXON) 'From the meadow on the hill'

Lawrence (LATIN) 'Crowned with laurels'. The victor's crown of bay leaves *(Labhras, Labhruinn, Larrance, Larry, Lars, Lauren, Laurence, Laurent, Lauric, Lauritz, Lawrance, Lawry, Lon, Lonnie, Loren, Lorenz, Lorenze, Lorenzo, Lori, Lorin, Lorne, Lorrie, Lorry)*

Lawson (ANGLO-SAXON) 'Son of Lawrence'

Lawton (ANGLO-SAXON) 'From the town on the hill' *(Laughton)*

Layton *see* **Leighton**

Lazar *see* **Eleazar**

Lazhar (ARABIC) 'Best appearance'

Leal (ANGLO-SAXON) 'Loyal, true and faithful' *(Loyal)*

Leander (GREEK) 'Like a lion' *(Leandro)*

Lear (CELTIC) 'One who keeps cattle'

Lech (POLISH) 'Woodland spirit'

Ledyard (TEUTONIC) 'Nation's guardian'

Lee (ANGLO-SAXON) 'From the meadow' (GAELIC) 'poetic' *(Leigh) see also* **Ashley**, **Bradley**, **Finlay** or **Leroy**

Leger (TEUTONIC) 'People's spear'

Leggett (FRENCH) 'Envoy or ambassador' *(Leggitt, Liggett)*

Leif (NORSE) 'The beloved one'

Leigh *see* **Lee** or **Bradley**

Leighton (ANGLO-SAXON) 'One who lives at the farm by the meadow' *(Layton)*

Leith (CELTIC) 'Broad, wide river'

Leland (ANGLO-SAXON) 'One who lives by the meadow land' *(Lealand, Leyland)*

Lemuel (HEBREW) 'Consecrated to God' *(Lem, Lemmie)*

Len *see* **Leonard**

Lenno (NATIVE AMERICAN) 'Man'

Lennon (GAELIC) 'Little cloak'

Lennox (CELTIC) 'Grove of elm trees'

Leo (LATIN) 'Lion' *(Lev) see also* **Leopold**

Leon (FRENCH) 'Lion-like'

Leonard (LATIN) 'Lion brave'. One with all the courage and tenacity of the king of beasts *(Len, Lenard, Lennard, Lennie, Lenny, Leoner, Leonardo, Leonhard, Leonid, Leonidas, Lonnard)*

Leonardo *see* **Leonard**

Leonidas (GREEK) 'Son of the lion' *see also* **Leonard**

Leopold (TEUTONIC) 'Brave for the people'. One who fights for his countryman *(Leo, Lepp)*

Leroy (FRENCH) 'The king' *(Lee, Leroi, Roy Les see Leslie)*

Leslie (CELTIC) 'From the grey fort' *(Les, Lesley)*

Lester (ANGLO-SAXON) 'From the army camp' *(Leicester)*

Leverett (FRENCH) 'The young hare'

Leverton (ANGLO-SAXON) 'From the rush farm'

Levi (HEBREW) 'United' *(Levin)*

Lewis (TEUTONIC) 'Famous battle warrior' *(Lew, Lewes, Lou, Louis, Ludo, Ludovic, Ludovick, Ludwig, Lugaidh, Luigi, Luis, Luthais) see also* **Aloysius** or **Clovis**

Liall *see* **Lyle**

Liam (CELTIC) 'Determined protector' *see also* **William**

Lin *see* **Lynn**

Lincoln (CELTIC) 'From the place by the pool'

Lind (ANGLO-SAXON) 'From the lime tree' *(Linden, Lindon, Lyndon) see also* **Lindsey**

Lindberg (TEUTONIC) 'Lime tree hill'

Lindell (ANGLO-SAXON) 'One who lives by the lime tree in the valley'

Lindley (ANGLO-SAXON) 'By the lime tree in the meadow'

Lindo (LATIN) 'Handsome man'

Lindsey (ANGLO-SAXON) 'Pool island' *(Lind, Lindsay, Linsay, Linsey)*

Linford (ANGLO-SAXON) 'From the lime tree ford'

Linfred (TEUTONIC) 'Gentle and gracious'

Lingard (CELTIC) 'The sea guard'

Link (ANGLO-SAXON) 'From the bank or edge'

Linley (ANGLO-SAXON) 'From the flax field'

Linton (ANGLO-SAXON) 'From the flax farm'

Linus (GREEK) 'Flax-coloured hair'

Lionel (FRENCH) 'The young lion' *(Lion, Lionello)*

Lisle *see* **Lyle**

Litton (ANGLO-SAXON) 'Farm on the hillside'

Livingston (OLD ENGLISH) 'From Leif's town'

Lleufer (WELSH) 'Splendid'

Llewellyn (WELSH) 'Lion-like', 'like a ruler'

Lloyd (WELSH) 'Grey haired' *(Floyd)*

Locke (ANGLO-SAXON) 'One who lives in the stronghold' *(Lockwood)*

Logan (CELTIC) 'Little hollow'

Lok (CHINESE) 'Happiness'

Loman (CELTIC) 'Enlightened'

Lombard (LATIN) 'Long-bearded'

Lon (GAELIC) 'Strong, fierce' *see also* **Lawrence**

London (MIDDLE ENGLISH) 'Fortress of the moon'

Lonny *see* **Zebulon**

Lorenz *see* **Lawrence**

Lorimer (LATIN) 'Harness-maker'

Loring (TEUTONIC) 'Man from Lorraine'

Lorne *see* **Lawrence**

Lorus (LATIN) 'Laurel bush'

Lothar *see* **Luther**

Lou *see* **Lewis**

Louis *see* **Lewis** or **Aloysius**

Lovell *see* **Lowell**

Lowell (ANGLO-SAXON) 'The beloved one' *(Lovel, Lovell, Lowe)*

Loyal *see* **Leal**

Lubin (OLD ENGLISH) 'Dear friend'

Lucian *see* **Lucius**

Lucius (LATIN) 'Light' *(Luc, Lucais, Lucas, Luce, Lucian, Lucio, Luck, Lukas, Luke, Lukey)*

Ludlow (ANGLO-SAXON) 'From the hill of the prince'

Ludo *see* **Lewis**

Ludolf (OLD GERMAN) 'Famous wolf'

Ludwig *see* **Aloysius** or **Lewis**

Ludovic *see* **Lewis**

Ludwig *see* **Lewis**

Lugaidh *see* **Lewis**

Luigi *see* **Lewis**

Luke (LATIN) 'Light' *see also* **Lucius**

Luman (LATIN) 'Radiant'

Lundy (FRENCH) 'Born on Monday'

Lunn (GAELIC) 'From the grove'

Lunt (NORSE) 'Strong and fierce'

Luther (TEUTONIC) 'Famous warrior' *(Lothaire, Lothar, Lothario, Lute)*

Lycidas (GREEK) 'Wolf son'

Lydell (GREEK) 'Man from Lydia'

Lyle (FRENCH) 'From the island' *(Liall, Lisle, Lyall, Lyell)*

Lyman (ANGLO-SAXON) 'Man from the meadow' *(Leyman)*

Lynfa (WELSH) 'From the lake'

Lynn (WELSH) 'From the pool or waterfall' *(Lin, Linn, Lyn)*

Lysander (GREEK) 'The liberator' *(Sandy)*

M

BOYS

Mabon (WELSH) 'Youth'

Mac (CELTIC) Used in many Scots and Irish names and meaning 'son of'. Also used in the form 'Mc'. For instance Macadam (son of Adam), McDonald (son of Donald) and so on

Macaire (GREEK) 'Happy one'

Macarius (LATIN) 'Blessed'

Mackenzie (IRISH GAELIC) 'Son of the wise leader' *(Mack)*

Macnair (CELTIC) 'Son of the heir'

Macy (FRENCH) 'From Matthew's estate'

Madaan (ARABIC) 'Striving'

Maddison *see* **Madison**

Maddock (WELSH) 'Beneficent' *(Maddox, Madoc, Madock, Madog)*

Maddox *see* **Maddock**

Madhur (SANSKRIT) 'Sweet'

Madison (ANGLO-SAXON) 'Mighty in battle' *(Maddison)*

Madjid (ARABIC) 'Glorious'

Maelgwyn (WELSH) 'Metal chief'

Magee (GAELIC) 'Son of the fiery one'

Magloire (FRENCH) 'My glory'

Magna (NATIVE AMERICAN) 'The coming moon'

Magnus (LATIN) 'The great one'. One who excels all others

Maher (HEBREW/ARABIC) 'Clever, industrious and skilful'

Mahfuz (ARABIC) 'Guardian'

Mahin (SANSKRIT) 'Royal' *(Mahish)*

Mahon (CELTIC) 'Chief'

Maitland (ANGLO-SAXON) 'One who lives in the meadow land'

Majnoon (PERSIAN) Legendary hero like Romeo (from the story of Majnoon and Leila)

Major (LATIN) 'Greater'. Anything you can do, he can do better!

Malachi (HEBREW) 'Angel'

Malchus (HEBREW) 'King'

Malcolm (CELTIC) 'The dove', 'follower of St Columba'

Malik (MUSLIM) 'Master'

Malin (ANGLO-SAXON) 'Little warrior'

Malise (GAELIC) 'Servant of Jesus'

Malkawn (HEBREW) 'Their king'

Mallard (TEUTONIC) 'Strong advisor'

Mallory (ANGLO-SAXON) 'Army counsellor' (LATIN) 'unlucky' *see also* **Malory**

Maloney (GAELIC) 'Believer in the Sabbath'

Malory (OLD FRENCH) 'Unfortunate' *(Mallory)*

Malvin (CELTIC) 'Polished chief' *(Mal, Mel, Melva, Melvin)*

Mamoun (ARABIC) 'Trustworthy'

Manassa (ARABIC) 'Causes to forget'

Manasseh (HEBREW) 'Making one forget'

Manchu (CHINESE) 'Pure one'

Mandel (TEUTONIC) 'Almond'

Mander (OLD FRENCH) 'Stable lad'

Manfred (ANGLO-SAXON) 'Peaceful hero' *(Manfried)*

Manik (SANSKRIT)
'Precious ruby'

Manish (SANSKRIT) 'Intelligent'

Manleich *see* **Manley**

Manley (ANGLO-SAXON) 'The hero's meadow' *(Manleich)*

Mannie *see* **Chaim, Chapman** or **Emmanuel**

Manning (ANGLO-SAXON) 'Hero's son'

Manny *see* **Chaim, Chapman** or **Emmanuel**

Manolo *see* **Emmanuel**

Mansfield (ANGLO-SAXON) 'Hero's field'

Mansoor (ARABIC) 'Victorious'

Manton (ANGLO-SAXON) 'Hero's farm'

Manuel *see* **Emmanuel**

Manville (FRENCH) 'From the great estate' *(Manvil)*

Marc *see* **Mark**

Marcel (LATIN) 'Little follower of Mars'. A war-like person

Marcellus *see* **Marcel**

Marcius (LATIN) 'Martial'

Marcus *see* **Mark**

Marden (ANGLO-SAXON) 'From the pool in the valley'

Mardon (TEUTONIC) 'Famous leader'

Marino (ITALIAN FROM LATIN) 'Sea'

Mario *see* **Marius**

Marion (FRENCH) 'Bitter'. A French form of Mary, often given as a boy's name in compliment to the Virgin

Marius (LATIN) 'The martial one' *(Mario)*

Marjan (ARABIC) 'Small pearls'

Mark (LATIN) 'Follower of Mars, the warrior' *(Marc, Marco, Marcus)*

Marland (ANGLO-SAXON) 'One who lives in the lake land'

Marlen *see* **Merlin**

Marley (ANGLO-SAXON) 'From the lake in the meadow' *(Marly)*

Marlon *see* **Merlin**

Marlow (ANGLO-SAXON) 'From the lake on the hill' *(Marlowe)*

Marmaduke (CELTIC) 'Sea leader' *(Duke)*

Marmion (FRENCH) 'Very small one'

Marques (PORTUGUESE) 'Nobleman'

Marsden (ANGLO-SAXON) 'From the marshy valley' *(Marsdon)*

Marsh (ANGLO-SAXON) 'From the marsh'

Marshall (ANGLO-SAXON) 'The steward'. The man who looked after the estate of a nobleman

Marston (ANGLO-SAXON) 'From the farm by the lake'

Martainn *see* **Martin**

Martel (OLD FRENCH) 'Hammer of war'

Martial (LATIN) 'War-like'

Martin (LATIN) 'War-like person'. A follower of Mars *(Mart, Martainn, Marten, Martie, Martino, Marton, Marty)*

Marvin (ANGLO-SAXON) 'Famous friend' *(Marwin, Mervin, Merwin, Merwyn)*

Marwood (ANGLO-SAXON) 'From the lake in the forest'

Maska (NATIVE AMERICAN) 'Powerful one'

Maskil (HEBREW) 'Enlightened, educated'

Maslin (FRENCH) 'Small Thomas' *(Maslen, Maslon)*

Mason (LATIN) 'Worker in stone' *(Massey)*

Massey *see* **Mason** or **Thomas**

Math (WELSH) 'Treasure'

Mather (ANGLO-SAXON) 'Powerful army'

Mathias *see* **Matthew**

Matmon (HEBREW) 'Treasure'

Matthew (HEBREW) 'Gift of God'. One of the 12 apostles *(Mat, Mata, Mathew, Mathias, Matt, Mattie, Matty, Matthias, Mattias)*

Maurice (LATIN) 'Moorish-looking, dark-complexioned' *(Maury, Maurey, Mauricio, Maurizio, Mo, Morel, Morey, Morice, Moritz, Morrell, Morrie, Morris, Morry, Morys)*

Maximilian (LATIN) 'The greatest, the most excellent'. One without equal *(Max, Maxey, Maxie, Maxim, Maximilien, Maxy)*

Maxwell (ANGLO-SAXON) 'Large spring of fresh water' *(Max, Maxi, Maxie)*

Mayer (LATIN) 'Greater' *(Myer)*

Mayfield (ANGLO-SAXON) 'From the field of the warrior'

Mayhew (FRENCH) 'Gift of God'. Another form of **Matthew**

Maynard (TEUTONIC) 'Powerfully strong and brave' *(Menard)*

Mayne *(Teutonic)* 'Mighty one'

Mayo *(Gaelic)* 'From the plain of the yew trees'

Mead *(Anglo-Saxon)* 'From the meadow'

Medwin *(Teutonic)* 'Strong and powerful friend'

Megha *(Sanskrit)* 'Star'

Mehrdad *(Persian)* 'Gift of the sun'

Meilyr *(Welsh)* 'Man of iron'

Mekuria *(Ethiopian)* 'Pride'

Melbourne (ANGLO-SAXON) 'From the mill stream' *(Melburn, Melburne, Milbourn, Milbourne, Milburn, Milburne, Pierrot)*

Melchior (PERSIAN) 'King of light'

Meldon (ANGLO-SAXON) 'From the mill on the hill'

Melmoth (CELTIC) 'Servant of Math'

Melvern (NATIVE AMERICAN) 'Great leader'

Melville (FRENCH) 'From the estate of the industrious' *(Mel, Melvil)*

Menachin (HEBREW) 'Comforter' *(Menahem)*

Mendel (SEMITIC) 'Wisdom'

Mercer (ANGLO-SAXON) 'Merchant'

Meredith (WELSH) 'Guardian from the sea' *(Meredydd, Meredyth, Merideth, Meridith, Meridyth, Merry)*

Merle (LATIN) 'The blackbird', 'the black-haired one'

Merlin (ANGLO-SAXON) 'The falcon'. The legendary wizard of King Arthur's court *(Marl, Marlin, Marlen, Marlon, Merl)*

Meron (HEBREW) 'Army'

Merrill (FRENCH) 'Little famous one' *(Merritt) see also* **Myron**

Merry *see* **Meredith**

Merton (ANGLO-SAXON) 'From the farm by the sea'

Meryll (FRENCH FROM OLD GERMAN) 'King'

Methuselah (HEBREW) 'Man of the javelin'

Metis (GREEK) 'Counsellor', 'adviser'

Meven (CELTIC/FRENCH) 'Agile'

Meyer (TEUTONIC) 'Steward'

Michael (HEBREW) 'Like the Lord' *(Micah, Mich, Michel, Mickie, Micky, Mike, Mischa, Mitch, Mitchell, Mithell)*

Milan (SLAVIC) 'Beloved'

Milburn (OLD ENGLISH) 'Mill stream' *see also* **Melbourne**

Miles (GREEK/LATIN) 'The soldier' *(Myles)*

Milford (ANGLO-SAXON) 'From the mill ford' *(Millford)*

Millard (FRENCH) 'Strong and victorious'

Miller (ANGLO-SAXON) 'Grain grinder'

Milo (LATIN) 'The miller' *(Mylo)*

Milton (ANGLO-SAXON) 'From the mill town' *(Milt)*

Milward (ANGLO-SAXON) 'The mill-keeper'

Miner (LATIN/FRENCH) 'Young person' *(Minor)*

Miroslav (SLAVONIC) 'Peace', 'glory'

Mischa *see* **Michael**

Mitch *see* **Michael**

Mitchell *see* **Michael**

Mo *see* **Maurice**

Modred (ANGLO-SAXON) 'Brave counsellor'. One who advised honestly without fear of reprisal

Moelwyn (WELSH) 'Fair haired'

Mohammed (ARABIC/ SANSKRIT) 'Praised', 'Prophet of Islam' *(Mohammed, Muhammad)*

Mokbil (ARABIC) 'The approaching one'

Mokhtar (ARABIC) 'Chosen'

Monroe (CELTIC) 'From the red swamp' *(Monro, Munro, Munroe)*

Montague (FRENCH) 'From the jagged mountain' *(Montagu, Monte, Monty)*

Montega (NATIVE AMERICAN) 'New arrows'

Montgomery (FRENCH) 'The mountain hunter' *(Monte, Monty)*

Moore (FRENCH) 'Dark complexioned, a Moor' *(More)*

Mordecai (HEBREW) 'Belonging to Marduk' *(Mort)*

Moreland (ANGLO-SAXON) 'From the moors'

Morfin *see* **Morven**

Morey *see* **Maurice**

Morgan (WELSH) 'White sea'. The foam-flecked waves *(Morganica, Morganne, Morgen)*

Moriah (HEBREW) 'Man chosen by Jehovah'

Moritz *see* **Maurice**

Morley (ANGLO-SAXON) 'From the moor meadow'

Morrell (LATIN) 'Dark'

Morris *see* **Maurice**

Morrison (ANGLO-SAXON) 'Maurice's son' *(Morison)*

Morse (ANGLO-SAXON) 'Maurice's son'

Mort *see* **Mordecai**

Mortimer (FRENCH) 'From the quiet water' *(Mortemer, Mortermer, Morthermer)*

Morton (ANGLO-SAXON) 'From the farm on the moor' *(Morten)*

Morven (GAELIC) 'Blond giant' *(Morfin)*

Morys (WELSH) Form of **Maurice**

Moses (HEBREW) 'Saved from the water'. The great prophet of Israel *(Moe, Moise, Mose, Mosie, Moss)*

Moss *see* **Moses**

Mostyn (WELSH) 'Fortress'

Moustapha (ARABIC) 'Chosen' *(Mustapha)*

Mubarak (ARABIC) 'Blessed'

Muhammad *see* **Mohammed**

Muir (CELTIC) 'From the moor'

Mungo (GAELIC) 'Lovable'

Munir (ARABIC) 'Illuminating, light'

Murad (ARABIC) 'Desired', 'wanted'

Murdoch (CELTIC) 'Prosperous from the sea' *(Murdock, Murtagh)*

Murphy (GAELIC) 'Sea warrior'

Murray (CELTIC) 'The mariner, a sea fighter'

Murtagh *see* **Murdoch**

Myles *see* **Miles**

Mylor (CELTIC) 'Ruler, prince'

Myron (GREEK) 'Sweet-smelling' 'the fragrant oil' *(Merrill)*

N

BOYS

Naaman (HEBREW) 'Pleasant one'

Nabil (ARABIC) 'Noble'

Nadabb (HEBREW) 'One with wide-ranging ideas'

Nadim (ARABIC) 'Repentant'

Nadir (ARABIC/SANSKRIT) 'Rare', 'precious', 'the pinnacle'

Nadiv (HEBREW) 'Noble'

Nahum (HEBREW) 'Comfort'

Naim (ARABIC) 'Contented'

Nairn (CELTIC) 'One who lives by the alder tree'

Najibullah (ARABIC) 'God-given intelligence'

Naldo see **Reginald**

Namir (HEBREW) 'Leopard'

Napoleon (GREEK) 'Lion of the woodland dell'

Narcissus (GREEK) 'Daffodil'. A Greek youth who fell in love with his own image

Nash (OLD FRENCH) 'Cliff'

Nashif (ARABIC) 'Hard'

Nasim (PERSIAN) 'Breeze'

Nathan (HEBREW) 'Gift of God' *(Nat, Nataniel, Nate, Nathaniel, Nattie)*

Nayan (SANSKRIT) 'Lovely eyes'

Neacail see **Nicholas**

Neal (Gaelic) 'The champion' *(Neale, Neall, Neel, Neil, Neill, Nels, Niall, Niels, Niles, Nils) see also* **Cornelius**

Ned Diminutive of many names beginning with Ed *see* **Edgar, Edmund** or **Edward**

Needham (TEUTONIC) 'Tyrant'

Neel *see* **Cornelius** or **Neal**

Nehemiah (HEBREW) 'Consolation of the Lord'

Neil *see* **Neal**

Nels *see* **Neal** or **Nelson**

Nelson (CELTIC) 'Son of Neal' *(Nels, Nils, Nilson)*

Nemo (GREEK) 'From the glen'

Nennog (WELSH) 'One from heaven'

Neo (GREEK) 'Born'

Nero (LATIN) 'Dark-complexioned', 'black-haired' *(Neron)*

Nestor (GREEK) 'Ancient wisdom'

Neville (LATIN) 'From the new town' *(Nev, Nevil, Nevile)*

Nevin (GAELIC) 'Worshipper of saints' (ANGLO-SAXON) 'nephew' *(Nefen, Nevins, Niven, Nivens)*

Nevlin (CELTIC) 'Sailor'

Newbern (TEUTONIC) 'The new leader'

Newbold (OLD ENGLISH) 'From the new building'

Newcomb (ANGLO-SAXON) 'Stranger'

Newel *see* **Noel**

Newell (ANGLO-SAXON) 'From the new hall' *(Newall) see also* **Noel**

Newland (ANGLO-SAXON) 'From the new lands' *(Newlands)*

Newlin (CELTIC) 'One who lives by the new pool' *(Newlyn)*

Newman (ANGLO-SAXON) 'The newcomer', 'the new arrival'

Newton (ANGLO-SAXON) 'From the new estate'

Niall *see* **Neal**

Nic *see* **Dominic, Nicholas**

Nicander (GREEK) 'Man of victory'

Nicholas (GREEK) 'Victorious people's army'. The leader of the people *(Claus, Cole, Colin, Colley, Klaus, Neacail, Nic, Niccolo, Nichol, Nicholl, Nick, Nickie, Nicky, Nicol, Nicolai, Nicolas, Nik, Nikki, Nikos, Niles)* see also **Colin**

Nick *see* **Dominic, Nicholas** or **Nicodemus**

Nico (GREEK) 'Victory'

Nicodemus (GREEK) 'Conqueror for the people' *(Mikki, Nick, Nickie, Nicky, Nik, Nikki, Nikky)*

Nicol *see* **Nicholas**

Nicolai *see* **Nicholas**

Nicomede (GREEK) 'Victorious leader'

Niels *see* **Neal**

Nigel (LATIN) 'Black-haired one'

Niger (LATIN) 'Black'

Nik *see* **Nicholas** or **Nicodemus**

Nikhat (SANSKRIT) 'Fragrant'

Nikki *see* **Nicholas** or **Nicodemus**

Nikos *see* **Nicholas**

Nilay (SANSKRIT) 'Home'

Niles *see* **Nicholas** or **Neal**

Nimrod (HEBREW) 'Valiant'

Niran (THAI) 'Eternal'

Nixon (ANGLO-SAXON) 'Nicholas's son' *(Nickson)*

Noach *see* **Noah**

Noah (HEBREW) 'Rest, comfort and peace' *(Noach)*

Noam (HEBREW) 'Sweetness', 'friendship'

Noble (LATIN) 'Noble and famous' *(Nobel, Nolan, Noland)*

Noda (HEBREW) 'Famous'

Nodas (HEBREW) 'Son of the leader'

Nodin (NATIVE AMERICAN) 'Wind'

Noel (FRENCH) 'Born at Christmas'. A suitable name for a boy born on Christmas Day *(Natal, Natale, Newel, Newell, Nowell)*

Nolan *see* **Noble**

Nollie *see* **Oliver**

Norbert (TEUTONIC) 'Brilliant sea hero'. The courageous commander of ships *(Norbie)*

Norman (FRENCH) 'Man from the north, a Northman'. The bold Viking from Scandinavia *(Norm, Normand, Normie, Norris)*

Norris *see* **Norman**

Northcliffe (ANGLO-SAXON) 'Man from the north cliff' *(Northcliff)*

Northrop (ANGLO-SAXON) 'From the northern farm' *(North, Northrup, Nortrop, Nortrup)*

Norton (ANGLO-SAXON) 'From the north farm'

Norua (TEUTONIC) 'Divine strength'

Norval (OLD FRENCH) 'Northern valley'

Norville (FRENCH) 'From the north town' *(Norvel, Norvie, Norvil)*

Norvin (ANGLO-SAXON) 'Friend from the north' *(Norwin, Norwyn)*

Norward (ANGLO-SAXON) 'Guardian from the north'

Norwell (Anglo-Saxon) 'From the north well'

Norwood (ANGLO-SAXON) 'From the north forest'

Notos (GREEK) 'The south wind'

Nova (LATIN) 'New'

Nuncio (ITALIAN FROM LATIN) 'Messenger' (*Ninzio*)

Nuri (HEBREW) 'Fire' *(Nuriel, Nuris)*

Nye *see* **Aneurin**

BOYS

Oakes (ANGLO-SAXON) 'One who lives by the oak tree'

Oakley (ANGLO-SAXON) 'From the oak tree meadow' *(Okely)*

Oates *see* **Otis**

Obadiah (HEBREW) 'Servant of the Lord'. The obedient one *(Obadias)*

Obed (HEBREW) 'Worshipper of the Lord'

Oberon *see* **Auberon**

Obert (TEUTONIC) 'Wealthy and brilliant'

Octavian *see* **Octavius**

Octavius (LATIN) 'The eighth born' *(Octavian, Octave, Octavus, Tavey)*

Odagoma (NATIVE AMERICAN) 'One with iron nerves'

Odell (TEUTONIC) 'Wealthy one' *(Odie, Odin, Odo)*

Odmar (TEUTONIC) 'Rich and famous'

Odo *see* **Odell**

Odolf (TEUTONIC) 'The wealthy wolf'

Odwin (TEUTONIC) 'Rich friend' *(Ortwin)*

Ogden (ANGLO-SAXON) 'From the oak valley' *(Ogdan)*

Ogilvie (CELTIC) 'From the high peak'

Oglesby (ANGLO-SAXON) 'Awe-inspiring'

Ogmund (TEUTONIC) 'Impressive protector'

Ola (HEBREW) 'Eternity'

Olaf (SCANDINAVIAN) 'Ancestral relic', 'peaceful reminder' *(Amhlaoibh, Olav, Olen, Olin)*

Olave (SCANDINAVIAN) 'Relic of our ancestors'

Olcott (TEUTONIC) 'One who lives in the old cottage'

Ole (SCANDINAVIAN) 'Squire'

Olin *see* **Olaf**

Oliver (LATIN) 'Symbol of peace'. The olive branch *(Noll, Nollie, Nolly, Olivero, Oliviero, Ollie, Olvan)*

Olney (ANGLO-SAXON) 'Olla's island'

Olvan *see* **Oliver**

Olvidio (SPANISH) 'The forgetful one'

Oman (SCANDINAVIAN) 'High protector'

Omanisa (NATIVE AMERICAN) 'The wanderer'

Omar (ARABIC/SANSKRIT) 'The first son', 'most high follower of the prophet'

On (CHINESE) 'Peace'

Onilwyn (WELSH) 'Ash grove' *(Onllwyn)*

Onslow (ANGLO-SAXON) 'Hill of the zealous one'

Oram (ANGLO-SAXON) 'From the enclosure by the riverbank'

Oran (GAELIC) 'Pale-skinned man' *(Oren, Orin, Orran, Orren, Orrin)*

Orban (FRENCH FROM LATIN) 'Globe'

Ordway (ANGLO-SAXON) 'The spear fighter'

Orel (LATIN) 'The one who listens'

Orestes (GREEK) 'The mountain climber'

Orford (ANGLO-SAXON) 'One who lives at the cattle ford'

Orien (LATIN) 'The dawn'

Orion (GREEK) 'The son of light'

Orlan (ANGLO-SAXON) 'From the pointed land' *(Orlando)*

Orlando *see* **Roland**

Orlin (LATIN) 'Golden and bright'

Ormond (TEUTONIC) 'Spearman', 'shipman' *(Orman, Ormand, Ormen, Ormin)*

Ornette (HEBREW) 'Light', 'cedar tree'

Oro (SPANISH) 'Golden-haired one'

Orrick (ANGLO-SAXON) 'One who lives by the ancient oak tree'

Orris (OLD FRENCH) 'Gold or silver lace'

Orson (ANGLO-SAXON) 'Son of the spearman' (LATIN) 'little bear' *(Urson)*

Ortensio (LATIN) 'The gardener'

Orton (ANGLO-SAXON) 'From the shore-farmstead'

Orval (ANGLO-SAXON) 'Mighty with a spear'

Orville (FRENCH) 'From the golden town' *(Orvil)*

Orvin (ANGLO-SAXON) 'Spear friend'

Osbert (ANGLO-SAXON) 'Divinely bright warrior' *(Bert, Bertie, Berty, Oz, Ozzie)*

Osborn (ANGLO-SAXON) 'Divine warrior' *(Osborne, Osbourn, Osbourne, Osburn, Osburne)*

Oscar (ANGLO-SAXON) 'Divine spearman'. A fighter for God *(Os, Oskar, Ossie, Oz, Ozzie)*

Osgood (SCANDINAVIAN) 'The divine Goth'

Oslac (SCANDINAVIAN) 'Divine sport'

Osman (SANSKRIT) 'God's slave' *(Usman)*

Osmar (ANGLO-SAXON) 'Divinely glorious'

Osmond (ANGLO-SAXON) 'Divine protector'

Osred (ANGLO-SAXON) 'Divine counsellor'

Osric (SCANDINAVIAN) 'Divine ruler'

Oswald (ANGLO-SAXON) 'Divinely powerful'

Oswin (OLD ENGLISH) 'Friend of God'

Otadan (NATIVE AMERICAN) 'Plenty'

Othman (TEUTONIC) 'The prosperous one'

Otho *see* **Otto**

Otis (GREEK) 'Keen of sight and hearing' *(Oates)*

Ottavio (ITALIAN FROM LATIN) 'Eighth'

Otte (TEUTONIC) 'Happy one'

Otto (TEUTONIC) 'Wealthy, prosperous man' *(Otho)*

Ottokar (GERMAN) 'Happy warrior'

Otway (TEUTONIC) 'Fortunate in battle' *(Ottway)*

Ouray (NATIVE AMERICAN) 'Arrow'

Owen (CELTIC) 'The young, well-born warrior' *(Owain)* *see also* **Evan**

Oxford (ANGLO-SAXON) 'From the ford where oxen crossed'

Oxton (ANGLO-SAXON) 'From the town where the oxen graze'

Ozul (HEBREW) 'Shadow'

P

BOYS

Pablo *see* Paul

Pacian (LATIN) 'Man of peace'

Paco (NATIVE AMERICAN) 'Brave eagle'

Padarn (WELSH) 'Fatherly'

Paddy *see* Patrick

Padgett (FRENCH) 'The young attendant, a page' *(Padget, Page, Paget, Paige)*

Paine (LATIN) 'The country rustic', 'a pagan' *(Payne)*

Paisley (LATIN) 'From the country'

Pakavi (NATIVE AMERICAN) 'A reed from the river bank'

Palladin (NATIVE AMERICAN) 'Fighter'

Palmer (LATIN) 'The palm-bearing pilgrim' *(Palm)*

Pancras (GREEK) 'All strength'

Paolo *see* Paul

Parakram (SANSKRIT) 'Strong one'

Pari (FRENCH) 'Fatherly'

Parish *see* Parrish

Park (ANGLO-SAXON) 'From the park' *(Parke)*

Parker (ANGLO-SAXON) 'The park-keeper'. One who guarded the park lands

Parkin (ANGLO-SAXON) 'Little Peter' *(Perkin, Peterkin)*

Parlan *see* **Bartholomew**

Parnell *see* **Peter**

Parr (ANGLO-SAXON) 'One who lives by the cattle pen'

Parrish (ANGLO-SAXON) 'From the church parish' *(Parish)*

Parry (FRENCH/CELTIC) 'Protector'

Parsifal *see* **Percival**

Pascal (ITALIAN) 'Easter born'. The new-born pascal lamb *(Pasquale)*

Pasquale *see* **Pascal**

Pat *see* **Fitzpatrick** or **Patrick**

Patera (SANSKRIT) 'A bird'

Patrick (LATIN) 'The noble patrician'. One of noble birth and from a noble line *(Paddy, Padraic, Padraig, Padruig, Pat, Patric, Patrice, Patricio, Patrizio, Patrizius, Patsy, Peyton, Rick) see also* **Fitzpatrick**

Patton (ANGLO-SAXON) 'From the warrior's farm' *(Patin)*

Patu (SANSKRIT) 'Protector'

Paul (LATIN) 'Little' *(Pablo, Paley, Paolo, Pauley, Paulie, Pavel)*

Pavel *see* **Paul**

Pax (LATIN) 'Peace'

Paxton (ANGLO-SAXON) 'From the warrior's estate'

Payne *see* **Paine**

Payton (ANGLO-SAXON) 'One who lives on the warrior's farm' *(Peyton)*

Pedro *see* **Peter**

Pelex (GREEK) 'Warrior's helmet'

Pell (ANGLO-SAXON) 'Scarf'

Pelton (ANGLO-SAXON) 'From the farm by the pool'

Pembroke (CELTIC) 'From the headland'

Penley (ANGLO-SAXON) 'From the enclosed meadow'

Penn (ANGLO-SAXON) 'Enclosure'

Penrod (TEUTONIC) 'Famous commander'

Penrose (CELTIC) 'Mountain promontory'

Penwyn (WELSH) 'Fair headed'

Pepin (TEUTONIC) 'The petitioner', 'the persevered' *(Pepi, Peppi, Peppin)*

Percival (FRENCH) 'Valley piercer' *(Parsefal, Parsifal, Perc, Perce, Perceval, Percy, Purcell)*

Percy *see* **Percival** *(Perry)*

Peregrine (LATIN) 'The wanderer' *(Perry)*

Pericles (GREEK) 'Far famed'

Perrin *see* **Peter**

Perry (ANGLO-SAXON) 'From the pear tree' *see also* **Peregrine**

Perseus (GREEK) 'Destroyer'

Perth (CELTIC) 'Thorn bush thicket'

Peter (LATIN) 'The stone, the rock'. The first pope *(Parnell, Peadar, Pearce, Pedro, Pernell, Perrin, Pete, Petrie, Pierce, Piero, Pierre, Pierro, Pierrot, Piers, Pietro)*

Petros (GREEK) 'Made of stone'

Peverall (FRENCH) 'The piper' *(Peveral, Peverel, Peverell, Peveril, Peverill)*

Phaon (GREEK) 'Brilliant'

Pharamond (GERMAN) 'Journey protection'

Pharaol (EGYPTIAN) 'The sun'

Pharos (GREEK) 'Beacon of light'

Phelan (GAELIC) 'Brave as the wolf'

Phelps (ANGLO-SAXON) 'Son of Philip' *see also* **Philip**

Philander (GREEK) 'The man who loves everyone'

Philaret (GREEK) 'One who loves virtue'

Philbert (TEUTONIC) 'Brilliant' *(Filbert)*

Philemon (GREEK) 'Kiss'

Philetas (GREEK) 'Beloved one' *(Philetus)*

Philip (GREEK) 'Lover of horses' *(Filib, Filip, Filli, Phelps, Phill, Phillie, Philly, Philipp, Phillip, Phillopa, Pilib)*

Phillips (ANGLO-SAXON) 'Phillip's son' *(Felips, Fellips, Phelips, Phellips, Phellipps, Philips, Phillipps)*

Philo (GREEK) 'Friendly love'

Phineas (GREEK) 'Mouth of brass'

Pickford (ANGLO-SAXON) 'From the ford at the peak'

Pickworth (ANGLO-SAXON) 'From the estate of the hewer'

Pierce *see* **Peter**

Piers *see* **Peter**

Pierrot *see* **Melbourne** or **Peter**

Pierson (FRENCH) 'Son of Pierre'

Pippin (DUTCH FROM TEUTONIC) 'Father'

Pitney (DUTCH FROM TEUTONIC) 'Preserving one's island'

Pitt (ANGLO-SAXON) 'From the hollow'

Placido (SPANISH) 'Serene' *(Placide)*

Plato (GREEK) 'The broad-shouldered one'. The great philosopher

Platt (FRENCH) 'From the plateau'

Poldo (TEUTONIC) 'Prince of the people'

Pollard (OLD GERMAN) 'Cropped hair'

Pollock (ANGLO-SAXON) 'Little Paul'

Pollux (GREEK) 'Crown'

Pomeroy (FRENCH) 'From the apple orchard'

Porter (FRENCH) 'Gatekeeper'

Powa (NATIVE AMERICAN) 'Rich one'

Powell (CELTIC) 'Alert', 'son of Howell'

Prahlad (SANSKRIT) 'Joy'

Pranjal (SANSKRIT) 'Straight and simple'

Pravat (THAI) 'History'

Prentice (ANGLO-SAXON) 'A learner or apprentice' *(Prentiss)*

Prescott (ANGLO-SAXON) 'From the priest's house' *(Prescot)*

Preston (ANGLO-SAXON) 'From the priest's farm'

Prewitt (FRENCH) 'Little valiant warrior' *(Prewet, Prewett, Prewit, Pruitt)*

Price (CELTIC) 'Son of a loving man'

Primo (LATIN) 'The first-born son'

Prince (LATIN) 'Chief'

Prior (LATIN) 'The Father Superior' *(Pryor)*

Probus (LATIN) 'Honest'

Proctor (LATIN) 'The administrator'

Prosper (LATIN) 'Fortunate'

Purcell *see* **Percival**

Purdy (HINDI) 'Recluse'

Purvis (ENGLISH) 'To provide food'

Putnam (ANGLO-SAXON) 'From the pit estate'

Pwyll (WELSH) 'Prudence'

Qabil (ARABIC) 'Able'

Qadim (ARABIC) 'Ancient'

Qadir (ARABIC) 'Powerful'

Quennel (FRENCH) 'One who lives by the little oak'

Quentin (LATIN) 'The fifth born' *(Quent, Quinton, Quintin, Quintus)*

Quigley (GAELIC) 'Distaff'

Quillan (GAELIC) 'Cub'

Quillon (LATIN) 'Sword'

Quimby (NORSE) 'From the woman's estate' *(Quemby, Quenby, Quinby)*

Quincy (FRENCH/LATIN) 'From the fifth son's estate'

Quinlan (GAELIC) 'The well formed one'. One with the body of an Adonis

Quinn (GAELIC) 'Wise and intelligent' *see also* **Conan**

R

BOYS

Rab *see* **Robert**

Race *see* **Horace**

Rachid (ARABIC) 'Wise'

Rad (ANGLO-SAXON) 'Counsellor', 'adviser' *see also* **Radcliffe**

Radbert (TEUTONIC) 'Brilliant counsellor'

Radborne (ANGLO-SAXON) 'From the red stream' *(Radbourn, Radbourne, Redbourn, Redbourne)*

Radcliffe (ANGLO-SAXON) 'From the red cliff' *(Rad, Radcliff, Redcliff, Redcliffe)*

Radford (ANGLO-SAXON) 'From the red ford' *(Radvers, Redford, Redvers)*

Radi (ARABIC) 'Content'

Radley (ANGLO-SAXON) 'From the red meadow' *(Radleigh, Redley, Ridley)*

Radman (SLAVIC) 'Joy' *(Radmen)*

Radnor (ANGLO-SAXON) 'From the red shore'

Radolf (ANGLO-SAXON) 'Wolf counsellor'. Wolf is used in the sense 'brave man'

Rafe *see* **Ralph** or **Raphael**

Rafferty (GAELIC) 'Prosperous and rich'

Raffi (ARABIC) 'Exalting' *(Raffin see also Raphael)*

Raghib (ARABIC) 'Willing'

Ragmar (TEUTONIC) 'Wise warrior'

Ragnold (TEUTONIC) 'Powerful judge'

Raheem (ARABIC) 'Kind'

Rainart (GERMAN) 'Strong judgement'

Rajendra (SANSKRIT) 'Royal one'

Raleigh (ANGLO-SAXON) 'One who lives in the meadow of the roe deer' *(Ralegh, Rawleigh, Rawley)*

Ralph (ANGLO-SAXON) 'Counsel wolf' *(Rafe, Raff, Ralf, Raoul, Raul, Rolf, Rolph)*

Ralston (ANGLO-SAXON) 'One who lives on Ralph's farm'

Rama (SANSKRIT) 'One who brings joy'

Rambert (TEUTONIC) 'Brilliant and mighty'

Ramiro (SPANISH) 'Great judge'

Ramsden (ANGLO-SAXON) 'Ram's valley'

Ramsey (ANGLO-SAXON) 'From Ram's island', 'from the raven's island'

Rana (SANSKRIT) 'Prince'

Rance (AFRICAN) 'Borrowed all' *(Ransell)*

Randal (OLD ENGLISH) 'Shield wolf' *(Rand, Randall, Randolf, Randolph, Randy, Ranulf, Rolf)*

Ranger (FRENCH) 'Keeper of the forest'. The gamekeeper who looked after the trees and the wildlife

Ranjit (SANSKRIT) 'Victorious'

Rankin (ANGLO-SAXON) 'Little shield'

Ransford (ANGLO-SAXON) 'From the raven's ford'

Ransley (ANGLO-SAXON) 'From the raven's meadow'

Ransom (ANGLO-SAXON) 'Shield warrior's son

Ranulf *see* **Randal**

Raoul *see* **Ralph**

Raphael (HEBREW) 'Healed by God' *(Rafael, Rafaello, Rafe, Raff, Raffaello, Raffi)*

Ras *see* **Erasmus** or **Erastus**

Rashid (ARABIC) 'Director', 'pious'

Ravi (SANSKRIT/HINDI) 'The sun'

Rawlins (FRENCH) 'Son of the wolf counsellor'

Rawson (ANGLO-SAXON) 'Son of the little wolf'

Ray (FRENCH) 'The sovereign' *see also* **Raymond**

Rayburn (OLD ENGLISH) 'From the deer brook'

Raymond (TEUTONIC) 'Wise protection' *(Raimond, Ramon, Ray, Raymon, Raymund, Reamonn)*

Raynard *see* **Reynard**

Raynor (SCANDINAVIAN) 'Mighty army' *(Rainer, Rainier)*

Reade (ANGLO-SAXON) 'The red-headed one' *(Read, Reed, Reede, Reid)*

Reading (ANGLO-SAXON) 'Son of the red-haired one' *(Redding)*

Reagen *see* **Regan**

Rearden *see* **Riordan**

Redbourne *see* **Radbourne**

Redcliff *see* **Radcliffe**

Redman (ANGLO-SAXON) 'Counsellor', 'advice-giver'

Redmond (ANGLO-SAXON) 'Counsellor', 'protector', 'advisor' *(Radmund, Redmund)*

Redvers *see* **Radford**

Redwald (ANGLO-SAXON) 'Mighty counsellor'

Reece (CELTIC) 'The ardent one'. One who loves living *(Rhett)* *see also* **Rhys**

Reeve (ANGLO-SAXON) 'The steward'. One who looked after a great lord's affairs

Regan (GAELIC) 'Royalty', 'a king' *(Reagan, Reagen, Regen)*

Reginald (TEUTONIC) 'Mighty and powerful ruler' *(Naldo, Raghnall, Raynold, Reg, Reggie, Reggy, Reinhold, Renaldo, Renato, Renaud, Renault, Rene, Reynold, Rinaldo, Ron, Ronald, Ronnie, Ronny)*

Rehard *see* **Reynard**

Reinhart (TEUTONIC)
 'Incorruptible' (*Reinhard*)

Remington (ANGLO-SAXON)
 'From the farm where the
 blackbirds sing'

Remus (LATIN) 'Fast rower'. A
 speedy oarsman

Renaldo *see* **Reginald**

Renaud *see* **Reynard**

Rennard *see* **Reynard**

Renfred (ANGLO-SAXON) 'Mighty
 and peaceful'. A peaceful
 warrior who could fight
 when necessary

Renfrew (CELTIC) 'From the
 still river'

Renny (GAELIC) 'Little mighty
 and powerful' *see also*
 Reginald

Renshaw (ANGLO-SAXON) 'From
 the forest of the ravens'

Renton (ANGLO-SAXON) 'From
 the farm of the roe buck'

Renwick (TEUTONIC)
 'Raven's nest'

Reuben (HEBREW) 'Behold a son'
 (*Rube, Ruben, Rubey, Ruby*)

Rex (LATIN) 'The king'. The
 all-powerful monarch
 (*Rey, Roy*)

Rexford (ANGLO-SAXON) 'From
 the king's ford'

Reyhan (ARABIC) 'Favoured
 of God'

Reynard (TEUTONIC) 'Mighty
 courage', 'the fox' (*Raynard,
 Rehard, Reinhard, Renaud,
 Rennard*)

Reynold *see* **Reginald**

Reza (ARABIC) 'Resigned to life'

Rezon (HEBREW) 'Prince'

Rhain (WELSH) 'Lance'

Rhett *see* **Reece**

Rhodes (GREEK) 'The place
 of roses'

Rhun (WELSH) 'Grand'

Rhydwyn (WELSH) 'One who
 lives by the white ford'

Rhys (CELTIC) 'Hero'
 (*Reece, Rees*)

Ricardo *see* **Richard**

Rich *see* **Alaric** or **Richard**

Richard (TEUTONIC) 'Wealthy',
'powerful one' *(Diccon,
Dick, Dickie, Dickon, Dicky,
Ricard, Ricardo, Rich,
Richerd, Richie, Rick,
Rickert, Rickie, Ricky,
Riocard, Ritch, Ritchie)*

Richie *see* **Alaric, Richard**

Richmond (ANGLO-SAXON)
'Powerful protector'
(Richman)

Rick *see* **Alaric, Aric, Cedric,
Eric, Patrick, Richard** or
Roderick

Ricker (TEUTONIC)
'Powerful army'

Rickward (ANGLO-SAXON)
'Powerful guardian'
(Rickwood)

Riddock (GAELIC) 'From the
barren field'

Rider (ANGLO-SAXON) 'Knight',
'horse-rider' *(Ryder)*

Ridge (ANGLO-SAXON) 'From
the ridge'

Ridgeway (ANGLO-SAXON) 'From
the ridge road'

Ridgley (ANGLO-SAXON) 'From
the ridge meadow'

Ridpath (ANGLO-SAXON) 'From
the red path' *(Redpath)*

Rigby (ANGLO-SAXON) 'Valley of
the ruler'

Rigg (ANGLO-SAXON) 'From
the ridge'

Rijul (SANSKRIT) 'Innocent'

Riley (GAELIC) 'Valiant and
war-like' *(Reilly, Ryley)*

Rinaldo *see* **Reginald**

Ring (ANGLO-SAXON) 'A ring'

Riordan (GAELIC) 'Royal bard'
(Rearden, Reardon)

Rip (DUTCH) 'Ripe', 'full-grown'
see also **Ripley** or **Robert**

Ripley (ANGLO-SAXON) 'From the
valley of the echo' *(Rip)*

Risley (ANGLO-SAXON) 'From the
brushwood meadow'

Riston (ANGLO-SAXON) 'From the
brushwood farm'

Ritchie *see* **Richard**

Ritter (TEUTONIC) 'A knight'

Roald (TEUTONIC) 'Famous ruler'

Roan (ANGLO-SAXON) 'From the rowan tree' *(Rowan)*

Roarke (GAELIC) 'Famous ruler' *(Rorke, Rourke, Ruark)*

Robert (TEUTONIC) 'Bright, shining fame'. A man of brilliant reputation *(Bob, Bobbie, Bobby, Rab, Rabbie, Rabby, Rip, Rob, Robbie, Robby, Roberto, Robin, Rupert, Ruprecht)*

Robinson (ANGLO-SAXON) 'Son of Robert'

Rochester (ANGLO-SAXON) 'Camp on the rocks'

Rock (ANGLO-SAXON) 'From the rock' *(Roc, Rocky)*

Rockley (ANGLO-SAXON) 'From the rocky meadow' *(Rockly)*

Rockwell (ANGLO-SAXON) 'From the rocky well'

Roden (ANGLO-SAXON) 'From the valley of the reeds'

Roderick (TEUTONIC) 'Famous wealthy ruler' *(Broderic, Broderick, Brodrick, Rick, Rickie, Ricky, Rod, Rodd, Roddie, Roddy, Roderic, Roderigo, Rodric, Rodrick, Rory, Rurik)*

Rodhlann *see* **Roland**

Rodman (TEUTONIC) 'Famous hero' *(Rodmond, Rodmund)*

Rodney (TEUTONIC) 'Famous and renowned' *(Rod, Roddie, Roddy, Rodi)*

Rodwell (ANGLO-SAXON) 'From the Christian's well'

Roe (ANGLO-SAXON) 'Roe deer'

Rogan (GAELIC) 'The red-haired one'

Roger (TEUTONIC) 'Famous spearman', 'renowned warrior' *(Rodge, Rodger, Rog, Rogerio)*

Roland (TEUTONIC) 'From the famed land' *(Lanny, Orlando, Rodhlann, Roley, Rollin, Rollo, Rowe, Rowland)*

Rolph *see* **Ralph** or **Rudolph**

Rolt (TEUTONIC) 'Power and fame'

Roman (LATIN) 'From Rome' *(Roma, Romain)*

Romaric (GERMAN) 'Glorious king'

Rombaud (GERMAN) 'Bold glory'

Romeo (LATIN) 'Man from Rome'

Romero (LATIN) 'Wanderer'

Romford *see* **Rumford**

Romney (CELTIC) 'Curving river'

Romolo (LATIN/SPANISH) 'Fame'

Romulus (LATIN) 'Citizen of Rome'. According to mythology, Romulus and his twin brother Remus founded Rome

Ronald *see* **Reginald**

Ronan (GAELIC) 'Little seal'

Ronson (ANGLO-SAXON) 'Son of Ronald'

Rooney (GAELIC) 'The red one'. One with a ruddy complexion *(Rowney, Ruan)*

Roosevelt (OLD DUTCH) 'From the rose field'. Sometimes used in compliment to two US presidents

Roper (ANGLO-SAXON) 'Rope-maker'

Rory (GAELIC) 'Red king' *(Rorie, Rorry, Ruaidhri)* see also **Roderick**

Roscoe (SCANDINAVIAN) 'From the deer forest' *(Ros, Rosco, Roz)*

Roslin (FRENCH) 'Small red-haired one' *(Roslyn, Rosselin, Rosslyn)*

Ross (CELTIC) 'From the peninsula' (TEUTONIC) 'horse'

Rosslyn *see* **Roslin**

Roswald (TEUTONIC) 'Mighty steed' *(Roswall, Roswell)*

Roth (OLD GERMAN) 'Red hair'

Rothwell (NORSE) 'From the red well'

Rover (ANGLO-SAXON) 'A wanderer'

Rowan (GAELIC) 'Red haired'
(Rowe, Rowen) see also
Roan

Rowell (ANGLO-SAXON) 'From the
deer well'

Rowley (ANGLO-SAXON) 'From
the rough meadow'

Rowsan (ANGLO-SAXON) 'Rowan's
son'. Son of a red-haired man

Roxbury (ANGLO-SAXON) 'From
the fortress of the rock'

Roy (CELTIC) 'Red haired', 'the
king' *see also* **Conroy,
Leroy** or **Rex**

Royal (FRENCH) 'Regal one'

Royce (ANGLO-SAXON) 'Son of
the king'

Royd (NORSE) 'From the forest
clearing'

Roydon (NORSE) 'One who lives
on the rye hill'

Royston (ENGLISH) Place in
Yorkshire

Ruaidhri *see* **Rory**

Ruan *see* **Rooney**

Ruark *see* **Roarke**

Rube *see* **Reuben**

Ruben *see* **Reuben**

Ruck (ANGLO-SAXON) 'The rock'.
One with black hair

Rudd (ANGLO-SAXON) 'Ruddy
complexion'

Rudolph (TEUTONIC) 'Famous
wolf' *(Dolf, Dolph, Rodolf,
Rodolph, Rolf, Rolfe, Rollo,
Rolph, Rudolf, Rudy)*

Rudyard (ANGLO-SAXON) 'From
the red enclosure'

Ruff (FRENCH) 'The red-haired
one' *see also* **Rufus**

Rufford (ANGLO-SAXON) 'From
the rough ford'

Ruford (OLD ENGLISH) 'From the
red ford'

Rufus (LATIN) 'Red haired'
*(Griff, Griffin, Griffith,
Rufe, Ruff) see also* **Griffith**

Rugby (ANGLO-SAXON) 'From the
rook estate'

Rule (LATIN) 'The ruler' *(Ruelle)*

Rumford (ANGLO-SAXON) 'From
the wide ford' *(Romford)*

Rupert *see* **Robert**

Rush (FRENCH) 'Red haired'

Rushford (ANGLO-SAXON) 'From the rush ford'

Ruskin (TEUTONIC) 'Small red-haired one'

Russell (ANGLO-SAXON) 'Red as a fox' *(Rus, Russ, Russel, Rusty)*

Rust (ANGLO-SAXON) 'Red haired' *(Russet, Rusty)*

Rutherford (ANGLO-SAXON) 'From the cattle ford'

Rutland (NORSE) 'From the stump land'

Rutledge (ANGLO-SAXON) 'From the red pool' *(Routledge)*

Rutley (ANGLO-SAXON) 'From the stump meadow'

Ryan (GAELIC) 'Small king'

Rycroft (ANGLO-SAXON) 'From the rye field'

Rye (FRENCH) 'From the riverbank'

Rylan (ANGLO-SAXON) 'From the rye land' *(Ryland)*

Ryle (ANGLO-SAXON) 'From the rye hill'

Ryman (ANGLO-SAXON) 'The rye-seller'

Ryton (ANGLO-SAXON) 'From the rye farm'

BOYS

Saadi (PERSIAN) 'Wise one'

Sabas (HEBREW) 'Rest'

Sabeel (ARABIC) 'The way'

Saber (FRENCH) 'A sword'

Sabin (LATIN) 'Man from the Sabines'

Sadik (ARABIC) 'Truthful'

Sadoc (HEBREW) 'Sacred'

Safford (ANGLO-SAXON) 'From the willow ford'

Sahale (NATIVE AMERICAN) 'Above'

Sakima (NATIVE AMERICAN) 'King'

Saladin (ARABIC) 'Goodness of the faith'

Salah (ARABIC) 'Goodness'

Salim (ARABIC) 'Safe', 'healthy', 'peace'

Salisbury (OLD ENGLISH) 'Fortified stronghold'

Salman (ARABIC) 'Safe', 'unharmed'

Salomon (HEBREW) 'Peaceful' *see also* **Solomon**

Salton (ANGLO-SAXON) 'From the willow farm'

Salvador (LATIN) 'The saviour' *(Salvadore, Salvator, Salvatore, Salvidor)*

Salvestro (ITALIAN) 'Woody'

Sam *see* **Sampson** or **Samuel**

Sama (SANSKRIT) 'Tranquillity'

Samir (ARABIC) 'Entertaining companion'

Sampson (HEBREW) 'Sun's man' (*Sam, Sammy, Samson, Sansom, Sim, Simpson, Simson*)

Samuel (Hebrew) 'His name is God' (*Sam, Sammie, Sammy*)

Samula (SANSKRIT) 'Foundation'

Sanborn (ANGLO-SAXON) 'From the sandy brook' (*Samborn*)

Sanchia (SPANISH) 'Holy'

Sancho (SPANISH) 'Sincere and truthful'

Sanders (ANGLO-SAXON) 'Son of Alexander' (*Sanderson, Sandie, Sandy, Saunders, Saunderson*)

Sanderson *see* **Sanders**

Sandford (ANGLO-SAXON) 'Sandy ford'

Sandie *see* **Alexander** or **Sanders**

Sandy *see* **Alexander, Lysander** or **Sanders**

Sanford (ANGLO-SAXON) 'From the sandy ford'

Sanjay (SANSKRIT) 'Triumphant'

Santo (ITALIAN) 'Saint-like'

Santon (ANGLO-SAXON) 'From the sandy farm'

Sanuya (NATIVE AMERICAN) 'Cloud'

Sanzio (ITALIAN) 'Holy'

Sardis (HEBREW) 'Prince of joy'

Sarge *see* **Sargent**

Sargent (LATIN) 'A military attendant' (*Sarge, Sargie, Serge, Sergeant, Sergent, Sergio*)

Sarid (HEBREW) 'Survivor'

Sasha *see* **Alexander**

Saul (HEBREW) 'Called by God' (*Zollie, Zolly*)

Saunders *see* **Alexander** or **Sanders**

Saunderson *see* **Sanders**

Savero (ARABIC) 'Bright one'

Saville (FRENCH) 'The willow estate' *(Savile)*

Sawa (NATIVE AMERICAN) 'Rock'

Sawyer (ANGLO-SAXON) 'A sawyer of wood'

Saxon (ANGLO-SAXON) 'People of the swords' *(Saxe)*

Sayer (CELTIC) 'Carpenter' *(Sayers, Sayre, Sayres)*

Scanlon (GAELIC) 'A snarer of hearts'

Schuyler (DUTCH) 'A scholar', 'a wise man', 'to shield'

Scipio (LATIN) 'Walking stick'

Scott (CELTIC) 'Tattooed warrior' (LATIN) 'from Scotland' *(Scot, Scottie, Scotty)*

Scoville (FRENCH) 'From the Scottish estate'

Scully (GAELIC) 'Town crier'. The bringer of news in the days before mass media

Seabert (ANGLO-SAXON) 'Sea glorious' *(Seabright, Sebert)*

Seabrook (ANGLO-SAXON) 'From a brook by the sea' *(Sebrook)*

Seain *see* **John**

Seamus *see* **Jacob**

Sean *see* **John**

Searle (TEUTONIC) 'Armed warrior' *(Searl)*

Seaton (FRENCH) 'From the Say's farm' *(Seadon, Seeton, Seetin, Seton)*

Sebald (OLD ENGLISH) 'Bold in victory'

Sebastian (LATIN) 'Reverenced one'. An august person *(Seb, Sebastiano, Sebastien)*

Sebert (OLD ENGLISH) 'Famous for victory' *see also* **Seabert**

Secundus (LATIN) 'Second'

Sedgley (ANGLO-SAXON) 'From the swordsman's meadow' *(Sedgeley)*

Sedgwick (ANGLO-SAXON) 'From the sword grass place'

Seeley (ANGLO-SAXON) 'Happy and blessed' *(Sealey, Seely)*

Seger (ANGLO-SAXON) 'Sea warrior' *(Seager, Segar)*

Seigneur *see* **Senior**

Selby (TEUTONIC) 'From the manor farm'

Selden (ANGLO-SAXON) 'From the valley of the willow tree' *(Seldon, Sheldon)*

Selig (TEUTONIC) 'Blessed happy one'

Selvac (CELTIC) 'One who has many cattle'

Selwyn (TEUTONIC) 'Friend at the manor house' *(Selwin)*

Senior (FRENCH) 'Lord of the manor' *(Seigneur)*

Sennett (FRENCH) 'Old and wise'. The all-knowing seer

Seosaidh *see* **Joseph**

Septimus (LATIN) 'Seventh-born son'

Sergio *see* **Sargent**

Serle (TEUTONIC) 'Bearer of arms and weapons'

Seth (HEBREW) 'The appointed by God'

Seton (ANGLO-SAXON) 'From the farm by the sea' *see also* **Seaton**

Severn (ANGLO-SAXON) 'The boundary'

Seward (ANGLO-SAXON) 'The sea defender'

Sewell (ANGLO-SAXON) 'Sea powerful' *(Sewald, Sewall, Siwald)*

Sexton (ANGLO-SAXON) 'Sacristan'. A church official

Sextus (LATIN) 'Sixth-born son'

Seyed (ARABIC) 'Master'

Seymour (ANGLO-SAXON/ FRENCH) 'From the moor by the sea'

Shadwell (ANGLO-SAXON) 'From the well in the arbour'

Shafiq (ARABIC) 'Kind', 'compassionate'

Shalom (HEBREW) 'Peace' *(Sholom)*

Shamus (IRISH) Irish form of **James**

Shanahan (GAELIC) 'The wise one'

Shandy (ANGLO-SAXON) 'Little boisterous one'

Shane (CELTIC) Celtic form of John *see also* **John**

Shanley (GAELIC) 'The venerable hero'

Shannon (GAELIC) 'Old wise one' *(Shanan)*

Sharif (ARABIC) 'Eminent', 'honourable'

Shattuck (ANGLO-SAXON) 'Little shad-fish'

Shaw (ANGLO-SAXON) 'From the grove'

Shea (GAELIC) 'Stately, courteous, and inventive person'. A man of many parts *(Shay)*

Sheean (CELTIC) 'Polite', 'courteous'

Sheehan (GAELIC) 'Peaceful one'

Sheffield (ANGLO-SAXON) 'From the crooked field'

Shelby (ANGLO-SAXON) 'From the estate on the cliff edge'

Sheldon (ANGLO-SAXON) 'From the hill ledge' *see also* **Selden**

Shelley (ANGLO-SAXON) 'From the meadow on the hill ledge'

Shelton (ANGLO-SAXON) 'From the farm on the hill ledge'

Shem (HEBREW) 'Renown'

Shepard (ANGLO-SAXON) 'The sheep tender, the shepherd' *(Shep, Shepherd, Shepp, Sheppard, Shepperd, Sheppy)*

Shepley (ANGLO-SAXON) 'From the sheep meadow'

Sherborne (ANGLO-SAXON) 'From the clear stream' *(Sherbourn, Sherbourne, Sherburn, Sherburne)*

Sheridan (GAELIC) 'Wild savage'

Sherlock (ANGLO-SAXON) 'White-haired man'

Sherman (ANGLO-SAXON) 'Wool shearer', 'sheep shearer'

Sherwin (ANGLO-SAXON) 'Loyal friend', 'swift-footed' *(Sherwynd)*

Sherwood (ANGLO-SAXON) 'Bright forest'

Shing (CHINESE) 'Victory'

Shipley (ANGLO-SAXON) 'From the sheep meadow'

Shipton (ANGLO-SAXON) 'From the sheep farm'

Sholom *see* **Shalom**

Sholto (GAELIC) 'The wild duck'

Sian *see* **John**

Siddell (ANGLO-SAXON) 'From a wide valley'

Sidney (FRENCH) 'A follower of St Denis', 'man from Sidon' *(Sid, Syd, Sydney)*

Siegfried *see* **Sigfrid**

Sigfrid (TEUTONIC) 'Peace after victory' *(Siegfried, Siegrid, Sigfried)*

Sigmund (TEUTONIC) 'Victorious protector' *(Sigismond, Sigismund, Sigmond)*

Sigurd (SCANDINAVIAN) 'Victorious guardian' *(Sigerd)*

Sigwald (TEUTONIC) 'Victorious ruler'

Silas (LATIN) 'From the forest' *(Si, Silvan, Silvano, Silvanus, Silvester, Sly, Sylvan, Sylvester)*

Simeon *see* **Simon**

Simon (HEBREW) 'One who hears' *(Sim, Simeon, Siomonn, Ximenes)*

Sinclair (FRENCH) 'From St Clair', 'shining light' *(St Clair)*

Siân *see* **John**

Siward (TEUTONIC) 'Conquering guardian'

Skeets (ANGLO-SAXON) 'The swift' *(Skeat, Skeet, Skeeter)*

Skelly (GAELIC) 'Historian'

Skelton (ANGLO-SAXON) 'From the farm on the hill ledge'

Skerry (SCANDINAVIAN) 'From the rocky island'

Skip (SCANDINAVIAN) 'Owner of the ship' *(Skipp, Skippy)*

Skipton (ANGLO-SAXON) 'From the sheep farm'

Slade (ANGLO-SAXON) 'Valley dweller'

Slevin (GAELIC) 'The mountain climber' *(Slaven, Slavin, Sleven)*

Sloan (GAELIC) 'Warrior' *(Sloane)*

Sly *see* **Silas**

Smedley (ANGLO-SAXON) 'From the flat meadow' *(Smedly)*

Smith (ANGLO-SAXON) 'The blacksmith'

Snowden (ANGLO-SAXON) 'From the snowy hill'. Man from the snowcapped mountains

Socrates (GREEK) 'Self-restrained'

Sol (LATIN) 'The sun' *see also* **Solomon**

Solomon (HEBREW) 'Wise and peaceful' *(Salomon, Sol, Solamon, Sollie, Solly, Soloman, Zollie, Zolly)*

Solon (GREEK) 'Wise man'. Greek form of Solomon

Somerled (TEUTONIC) 'Summer wanderer'

Somerset (ANGLO-SAXON) 'From the summer place'. The place where wanderers rested for the summer

Somerton (ANGLO-SAXON) 'From the summer farm'

Somerville (ANGLO-SAXON) 'From the summer estate' *(Sommerville)*

Sonny *see* **Bronson** or **Tyson**

Sophocles (GREEK) 'Glory of wisdom'

Sorrel (FRENCH) 'With brownish hair'

Southwell (ANGLO-SAXON) 'From the south well'

Spalding (ANGLO-SAXON) 'From the split meadow' (SPAULDING)

Spangler (TEUTONIC) 'The tinsmith

Spark (ANGLO-SAXON) 'Gay gallant'. The man about town'

Speed (ANGLO-SAXON) 'Success, prosperity'

Spencer (FRENCH) 'Shopkeeper', 'dispenser of provisions' *(Spence, Spenser)*

Spiro (GREEK) 'Breath of the gods'

Sprague (OLD FRENCH) 'Lively'

Sproule (ANGLO-SAXON) 'Energetic, active person *(Sprowle)*

Squire (ANGLO-SAXON) 'Knight's shield-bearer'

St Clair *see* **Sinclair**

St John (ENGLISH) A contraction of Saint John

Stacey (LATIN) 'Prosperous and stable' *(Stacy)*

Stafford (ANGLO-SAXON) 'From the ford by the landing place' *(Staffard)*

Stamford (ANGLO-SAXON) 'From the stony crossing' *(Stanford)*

Stanbury (ANGLO-SAXON) 'From a stone fortress' *(Stanberry)*

Stancliffe (ANGLO-SAXON) 'From the rocky cliff' *(Stancliff, Standcliff, Standcliffe)*

Standish (ANGLO-SAXON) 'From the stony park'

Stanfield (ANGLO-SAXON) 'From the stony field'

Stanhope (ANGLO-SAXON) 'From the stony hollow'

Stanislaus (SLAVIC) 'Stand of glory' *(Aineislis, Stan, Stanislas, Stanislav, Stanislaw)*

Stanley (ANGLO-SAXON) 'From the stony meadow', (SLAVIC) 'pride of the camp' *(Stan, Stanleigh, Stanly)*

Stanton (ANGLO-SAXON) 'From the rocky lake', 'from the stony farm'

Stanway (ANGLO-SAXON) 'From the stony road'

Stanwick (ANGLO-SAXON) 'From the stony village'

Stanwood (ANGLO-SAXON) 'From the stony forest'

Starling (ANGLO-SAXON) 'The starling', from the bird

Starr (ANGLO-SAXON) 'A star'

Staton (TEUTONIC) 'One who lives in the stone house'

Stavros (GREEK) 'Cross'

Stedman (ANGLO-SAXON) 'Farm owner'. One who owns the land he tills

Stefan *see* **Stephen**

Stein (TEUTONIC) 'The stone'

Stephen (GREEK) 'The crowned one'. A man who wears the victor's laurel wreath *(Etienne, Istran, Stefan, Steffen, Stephanus, Stephenson, Steve, Steven, Stevenson, Stevie)*

Sterling (TEUTONIC) 'Good', 'honest', 'worthy' *(Stirling)*

Sterne (ANGLO-SAXON) 'The austere one', 'an ascetic' *(Stearn, Stearne, Stern)*

Stevenson *see* **Stephen**

Stewart (ANGLO-SAXON) 'The steward'. Name of the Royal House of Scotland *(Stew, Steward, Stu, Stuart)*

Stillman (ANGLO-SAXON) 'Quiet and gentle man' *(Stilman)*

Stinson (ANGLO-SAXON) 'Son of stone'

Stockley (ANGLO-SAXON) 'From the cleared meadow'

Stockton (ANGLO-SAXON) 'From the farm in the clearing'

Stockwell (ANGLO-SAXON) 'From the well in the clearing'

Stoddard (ANGLO-SAXON) 'The horse-keeper'

Stoke (ANGLO-SAXON) 'A village'

Storm (ANGLO-SAXON) 'The tempest'

Storr (SCANDINAVIAN) 'Great man'

Stowe (ANGLO-SAXON) 'From the place'

Strahan (GAELIC) 'The poet'

Stratford (ANGLO-SAXON) 'The street crossing the ford'

Strephon (GREEK) 'One who turns'

Stroud (ANGLO-SAXON) 'From the thicket'

Struthers (GAELIC) 'From the rivulet' *(Strothers)*

Stuart *see* **Stewart**

Styles (ANGLO-SAXON) 'From the dwelling by the stile' *(Stiles)*

Suffield (ANGLO-SAXON) 'From the south field'

Sujit (SANSKRIT) 'Winner'

Sulien (WELSH) 'Sun-born'

Sullivan (GAELIC) 'Man with black eyes' *(Sullie, Sully)*

Sully (ANGLO-SAXON) 'From the south meadow' *see also* **Sullivan**

Sulwyn (WELSH) 'Fair from the sun'

Sumitra (SANSKRIT) 'Good friend'

Sumner (LATIN) 'One who summons'. The church official who summoned the congregation to prayer

Sunil (SANSKRIT) 'Very dark blue'

Sunny (ENGLISH) 'Cheery'

Supriya (SANSKRIT) 'Loved'

Surinder (HINDI) 'Mightiest of the gods'

Sushil (SANSKRIT) 'Well behaved'

Sutcliffe (ANGLO-SAXON) 'From the south cliff' *(Sutcliff)*

Sutherland (SCANDINAVIAN) 'From a southern land'

Sutton (ANGLO-SAXON) 'From the south town'

Sven (SCANDINAVIAN) 'Youth'

Swain (ANGLO-SAXON) 'Herdsman', 'knight's attendant' *(Swayne, Sweyn)*

Swami (SANSKRIT) 'Master'

Sweeney (GAELIC) 'Little hero'

Swinton (ANGLO-SAXON) 'From the pig farm'

Swithin (OLD ENGLISH) 'Strong' *(Swithun)*

Sydney *see* **Sidney**

Syena (SANSKRIT) 'Falcon'

Sylvester *see* **Silas**

Symington (ANGLO-SAXON) 'From Simon's farm'

T

BOYS

Tab (TEUTONIC) 'The drummer' *(Tabb, Tabby, Taber)*

Tabib (TURKISH) 'Physician'

Tabor (TURKISH) 'The encampment'

Tad *see* **Tadd** or **Thaddeus**

Tadd (CELTIC) 'Father' *(Tad)* *see also* **Thaddeus** or **Theodore**

Taddeo *see* **Thaddeus**

Tadeo (SPANISH/LATIN) 'Praise' *(Tadeas)*

Taffy (CELTIC) Welsh form of **David**

Tafryn (WELSH) 'Brow of the hill'

Taggart (GAELIC) 'Son of the prelate'

Tahurer (ENGLISH) 'Drummer'

Taiesin (WELSH) 'Radiant brow'

Tait (SCANDINAVIAN) 'Cheerful' *(Tate)*

Tal (ENGLISH) 'Tail'

Talbot (FRENCH) 'The looter' *(Talbert)*

Talfryn (WELSH) 'Brow of the hill'

Taliesin (WELSH) 'Radiant brow'

Tallon (ENGLISH) 'Tall'

Talmadge (ENGLISH) 'Tall'

Talon (ENGLISH) 'Claw'

Tam *see* **Thomas**

Tama (NATIVE AMERICAN) 'Thunderbolt'

Tamal (SANSKRIT) 'Tree with the black bark'

Tamar (HEBREW) 'Palm tree'

Tamtun (ENGLISH) 'From the quiet river farm'

Tancred (OLD GERMAN) 'Thoughtful adviser'

Tangwyn (WELSH) 'Blessed peace' *(Tanigwyn)*

Tanner (ANGLO-SAXON) 'Leather worker' *(Tann, Tannere)*

Tanton (ANGLO-SAXON) 'From the quiet river farm'

Tarak (SANSKRIT) 'Protector'

Tareesh (SANSKRIT) 'An expert', 'the ocean'

Tarik (SANSKRIT) 'He who crosses the river of life'

Tariq (ARABIC) 'Conqueror'

Tarleton (ANGLO-SAXON) 'Thor's farm'

Taro (JAPANESE) 'First-born male'

Tarrance (LATIN) Roman clan name

Tarrant (OLD WELSH) 'Thunder'

Tarrin (ENGLISH) 'Man of the earth' *(Taron, Terran, Terron)*

Taru (SANSKRIT) 'Tree'

Tarun (SANSKRIT) 'Young'

Tassa (ENGLISH) 'Born at Christmas'

Tate (ANGLO-SAXON) 'Cheerful' *(Tait, Tayt, Tayte, Teyte)*

Tavey *see* **Octavius**

Tavis (CELTIC) 'Son of David'. Scottish form of **Thomas** *(Tavish, Tevis)*

Tay (WELSH) Form of **David**

Tayib (INDIAN) 'Good', 'delicate'

Taylan (ENGLISH) 'Tailor' *(Taylon, Taylor, Tayson)*

Taylor (ANGLO-SAXON) 'The Tailor' *see also* **Taylan**

Teague (CELTIC) 'The poet'

Tearlach *see* **Charles**

Tearle (ANGLO-SAXON) 'Stern', 'severe one'

Tecwyn (WELSH) 'Fair and white'

Ted *see* **Edgar, Edward, Theodore** or **Theodoric**

Teddy *see* **Edgar, Edward, Theodore** or **Theodoric**

Tedman (TEUTONIC) 'Protector of the nation'

Tedmond (ANGLO-SAXON) 'King's protector'

Tejeshwar (SANSKRIT) 'The sun'

Tejpal (SANSKRIT) 'Glorious'

Telford (French) 'Iron hewer' *(Taillefer, Telfer, Telfor, Telfour)*

Templeton (ANGLO-SAXON) 'Town of the temple'

Tennyson (ANGLO-SAXON) 'Son of Dennis' *(Tenison, Tennison)*

Teodorico *see* **Theodoric**

Terence (LATIN) 'Smooth, polished and tender' *(Terencio, Terrene, Terry, Torrance)*

Terrall (ENGLISH) 'Powerful'

Terrill (TEUTONIC) 'Follower of Thor' *(Terell, Terrel, Terrell, Tirell, Tirrel, Tirrell, Tyrell, Tyrrel, Tyrrell)*

Terry *see* **Terence**

Teyen (ANGLO-SAXON) 'From the enclosure'

Thacher (ENGLISH) 'Roofer' *(Thacker, Thackere)*

Thaddeus (GREEK) 'Courageous and stout hearted' (HEBREW) 'praise to God' *(Tad, Thad, Taddy, Taddeo)*

Thaine (ANGLO-SAXON) 'Warrior attendant' *(Thane, Thayne)*

Thatcher (ANGLO-SAXON) 'A thatcher of roofs' *(Thatch, Thaxter)*

Thaw (ANGLO-SAXON) 'Ice-breaker'

Thayer (GREEK) 'The nation's army'

Themistocles (GREEK) 'Law and right'

Theo Diminutive of all names beginning with 'Theo'

Theobald (TEUTONIC) 'Bold leader of the people' *(Thibaud, Thibaut, Tibbald, Tioboid, Tybalt)*

Theodore (GREEK) 'Gift of God' *(Dore, Feodor, Feodore, Teador, Ted, Teddie, Teddy, Tudor)*

Theodoric (TEUTONIC) 'Ruler of the people' *(Derek, Derk, Derrick, Dieter, Dietrich, Dirk, Ted, Teddie, Teddy, Tedric, Teodorico, Theodorick)*

Theodosius (GREEK) 'God given'

Theomund (ENGLISH) 'National protector'

Theon (GREEK) 'Godly man'

Theophilus (GREEK) 'Divinely loved'

Theron (GREEK) 'The hunter'

Thibaud (FRENCH) 'People's prince' *see also* **Theobald**

Thomas (HEBREW) 'The twin'. The devoted brother *(Massey, Tam, Tamas, Tammany, Tammy, Tavis, Thom, Tom, Tomas, Tomaso, Tomkin, Tomlin, Tommy)*

Thor (SCANDINAVIAN) 'God of thunder'. The ancient Norse god *(Thorin, Tor, Turpin, Tyrus)*

Thorald (SCANDINAVIAN) 'Thor's ruler'. One who ruled in the name of the thunder-god *(Terrell, Torald, Tyrell)* see also **Thorold**

Thorbert (SCANDINAVIAN) 'Brilliance of Thor' *(Torbert)*

Thorburn (SCANDINAVIAN) 'Thor's bear' *(Torburn)*

Thorley (ANGLO-SAXON) 'From Thor's meadow' *(Torley, Thurleah, Thurleigh)*

Thormund (ANGLO-SAXON) 'Protected by Thor' *(Thormond, Thurmond, Tormond, Tormund)*

Thorndyke (ANGLO-SAXON) 'From the thorny ditch'

Thorne (ANGLO-SAXON) 'From the thorn tree'

Thornley (ANGLO-SAXON) 'From the thorny meadow' *(Thorneley, Thornely, Thornly)*

Thornton (ANGLO-SAXON) 'From the thorny place' *(Thorn)*

Thorold (OLD ENGLISH) 'Thor's strength'

Thorpe (ANGLO-SAXON) 'From the small village' *(Thorp)*

Thurlow (ANGLO-SAXON) 'From Thor's hill'

Thurston (ANGLO-SAXON) 'Thor's jewel' *(Thorstein, Thurstan)*

Tibor (SLAVONIC) 'Holy place'

Tierman (GAELIC) 'Lord and master' *(Tierney)*

Tiernan (CELTIC) 'Kingly'

Tiffany (FRENCH) 'The divine appearance of God' *(Tiphani)*

Tilden (ANGLO-SAXON) 'From the fertile valley'

Tilford (ANGLO-SAXON) 'From the good man's farm'

Timon (GREEK) 'Honour', 'reward', 'value'

Timothy (GREEK) 'Honouring God' *(Tim, Timmie, Timmy, Timoteo, Timotheus, Tiomoid, Tymon)*

Tirtha (SANSKRIT) 'Holy place'

Titus (GREEK) 'Of the giants', (LATIN) 'saved' *(Tito)*

Tobias (HEBREW) 'God is good' *(Tioboid, Tobe, Tobiah, Tobit, Toby)*

Todd (LATIN) 'The fox'

Toft (ANGLO-SAXON) 'A small farm'

Tolland (ANGLO-SAXON) 'One who owns taxed land' *(Toland)*

Tolman (OLD ENGLISH) 'Tax collector'

Tomkin (ANGLO-SAXON) Diminutive of **Thomas**

Tony *see* **Anthony** or **Dalton**

Toole (CELTIC) 'Lordly', 'noble'

Torey (ANGLO-SAXON) 'From the craggy hills' *(Tory)*

Torin (GAELIC) 'Chief' *(Thorfinn)*

Torley *see* **Thorley**

Tormey (GAELIC) 'Thunder spirit' *(Tormy)*

Torquil (TEUTONIC) 'Thor's pledge'

Torr (ANGLO-SAXON) 'From the tower'

Torrance (GAELIC) 'From the little hills' *see also* **Terence**

Torrey (CELTIC) 'One who lives by the tower'

Tostig (WELSH) 'Sharp'

Townley (ANGLO-SAXON) 'From the town meadow' *(Towley, Townley, Townly)*

Townsend (ANGLO-SAXON) 'From the end of the town'

Tracy (LATIN) 'Bold and courageous'

Trahern (CELTIC) 'Iron strength' *(Trahearn, Trahearne, Trehearn, Trehearne, Trehern)*

Travers (LATIN) 'From the crossroads' *(Travis, Travus)*

Tredway (ANGLO-SAXON) 'Mighty warrior'

Trelawny (CORNISH) 'From the church town' *(Trelawney)*

Tremayne (CELTIC) 'From the house in the rock' *(Tremaine)*

Trent (LATIN) 'The torrent'

Trevelyan (CELTIC) 'From Elian's farm'. An old Cornish name *(Trevan, Treven, Trevian, Trevion, Trevyan, Trevyon)*

Trevor (GAELIC) 'Prudent, wise and discreet' *(Trefor)*

Trey (MIDDLE ENGLISH) 'The third'

Trigg (SCANDINAVIAN) 'True and faithful'

Trigun (SANSKRIT) 'Three-dimensional'

Tripp (ANGLO-SAXON) 'The traveller' *(Trip, Tripper)*

Tristan (CELTIC) 'The noisy one' *(Drostan, Tristen, Tristin)*

Tristram (CELTIC) 'The sorrowful one'. Do not confuse with **Tristan**

Trowbridge (ANGLO-SAXON) 'From the tree bridge'

Troy (FRENCH) 'From the land of the people with curly hair'

True (ANGLO-SAXON) 'Faithful and loyal'

Truesdale (ANGLO-SAXON) 'The home of the beloved one' *(Trusdale)*

Truman (ANGLO-SAXON) 'A faithful follower' *(Trueman, Trumane)*

Trumble (ANGLO-SAXON) 'Bold and strong'

Tucker (ANGLO-SAXON) 'Cloth thickener' *see also* **Fuller**

Tufan (SANSKRIT) 'Storm'

Tuhin (SANSKRIT) 'Snow'

Tulio (SPANISH) 'Lively'

Tully (GAELIC) 'Obedient to the will of God'

Tung (CHINESE) 'Everyone'

Tupper (ANGLO-SAXON) One who reared and tended sheep

Turner (LATIN) 'Lathe worker'

Turpin (SCANDINAVIAN) 'Thunder-like'. Finnish form of **Thor**

Tushar (SANSKRIT) 'Snow'

Tut (ARABIC) 'Strong and courageous'. Used to honour the Ancient Egyptian king Tutankamen

Tutankamen *see* **Tut**

Tuxford (SCANDINAVIAN) 'From the ford of the champion spear-thrower'

Twain (ANGLO-SAXON) 'Divided in two'. A co-heir

Twitchell (ANGLO-SAXON) 'From a narrow passageway'

Twyford (ANGLO-SAXON) 'From the twin river'

Tye (ANGLO-SAXON) 'From the enclosure'

Tyler (ANGLO-SAXON) 'Maker of tiles or bricks' *(Tiler, Ty)*

Tynam (GAELIC) 'Dark, grey' *(Tynan)*

Tyree (SCOTTISH) Island dweller

Tyrone (GREEK) 'The sovereign'

Tyson (TEUTONIC) 'Son of the German' *(Sonny, Ty)*

BOYS

Udell (ANGLO-SAXON) 'From the yew tree valley' *(Udale, Udall)*

Udo (LATIN) 'Hot and humid'

Udolf (ANGLO-SAXON) 'Prosperous wolf'

Uilliam *see* **William**

Uillioc *see* **Ulysses**

Uland (TEUTONIC) 'Noble land'

Ulbrecht (GERMAN) 'Noble splendour'

Ulfred (ANGLO-SAXON) 'Peace of the wolf'

Ulger (ANGLO-SAXON) 'Courageous wolf', 'spearman'

Ullock (ANGLO-SAXON) 'Sport of the wolf'

Ulmer (ANGLO-SAXON) 'Famous wolf' *(Ulmar)*

Ulric (TEUTONIC) 'Ruler of all' *(Alric, Ulrich)* see also **Alaric**

Ulrich *see* **Alaric** or **Ulric**

Ultann (WELSH) 'Saintly'

Ulysses (GREEK) 'The angry one', 'the hater' *(Uillioc, Ulick, Ulises)*

Umberto *see* **Humbert**

Umed (SANSKRIT) 'Hope'

Uno (LATIN) 'The one'

Unwin (ANGLO-SAXON)
'The enemy'

Upton (ANGLO-SAXON) 'From the hill farm'

Upwood (ANGLO-SAXON) 'From the hill forest'

Urban (LATIN) 'From the city'. A townsman *(Urbano)*

Uriah (HEBREW) 'The Lord is my light', 'the Lord's light' *(Uri, Urias, Uriel, Yuri)*

Urien (WELSH) 'Town-born'

Urlwin (TEUTONIC)
'Noble friend'

Ushakanta (SANSKRIT) 'The sun'

Usman (SANSKRIT) *see* **Osman**

Utsav (SANSKRIT) 'Celebration'

Uttam (SANSKRIT) 'The best'

Uziel (HEBREW) 'Strength', 'a mighty force'

Uzziah (HEBREW) 'Might of the Lord'

BOYS

Vachel (FRENCH) 'Little cow'

Vadim *see* **Vladimir**

Vail (ANGLO-SAXON) 'From the valley' *(Vale, Valle)*

Vailintin *see* **Valentine**

Val (TEUTONIC) 'Mighty power'. Also diminutive for any name beginning with 'Val'

Valarian (LATIN) 'Healthy' *(Valarius)*

Valdemar (TEUTONIC) 'Famous ruler' *(Valdimar, Waldemar)*

Valentine (LATIN) 'Healthy, strong and valorous' *(Vailintin, Valente, Valentin, Valentino, Valiant)*

Valerian (LATIN) 'Strong and powerful', 'belonging to Valentine'

Vallis (FRENCH) 'The Welshman'

Van (DUTCH) 'From' or 'of'. More generally used as a prefix to a surname, but occasionally found on its own as a forename

Vance (ANGLO-SAXON) 'From the grain barn'

Varden (ANGLO-SAXON) 'From a green hill' *(Vardon, Verden, Verdon)*

Varian (LATIN) 'Changeable'

Varick (TEUTONIC) 'Protecting ruler'

Vasilis (GREEK) 'Knightly', 'magnificent' *(Vasileior, Vasos)*

Vassily (SLAVIC) 'Unwavering protector' *see also* **Basil**

Vaughan (CELTIC) 'The small one' *(Vaughn, Vawn)*

Vawn *see* **Vaughan**

Venn (OLD ENGLISH) 'Handsome'

Verdon *see* **Varden**

Vere (LATIN) 'Faithful and true'. The loyal one

Verney (FRENCH) 'From the alder grove'

Vernon (LATIN) 'Growing', 'flourishing'. Like trees in spring *(Vern, Verne, Verner)*

Verrell (FRENCH) 'The honest one' *(Verill, Verrall, Verrill)*

Victor (LATIN) 'The conqueror' *(Vic, Vick, Victoir, Vince, Vincent, Vinny, Vittorio)*

Vidyut (SANSKRIT) 'Lightning'

Vijay (SANSKRIT) 'Victor', 'victory'

Vinny *see* **Vincent**

Vinson (ANGLO-SAXON) 'Son of Vincent'

Viresh (SANSKRIT) 'Brave leader'

Virgil (LATIN) 'Staff-bearer', 'strong and flourishing' *(Vergil, Virge, Virgie, Virgy)*

Vismay (SANSKRIT) 'Surprise'

Vito (LATIN) 'Alive', 'vital'

Vittorio *see* **Victor**

Vivien (LATIN) 'Lively one' *(Ninian, Vivian)*

Vladimir (SLAVIC) 'Royally famous' *(Vadim)*

Vladislav (SLAVIC) 'Glorious ruler'

Volney (TEUTONIC) 'Of the people'

Vychan (WELSH) 'Little'

Vyvyan (LATIN) 'Lively' *(Bibiano)*

BOYS

Wace (ANGLO-SAXON) 'A vassal'

Wade (ANGLO-SAXON) 'Mover, wanderer'

Wadley (ANGLO-SAXON) 'From the wanderer's meadow'

Wadsworth (ANGLO-SAXON) 'From the wanderer's estate'

Wagner (TEUTONIC) 'A waggoner'

Wahab (SANSKRIT) 'Big-hearted'

Waine *see* **Wayne**

Wainwright (ANGLO-SAXON) 'Waggon maker'

Waite (ANGLO-SAXON) 'A guard', 'a watchman'

Wake (ANGLO-SAXON) 'Alert and watchful' *see also* **Wakefield**

Wakefield (ANGLO-SAXON) 'From the west field' *(Wake)*

Wakeley (ANGLO-SAXON) 'From the wet meadow'

Wakeman (ANGLO-SAXON) 'Watchman'

Walbert (OLD ENGLISH) 'Bright power'

Walby (ANGLO-SAXON) 'From the ancient walls'

Walcott (ANGLO-SAXON) 'Cottage dweller'

Waldemar *see* **Valdemar**

Walden (ANGLO-SAXON) 'One who lives in the valley in the woods'

Waldo (TEUTONIC) 'The ruler'

Waldron (TEUTONIC) 'Strength of the raven'

Walford (OLD ENGLISH) 'Welshman's ford'

Walker (ANGLO-SAXON) 'The walker'

Wallace (ANGLO-SAXON) 'The Welshman', 'the stranger' *(Wallache, Wallie, Wallis, Wally, Walsh, Welch, Welsh)*

Walmond (TEUTONIC) 'Mighty protector' *(Walmund)*

Walsh *see* **Wallace**

Walstan (ANGLO-SAXON) 'Cornerstone'

Walter (TEUTONIC) 'Mighty warrior' *(Wally, Walt, Walters, Walther, Wat)*

Walton (ANGLO-SAXON) 'From the forest town'

Walworth (ANGLO-SAXON) 'From the stranger's farm'

Walwyn (ANGLO-SAXON) 'Friendly stranger'

Warand (TEUTONIC) 'Protecting'

Warburton (ANGLO-SAXON) 'From the castle town'

Ward (ANGLO-SAXON) 'Watchman', 'guardian' *(Warden see also Durward)*

Wardell (ANGLO-SAXON) 'From the hill watch'

Wardley (ANGLO-SAXON) 'From the watchman's meadow'

Ware (ANGLO-SAXON) 'Prudent one'. A very astute person

Warfield (ANGLO-SAXON) 'From the field by the weir'

Warford (ANGLO-SAXON) 'From the ford by the weir'

Waring *see* **Warren**

Warley (ANGLO-SAXON) 'From the meadow by the weir'

Warmund (TEUTONIC) 'Loyal protector' *(Warmond)*

Warner (TEUTONIC) 'Protecting army' *(Verner, Werner)*

Warren (TEUTONIC) 'The gamekeeper'. One who looked after the game preserves *(Waring)*

Warton (ANGLO-SAXON) 'From the farm by the weir'

Warwick (ANGLO-SAXON) 'Strong fortress' *(Warrick)*

Washburn (ANGLO-SAXON) 'From the river in spate'

Washington (ANGLO-SAXON) 'From the keen-eyed one's farm'

Watford (ANGLO-SAXON) 'From the hurdle by the ford'

Watkins (ANGLO-SAXON) 'Son of Walter' *(Watson)*

Waverley (ANGLO-SAXON) 'The meadow by the aspen trees' *(Waverly)*

Wayland (ANGLO-SAXON) 'From the pathway near the highway' *(Weylin)*

Wayne (TEUTONIC) 'Waggon maker' *(Wain, Waine)*

Webb (ANGLO-SAXON) 'A weaver' *(Webber, Weber, Webster)*

Webley (ANGLO-SAXON) 'From the weaver's meadow'

Webster (OLD ENGLISH) 'Weaver' *see also* **Webb**

Weddell (ANGLO-SAXON) 'From the wanderer's hill'

Welborne (ANGLO-SAXON) 'From the spring by the brook' *(Welbourne)*

Welby (ANGLO-SAXON) 'From the farm by the spring'

Welch *see* **Wallace**

Weldon (ANGLO-SAXON) 'From the well on the hill'

Welford (ANGLO-SAXON) 'From the ford by the spring'

Wellington (ANGLO-SAXON) 'From the rich man's farm'

Wells (ANGLO-SAXON) 'From the spring'

Welsh *see* **Wallace**

Welton (ANGLO-SAXON) 'From the farm by the spring'

Wenceslaus (SLAVIC) 'Wreath of glory' *(Wenceslas)*

Wendell (TEUTONIC) 'The wanderer' *(Wendall)*

Wentworth (ANGLO-SAXON) 'Estate belonging to the white-haired one'

Werner *see* **Warner**

Wes Diminutive of all names beginning with 'Wes'

Wesley (ANGLO-SAXON) 'From the west meadow' *(Wesleigh, Westleigh)*

Westbrook (ANGLO-SAXON) 'From the west brook'

Westby (ANGLO-SAXON) 'From the homestead in the west'

Westcott (ANGLO-SAXON) 'From the west cottage'

Westley (ANGLO-SAXON) 'From the west meadow'

Weston (ANGLO-SAXON) 'From the west farm'

Wetherell (ANGLO-SAXON) 'From the sheep hill' *(Wetherall, Wetherill)*

Wetherley (ANGLO-SAXON) 'From the sheep meadow' *(Wetherly)*

Weylin (CELTIC) 'Son of the wolf' *see also* **Wayland**

Wharton (ANGLO-SAXON) 'Farm in the hollow'

Wheatley (ANGLO-SAXON) 'From the wheat meadow'

Wheeler (ANGLO-SAXON) 'The wheel-maker'

Whistler (ANGLO-SAXON) 'The whistler', 'the piper'

Whitby (ANGLO-SAXON) 'From the white farmstead'

Whitcomb (ANGLO-SAXON) 'From the white hollow' *(Whitcombe)*

Whitelaw (ANGLO-SAXON) 'From the white hill'

Whitfield (ANGLO-SAXON) 'From the white field'

Whitford (ANGLO-SAXON) 'From the white ford'

Whitley (ANGLO-SAXON) 'From the white meadow'

Whitlock (ANGLO-SAXON) 'White-haired one'

Whitman (ANGLO-SAXON) 'White-haired man'

Whitmore (ANGLO-SAXON) 'From the white moor'

Whitney (ANGLO-SAXON) 'From the white island' *(Whitny, Witney, Witny)*

Whittaker (ANGLO-SAXON) 'One who dwells in the white field' *(Whitaker)*

Wiatt *see* **Guy**

Wickham (ANGLO-SAXON) 'From the enclosed field by the village' *(Wykeham)*

Wickley (ANGLO-SAXON) 'From the village meadow'

Wilbur (TEUTONIC) 'Resolute and brilliant'. A determined and clever person *(Wilbert)*

Wildon (OLD ENGLISH) 'From the wooden hill'

Wiley *see* **William**

Wilford (ANGLO-SAXON) 'From the willow ford'

Wilfred (TEUTONIC) 'Firm peace-maker'. Peace, but not at any price *(Fred, Freddie, Freddy, Wilfrid)*

Wilhelm *see* **William**

Wilkie *see* **William**

Willard (ANGLO-SAXON) 'Resolute and brave'

William (TEUTONIC) 'Determined protector'. The strong guardian *(Bill, Billie, Billy, Gwylim, Liam, Uilleam, Uilliam, Wiley, Wilhelm, Wilkes, Wilkie, Will, Willet, Williamson, Willie, Willis, Willy, Wilson)*

Willis *see* **William**

Willoughby (ANGLO-SAXON) 'From the farmstead by the willows'

Wilmer (TEUTONIC) 'Resolute and famous'. One renowned for his firmness *(Wilmot)*

Wilson (ANGLO-SAXON) 'Son of William' *see also* **William**

Wilton (ANGLO-SAXON) 'From the farm by the well'

Win Diminutive of all names containing 'Win'

Winchell (ANGLO-SAXON) 'The bend in the road'

Windsor (ANGLO-SAXON) 'The boundary bank'

Winfield (ANGLO-SAXON) 'From a friend's field'

Winfred (ANGLO-SAXON) 'Peaceful friend' *(Winifred)*

Wing (CHINESE) 'Glory'

Wingate (ANGLO-SAXON) 'From the winding lane'

Winslow (ANGLO-SAXON) 'From a friend's hill'

Winston (ANGLO-SAXON) 'From a friend's estate'

Winter (ANGLO-SAXON) 'Born during winter months'

Winthrop (TEUTONIC) 'From a friendly village'

Winton (ANGLO-SAXON) 'From a friend's farm'

Winward (ANGLO-SAXON) 'From the friendly forest' *(Winwald)*

Wirth (TEUTONIC) 'The master' *(Wirt)*

Witha (ARABIC) 'Handsome'

Witney *see* **Whitney**

Witram (GERMAN) 'Forest river'

Witter (TEUTONIC) 'Wise warrior' *(Witt)*

Witton (TEUTONIC) 'From a wise man's farm'

Wolcott (ANGLO-SAXON) 'From the cottage of the wolf' *(Wulcott)*

Wolfe (TEUTONIC) 'A wolf'. A man of courage

Wolfgang (TEUTONIC) 'The advancing wolf'. A warrior in the vanguard of the army

Wolfram (TEUTONIC) 'Respected and feared'

Woodley (ANGLO-SAXON) 'From the forest meadow' *(Woodly)*

Woodrow (ANGLO-SAXON) 'From the hedge in the wood'

Woodruff (ANGLO-SAXON) 'Forest bailiff'

Woodward (ANGLO-SAXON) 'Forest guardian'

Woody Familiar form of all names containing 'Wood'

Woolsey (ANGLO-SAXON) 'Victorious wolf' *(Wolseley, Wolsey)*

Worcester (ANGLO-SAXON) 'Camp in the forest of the alder trees' *(Wooster)*

Wordsworth (ANGLO-SAXON) 'From the farm of the wolf'

Worrall (ANGLO-SAXON) 'From the loyal man's manor' *(Worrell, Worrill)*

Worth (ANGLO-SAXON) 'The farmstead'

Worthington (ANGLO-SAXON) 'Riverside'

Worton (ANGLO-SAXON) 'From the vegetable farm'

Wray (SCANDINAVIAN) 'One who lives in the house on the corner'

Wren (CELTIC) 'The chief'

Wright (ANGLO-SAXON) 'Craftsman in woodwork', 'a carpenter'

Wulfstan (OLD ENGLISH) 'Wolf stone'

Wyatt *see* **Guy**

Wybert (OLD ENGLISH) 'Battle famous'

Wyborn (SCANDINAVIAN) 'Warrior bear' *(Wyborne)*

Wycliff (ANGLO-SAXON) 'From the white cliff'

Wylie (ANGLO-SAXON) 'The enchanter, the beguiler'

Wyman (ANGLO-SAXON) 'The warrior'

Wymer (ANGLO-SAXON) 'Renowned in battle'

Wyndham (ANGLO-SAXON) 'From the village with the winding path' *(Windham)*

Wynford (WELSH) 'White torrent'

Wynn (CELTIC) 'The fair one'

Wystand (OLD ENGLISH) 'Battle stone' *(Wystan)*

Wythe (ANGLO-SAXON) 'From the dwelling by the willow tree'

BOYS

Xanthus (LATIN) 'Golden haired'

Xavier (ARABIC/SPANISH) 'Bright' *(Javier)*

Xenek (GREEK) 'The stranger'

Xenophon (GREEK) 'Strong sounding'

Xenos (GREEK) 'The stranger'

Xerxes (PERSIAN) 'The king'

Ximenes *see* **Simon**

Xylon (GREEK) 'From the forest'

BOYS

Yahya (ARABIC) 'Living'

Yale (TEUTONIC/ANGLO-SAXON) 'The vanquished'

Yancy (NATIVE AMERICAN) 'The Englishman'. Name given to settlers which became Yankee *(Yance)*

Yardan (ARABIC) 'Merciful king'

Yardley (OLD ENGLISH) 'From the enclosed meadow'

Yarin (HEBREW) 'Understand'

Yasir (ARABIC) 'Easy', 'soft'

Yates (ANGLO-SAXON) 'One who lives at the gates'

Yehudi (HEBREW) 'Praise to the Lord'

Yemon (JAPANESE) 'The one who guards the gate'

Yeoman (ANGLO-SAXON) 'The tenant farmer'

Yestin (WELSH) 'Just'

Ynyr (WELSH) 'Honour'

Yorick *see* **George** or **York**

York (ANGLO-SAXON/CELTIC/LATIN) 'Sacred yew tree' *(Yorick, Yorke)*

Yul (MONGOLIAN) 'Beyond the horizon'

Yules (ANGLO-SAXON) 'Born at Christmas' *(Yule)*

Yuma (NATIVE AMERICAN) 'Son of a chief'

Yvon (TEUTONIC) 'The archer'

Ywain (CELTIC) 'Young warrior'

BOYS

Zabros (GREEK) 'Glutton'

Zach *see* **Zacharias**

Zachaeus (ARAMAIC) 'Pure'

Zacharias (HEBREW) 'The Lord has remembered' *(Zach, Zachariah, Zachary, Zack)*

Zack *see* **Zacharias**

Zadok (HEBREW) 'The righteous one' *(Zaloc)*

Zahid (SANSKRIT/ARABIC) 'Intelligent and pious'

Zahir (ARABIC) 'Splendid'

Zaloc *see* **Zadok**

Zane *see* **John**

Zarab (ARABIC) 'Protector against enemies'

Zared (HEBREW) 'The ambush'

Zebediah (HEBREW) 'Gift of the Lord' *(Zebedee)*

Zebulon (HEBREW) 'The dwelling place' *(Lonny, Zeb, Zebulen)*

Zechariah (HEBREW) 'The Lord is renowned'

Zedekiah (HEBREW) 'The Lord's justice'

Zeeman (DUTCH) 'The sailor'

Zeke *see* **Ezekiel**

Zel (PERSIAN) 'Cymbal'

Zelig (TEUTONIC) 'Blessed one'

Zelos (GREEK) 'Emulation'

Zelotes (GREEK) 'The zealous one'

Zenas (GREEK) 'Living being'

Zeno (GREEK) 'Stranger'

Zenos (GREEK) 'Gift from Jupiter'

Zephaniah (HEBREW) 'Treasured by the lord' *(Zephan)*

Zerah (HEBREW) 'Rising light'

Zeus (GREEK) 'Father of the gods'

Zia (SANSKRIT) 'Enlightened'

Zimraan (ARABIC) 'Celebrated'

Zolly *see* **Solomon**

Zuriel (HEBREW) 'The Lord is my rock and foundation' *(Zurial)*